CORNERSTONE

Building on Your Best

Concise Edition

RHONDA J. MONTGOMERY

The University of Nevada, Las Vegas

PATRICIA G. MOODY

The University of South Carolina

ROBERT M. SHERFIELD

The Community College of Southern Nevada

ALLYN AND BACON

Boston · London · Toronto · Sydney · Tokyo · Singapore

DEDICATION

Cornerstone is dedicated to our families and close friends who have helped us, nurtured us, believed in us, and encouraged us to become the best we can be.

For Rhonda:
   Mick Montgomery, Jackie Montgomery, Sharlene Redd, Charles and Sharon Delph

For Pat:
   My personal hero, my mother, Annie Laura Bryan Ginn

For Robb:
   Great friends in a new city, Curtis Roe, Lynn Forkos, William Pulse, Dell Griffin

Copyright © 1999 by Allyn and Bacon
A Viacom Company
160 Gould Street
Needham, MA 02194
www.abacon.com

Series editor: Virginia Lanigan
Series editorial assistant: Bridget Keane
Marketing manager: Richard Muhr
Composition and prepress buyer: Linda Cox
Manufacturing buyer: Megan Cochran
Cover administrator: Linda Knowles
Cover designer: Susan Paradise
Photo researchers: Susan Duane and Martha Shethar
Production administrator: Susan Brown
Editorial-Production service: Colophon
Text designer: Seventeenth Street Studios
Character illustrator: Christian O'Brien
Electronic Page Layout: Christine Thompson

0-205-28268-7

Printed in the United States of America
10 9 8 7 6 5 4 3 2 1   01   00   99   98

Photo Credits: p. 4 Brian Smith; p. 8 Robert Harbison; p. 9 Brian Smith; p. 14 Brian Smith; p. 21 Jacques Chenet/ Woodfin Camp & Associates; p. 23 P. Beringer/The Image Works; p. 26 Sports Chrome Inc.; p. 35 Wide World Photos; p. 39 North Wind Picture Archives; p. 58 C. J. Allen/Stock Boston; p. 63 C. J. Allen/Stock Boston; p. 79 Ellis Herwig/ Stock Boston; p. 82 Phyllis Picardi/Stock Boston; p. 91 Allstock/Tony Stone Images; p. 93 PhotoDisk, Inc.; p. 102 Gary Conner/PhotoEdit; p. 116 Paula Lerner/Woodfin Camp & Associates; p. 121 Esbin-Anderson/The Image Works; p. 122 Brian Smith; p. 135 Anthony Neste; p. 148 David H. Wells/The Image Bank; p. 152 Anthony Neste; p. 171 Brian Smith; p. 175 Brian Smith; p. 180 Brian Smith; p. 191 Brian Smith; p. 199 Brian Smith; p. 217 Robert Harbison; p. 223 Bob Daemmrich/The Image Works; p. 246 Phyllis Picardi/ Stock Boston; p. 256 Grantpix/Stock Boston; p. 258 Anthony Neste; p. 262 Spencer Grant/The Picture Cube; p. 268 Bob Daemmrich/Stock Boston; p. 278 Brian Smith.

CONTENTS

> Education is not preparation for life, education is life itself.
>
> John Dewey, educator

CORNERSTONE was born out of our desire to help new college students develop the skills that would enable them to be successful in college. Seldom will you read a textbook as honest and straightforward as we have tried to make this one. The words that you read and the activities provided in this work-text have not come easily to us. They are the result of our collective experiences over our many years of teaching and administration in higher education. We hope our words will touch you deeply and provide you insight that will enable you to make it to graduation and beyond.

We hope that our words will give you peace as well as cause you some discomfort; teach you and challenge you; hold you and let you go. It is also our hope that you will approach these activities with new eyes; yours is a different world now. To experience that world, you'll need to be open and willing to participate. Without your participation, the power of this worktext is lost. With your participation, it holds unlimited possibilities for bringing change, improving skills, and setting you off on a lifetime of success.

Within the pages of this worktext you will find many activities such as *At This Moment* and *The One Minute Journal,* which will help you explore where you are and where you are going. Each chapter includes a feature called *An Insider's View,* stories from students across the United States discussing issues found within the chapter. Each chapter ends with an *Internet Activity* that will both help you explore issues and actively learn to use one of the most powerful technological tools available today.

You will notice that the pages of *Cornerstone* are filled with cartoons. They are there for your enjoyment and to add a little comic relief (many of them are a howl!). The cartoons also tell a story. Get to know Cliff, Miho, Vasquez, Kate, and the others. Watch how they cope with their college experiences, how they're changed by them, and how they grow from them.

While this edition of *Cornerstone* is a condensed version of our larger book, we have added a couple of important new topics. There is an entirely new chapter, Chapter Four, *Think before You Leap: Using Critical Thinking Skills in College and Life.* The ability to think critically will help you succeed as a student and, perhaps more importantly, succeed as a member of society.

Chapter Eight, *Avoiding the All-Nighter: Studying for Success,* contains a new section of *Learning Styles.* Knowing that not everyone learns in the same way, and recognizing your own individual learning styles and preferences may help you immeasurably, especially when it comes time to prepare for tests.

Included with your book is a double entry journal, in which you are asked to respond to a variety of questions. When used properly, this journal can be a valuable communication tool between you, your peers, and your instructor. Take your time to reflect honestly and openly on the questions asked. Only through your own soul-searching and self-revelation will the features of this book help you improve your skills as a college student and assist you in becoming a productive citizen.

We wish you luck in building your future on the cornerstones that will carry you for the rest of your life.

Rhonda, Pat, and Robb

ACKNOWLEDGMENTS

Professional Acknowledgments   Dr. David Christianson, Dean, William F. Harrah College of Hotel Administration, University of Nevada, Las Vegas; Dr. John Duffy, Dean, College of Applied Professional Sciences, The University of South Carolina; Dr.Carol Harter, President, University of Nevada, Las Vegas; Dr. John Palms, President, The University of South Carolina; Patti Shock, Department Chair, Tourism and Convention Administration, University of Nevada, Las Vegas; and Dr. Don Smith, English Department Chair, Community College of Southern Nevada. Janette M. Ardito, Maria D'Angelo-Bray, Judy Grant, Melissa Godi, Jeanne L. Harmon, Dr. Billie Herrin, Maria P. Houston, Keith T. Jones, Doc Manning, Julie Messina, Lenora Elaine Nelson, Yasir Niazi, Dr. Sue Rigby, Gabe Salamanco, Samantha G. Seawright, Mary Simmons, Katie Sonefeld, and Kelvin W. Woods.

Special thanks to   Al Soprano, Steve Konowalow, and Patricia LaFlamme, The Community College of Southern Nevada

The following educators and students offered significant contributions to the development of this book with their insightful and constructive reviews: Joanne Bassett, Shelby State Community College; Carol Brooks, GMI Engineering and Management Institute; Deborah Daiek, Wayne State University; David DeFrain, Central Missouri State University; Earlyn G. Jordan, Fayetteville State University; Michael Laven, University of Southwestern Louisiana; Judith Lynch, Kansas State University; Susan Magun-Jackson, The University of Memphis; Charles William Martin, California State University, San Bernardino; Ellen Oppenberg, Glendale Community College; Lee Pelton, Charles S. Mott Community College; Robert Rozzelle, Wichita State University; James Stepp, University of Maine at Presque Isle; and Charles Washington, Indiana University–Purdue University.

The following people provided valuable suggestions for the development of this concise edition of *Cornerstone:* Kathy Carpenter, University of Nebraska-Kearney; Janet Cutshall, Sussex County Community College; Dwight Fontenot, The University of Michigan; Marnell L. Hayes, Lake City Community College; Michael S. Lavan, University of Southwest Louisiana; Brian Richardson, Arizona State University; Betty Smith, University of Nebraska-Kearney.

Students   David Barfield, Midlands Technical College; Robin Berghaus, Brookline High School, Massachusetts; William DePippo, Emerson College; Ellen Harder, Brandeis University; Julie Kikta, Midlands Technical College; Molly Moss, Arizona State University; Josh

Newman, Newton North High School, Massachusetts; Shawnee Price, Midlands Technical College; and Julie Weber, Ohio University.

Thanks to Christian O'Brien for creating the illustrations for this book. Christian is a graduate of Massachusetts College of Art in Boston. While there, he edited *The Rag,* an on-campus publication, and was a member of the Student Government Association. His work can be found in various small press publications.

Born in 1974, he grew up in Haverhill, Massachusetts, and spent much of his childhood drawing cartoons. Despite support from family and teachers, he often doubted he was capable of succeeding as an artist. At college, he honed his talents and learned to have faith in his ability.

And thanks to Jackie Romeo of Emerson College, who contributed her advice and her humor to the conceptualization of the illustrations.

ABOUT THE AUTHORS

Rhonda J. Montgomery

Rhonda Montgomery is the Assistant Dean of Student Affairs for the William F. Harrah College of Hotel Administration at the University of Nevada, Las Vegas and has been teaching in higher education for 10 years. Rhonda has been responsible for developing and incorporating first-year orientation/study skills curricula into existing introductory courses and programs.

Currently, Rhonda is teaching a first-year orientation/study skills course as well as hospitality education. Because she believes in the holistic development of first-year students, she volunteers to teach first-year students each semester and uses a variety of experiences such as field trips, exercises, and case studies to aid in their retention and success.

Rhonda is the co-author of five texts including two student success texts, *Cornerstone* and *365 Things I Learned in College* (Allyn & Bacon, 1996). She has also presented at The National Conference on the Freshman Year Experience and spoken extensively to first-year students and educators about building success into their curriculum.

Patricia G. Moody

Patricia G. Moody is a Professor and Chairman of the Department in Business and Marketing Education at the University of South Carolina, where she has been a faculty member for over twenty years. An award-winning educator, Pat has been honored as Distinguished Educator of the Year at her college, Collegiate Teacher of the Year by the National Business Education Association, and has been a top-five finalist for the Amoco Teaching Award at the University of South Carolina. In 1994, she was awarded the prestigious John Robert Gregg Award, the highest honor in her field of over 100,000 educators.

Pat frequently speaks to multiple sections of first-year students, incorporating personal development content from her trademark speech, "Fly Like an Eagle," as well as numerous strategies for building self-esteem and for achieving success in college. She also works with first-year classes on subjects such as goal setting, priority management, and diversity.

A nationally known motivation speaker, Pat has spoken in 42 states, has been invited to speak in several foreign countries, and frequently keynotes national and regional conventions. She has presented "Fly Like an Eagle" to thousands of people from Olympic athletes to corporate executives to high school students. Her topics include Thriving in the Changing Corporate Environment, Perception is Everything: Powerful Communications Strategies, Gold Star Customer Service, and The Great Balancing Act: Managing Time at Home and at Work.

An avid sports fan, she follows Gamecock athletics and chairs the University of South Carolina Athletics Advisory Committee.

Robert M. Sherfield

Robert Sherfield has been teaching public speaking, theater, and study skills and working with first-year orientation programs for over 15 years. Currently, he is on the full-time faculty at the Community College of Southern Nevada, teaching study skills, orientation courses, and drama.

Robb's extensive work with student success programs includes experience with the design and implementation of these programs—including one program that was presented at the International Conference on the Freshman Year Experience in Newcastle upon Tyne, England.

Some of Robb's responsibilities have also included serving as Coordinator of University 101, Director of Student and Cultural Activities, Director of Orientation Programs, and Director of Student Media at the University of South Carolina at Union. He also codesigned a student success course at Florence Darlington Technical College.

In addition to his coauthorship of *Cornerstone: Building on Your Best*, he has also coauthored *Roadways to Success* (Allyn & Bacon, 1997) and the trade book, *365 Things I Learned in College* (Allyn & Bacon, 1996).

Robb's interest in student success began with his own first year in college. Low SAT scores and a mediocre high school ranking denied him entrance into college. With the help of a success program, Robb was granted entrance into college, and went on to earn a doctorate and become a college faculty member. He has always been interested in the social, academic, and cultural development of students, and sees this book as his way to contribute to the positive development of first-year students across the nation.

CORNERSTONE

1

Nothing Stays the Same: Preparing for and Dealing with Change

Mark was the son of textile workers. Both of his parents had worked in the mills for almost 30 years. They lived in the rural south about 35 miles from the nearest metropolitan area. His high school graduated a small number of students yearly. Mark had decided to attend a community college some 30 miles from home for his first two years and then transfer

to a larger, four-year college. Money, time, grades, goals, and family commitments led to his decision.

Mark's first class that fall semester was English. The professor walked in, handed out the syllabus, called the roll, and began to lecture. Lord Byron was the topic for the day. The professor sat on a stool by the window, leaned his elbow on the ledge, and sipped a cup of coffee as he told the story of how Byron's foot had been damaged at birth. He continued to weave the details of Byron's life poetically, through quotes and parables, until the 50-minute period had quietly slipped away.

After an hour's break, Mark headed across campus for history. The professor entered with a dust storm behind her. She went over the syllabus, and before the class had a chance to blink, she was involved in the first lecture. "The cradle of civilization," she began, "was Mesopotamia." The class scurried to find notebooks and pens to begin taking notes. Already, they were behind, Mark included. Exactly 47 minutes after she had begun to speak, the professor took her first breath. "You are in history now. You elected to take this class and you will follow my rules," she told the first-year students sitting in front of her. "You are not to be late, you are to come to this class pre-pared, and you are to read your homework. If you do what I ask you to do, you will learn more about Western civilization than you ever thought possible. If you do not keep up with me,

He knew that because of one day in college, he would never be the same.

you will not know if you are in Egypt, Mesopotamia, or pure hell! Class dismissed!"

Without a moment to spare, Mark ran to the other end of campus for his next class. He walked into the room in a panic, fearing he was late. To his surprise, the instructor was not yet in class. The class waited for more than 10 minutes before the professor entered. "You need to sign this roster and read chapter one for Wednesday," he said. "You can pick up a syllabus on your way out." Mark was shocked. Was the class over? What about the bell? The students in the class looked at each other with dismay and quietly left the room, wondering what Wednesday would hold.

On the 30-mile trip home, Mark's mind was filled with new thoughts . . . Lord Byron, Mesopotamia, professors who talked too fast, professors who did not talk at all, the cost of tuition, the size of the library. He knew that something was different, something had changed. He couldn't put his finger on it. It would be years later before he would realize that the change was not his classes, not his schedule, not the people, not the professors—but himself; Mark had changed. In one day, he had tasted something intoxicating, something that was addictive. He had tasted a new world.

Mark had to go to work that afternoon, and even his job had changed. He had always known that he did not want to spend the rest of his life in the factory, but this day the feeling was stronger. His job was not enough, his family was not enough, the farm on which he had been raised was not enough anymore. There was a new light for Mark, and he knew that because of *one* day in college, he would never be the same. It was like tasting Godiva chocolate for the first time—Hershey's kisses were no longer enough. It was like seeing the ocean for the first time and knowing that the millpond would never be the same. He couldn't go back. What he knew before was simply not enough.

My name is Robert *Mark* Sherfield, and 22 years later, as I coauthor your text, I am still addicted to that new world. Spartanburg Methodist College changed my life, and I am still changing—with every day, every new book I read, every new class I teach, every new person I meet, and every new place to which I travel, I am changing.

Why Address Change?

Sometimes our fate resembles a fruit tree in winter. Who would think that those branches would turn green again and blossom, but we hope, we know it.
Goethe, German playwright

Take a minute and think about your life so far. You've already faced some major changes, haven't you? For some of you, graduating from high school recently was a big change. For others, returning to school after being out for five or ten years is a monumental change. For still others, the loss of your job or changing job requirements have caused you to return to college, and that is a major change. In the days, weeks, and months to come, you'll be faced with many more changes, changes that you perhaps did not or could not have expected. You will meet people whose religion, race, national origin, age, or sexual orientation differs from your own. You'll be asked to sit in groups with people who do not have the same values, morals, judgments, and actions as you. You'll be told and shown things by professors and peers that you never imagined possible. Some of these events will be positive, some shocking, some disturbing, some elevating, and some life altering. You are embarking on one of the most exciting rides of your life—so get ready!

In many of the situations that will arise in the coming days, you may not have to be involved or take any action, you may be only an observer. In some situations you will need to take immediate action. In other cases you'll have time to ponder and reflect on the appropriate action. This chapter will help you cope with change and make wise and healthy decisions. After completing this chapter, you will be able to

- Determine whether college is important to you

- Identify reasons for attending college

- Discuss how college changes people

- Analyze recent changes in your personal life

- Prepare for changes in the coming days

- Prepare for life changes

- Discuss the premises of change

- Recognize and deal with the physical and emotional effects of change

- Incorporate into your life the cornerstones for dealing with change

Why Cornerstone?

What Can This Book Do for You?

This book is intended to shake you up—to *cause* change! Yes, to cause change. We hope that this book will help you see more clearly the possibilities the future holds; that the activities included here will help you anticipate and cope with the many new situations you will face; that in the days and weeks to come you will use this book as a guide to help you contend with change, discover more about yourself, develop study and prioritizing skills, master the terminology of college life, develop higher order thinking skills, learn more about careers, cope with stress, and develop an appreciation for diversity. We hope that our words together—yours and ours—will

> Life is about change, and about movement, and about becoming something other than what you are at this very moment.
> Unknown

help you make your goals and dreams come true. This book is primarily about decisions: decisions that you will face in the days and months ahead, decisions that may affect the rest of your life, decisions that *you* will make. This book is about learning how to bring the best you have to each situation. *Cornerstone* is about building on your best!

We chose the title *Cornerstone* because a cornerstone is, according to the *American Heritage Dictionary,* "the indispensable and fundamental basis of something." We consider this course the cornerstone for your success in college. In a building, a cornerstone is laid to establish a firm foundation. Often, a ceremony attends the laying of a cornerstone, and treasured documents and valuables may be placed within the cornerstone. Today is a celebration; a celebration of your future, of your potential, and of the joys and triumphs yet to come. Today, you are laying the cornerstone for the rest of your life. Take your time, use only the best materials available to you, plan your structure carefully, let others help you along the way, and you will have built a lasting monument celebrating your achievements.

As you read about—and possibly struggle with—the concepts and challenges presented here, you will find many opportunities to write and personalize this worktext. Some of the activities may seem personal and may make you uncomfortable, but if you undertake them seriously, you will gain valuable tools that will help you be successful. The chapters contain many common elements: quotations; At This Moment, A Self-Assessment; interactive writing opportunities; activities; journal exercises; student testimonials; stories of students and graduates; and cornerstones for success.

There are 11 exercises called At This Moment, A Self-Assessment. These exercises are intended to assess where you stand "at this moment" in relation to materials covered in a chapter. Take a moment to determine where you are at this moment in dealing with change.

AT THIS MOMENT...

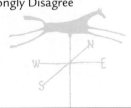

5 = Strongly Agree

4 = Agree

3 = Don't Know

2 = Disagree

1 = Strongly Disagree

1. I handle change easily.
   1 2 3 4 5

2. I deal with stress easily.
   1 2 3 4 5

3. I can make new friends quickly.   *1 2 3 4 5*

4. I had no trouble starting college (leaving my friends, spouse, children).
   1 2 3 4 5

5. I can recognize the physical and emotional symptoms caused by change.
   1 2 3 4 5

6. Change is good.
   1 2 3 4 5

7. I adapt to new situations easily.   *1 2 3 4 5*

8. I know how to promote change in my life.
   1 2 3 4 5

9. Change seems to be difficult for my friends.
   1 2 3 4 5

10. I do not fear change.
    1 2 3 4 5

A SELF-ASSESSMENT Total your points from these ten questions. Refer to the following rating scale to determine where you stand in relation to dealing with change.

0–10   You have a great deal of difficulty and anxiety when dealing with change.

11–20 You have a greater than normal amount of anxiety when dealing with change.

21–30 You have a considerable amount of anxiety when dealing with change.

31–40 You have some anxiety when dealing with change.

41–50 You deal with change very easily and with little anxiety.

Now, refer to your journal and respond in writing to your findings. Consider the following questions when writing in your journal.

1. Why is change hard (or easy) for me?

2. What makes me afraid (or unafraid) of change?

3. I suffer (or do not suffer) emotionally and physically from change.

Why College?

Well, here you are, in college. Time to party? Time to get away from the children? Time to find a significant other? Time to study? Time to ponder the meaning of life? All these may be reasons to attend college. There are more than three and a half million first-year students in the nation's colleges right now; each one may have a different reason for being there. Some students are pursuing a high-paying job, developing a specific skill, retraining for the job market, following an old dream. Others are recently divorced and trying to acquire skills that were not taught 15 years ago. Some are in college because of pressure from their parents. And yes, there are those who say that they are in college to party and have a good time. Perhaps you've met a few of them already. And let us not forget the tens of thousands who say they are enrolled to experience developmental, interactive pedagogy and scientific relativity . . . NOT!

> The real object of education is to give one resources that will endure as long as life endures; habits that time will not destroy; occupations that will render sickness tolerable; solitude pleasant; age venerable; life more dignified and useful; and death less terrible.
>
> S. Smith, author

The college experience is different for every person. Some people love every minute of it, some people see it as a necessary evil to getting that wonderful job. Some see the college experience as a way of expanding horizons, and others see it as a two- or four- (or five-) year prison sentence!

List the major reasons that you are in college today. Be honest with yourself!

1. _____

2. _____

3. _____

4. _____

Were all four blanks easy to fill? Did you do it quickly? As you discuss these reasons in class, you will find that many of your classmates are attending college for many of the same reasons you listed. If your class holds true to form, most of your classmates responded "to get a better job and make more money." In a poll conducted by *The Chronicle of Higher Education* (August 25, 1993) 78.5 percent of first-year students polled responded to this question with the answer "to be able to get a better job."

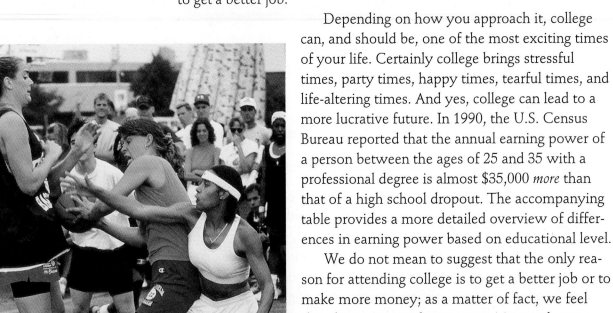

Depending on how you approach it, college can, and should be, one of the most exciting times of your life. Certainly college brings stressful times, party times, happy times, tearful times, and life-altering times. And yes, college can lead to a more lucrative future. In 1990, the U.S. Census Bureau reported that the annual earning power of a person between the ages of 25 and 35 with a professional degree is almost $35,000 *more* than that of a high school dropout. The accompanying table provides a more detailed overview of differences in earning power based on educational level.

We do not mean to suggest that the only reason for attending college is to get a better job or to make more money; as a matter of fact, we feel that this is a secondary reason. Many other considerations may be at least as important as money to a person's decision to attend college, among them knowledge, spiritual development, sports, socialization, peer or parental pressure, and job training. Some of these reasons are practical, and some have a more altruistic appeal. Were any of these items listed as one of *your* reasons for attending college?

Education level	Age Group			
	24–34	35–44	45–54	55–64
High school dropout	$12,527	$14,341	$17,301	$16,720
High school diploma	17,976	21,413	22,842	19,865
Bachelor's degree	28,896	37,214	39,122	36,853
Master's degree	34,351	41,737	46,837	38,972
Doctorate	38,443	55,176	63,536	56,549
Professional degree	47,192	87,816	83,358	82,887

Mean Annual Earning by Education Level

Change is certain to happen during your college years.

One response you probably won't find on your list of reasons for attending college—or on the lists of your classmates'—is "I want to change." Although most people do not come to college for the express purpose of changing, change is certain to happen during your college years. The key to dealing with change is to realize that change is the only thing in this world that is assured, short of death and taxes.

Whatever your reasons for attending college, if you embrace the notion that change is going to occur and respond to change by guiding it along, nurturing your new relationships with peers and professors, learning to study effectively, becoming involved in campus activities, and opening your mind to different views and ideologies, college will be a "moment in time" that you can carry with you for the rest of your life. You will be building on your best.

■ **AN INSIDER'S VIEW**

Kelvin Woods
Midlands Technical College
Columbia, South Carolina

Change for me is very difficult, so the decision to return to college as a mature student was not an easy one. I was worried about my age and I had to make several major changes in my life to accomplish my goals of working and acquiring an advanced education. I had to adapt my personal habits and ideas to fit the requirements of being a full-time college student.

It is difficult to juggle a full-time job and attend school full-time. I have to plan out a study schedule, which sometimes is any moment that I'm not at school or work. I had to change and learn how to study effectively. This was one of the biggest changes in my life. I am still amazed at the amount of time studying requires.

I also had to change my life to squeeze in time to be a husband and a home owner. It is not always easy to do this, and my wife has been very supportive in helping me obtain my goals. You have to change yourself and become self-disciplined in order to be successful.

I also found that I had to change how I felt about myself and others. This came about from being in the classroom with fellow students who were ten or more years my junior. This was not an easy thing to do, since I was a police officer for almost ten years. I felt I had more life-experience than they did, which caused some difficulty in accepting some of their ideas. Well!!! I was wrong in believing that the younger students couldn't teach me anything. I watched how they helped each other through tough assignments and I struggled on my own. I had to change and learn how to communicate with them. I had to learn how to learn from them. This was not easy, but it certainly has been rewarding.

Change is necessary for you if you are going to be successful in college and in life. You should never be afraid to change, just guide it along and make it work for your benefit. If your goals are to be successful in school, you should feel good about yourself, because you can be successful if you learn how to embrace change and put forth an honest effort.

> Education is the knowledge of how to use the whole of oneself. Many use one or two facilities out of a score with which they are endowed. One is educated who knows how to make a tool of every faculty; how to open it, how to keep it sharp, and how to apply it to all practical purposes.
>
> H. W. Beecher, educator

The Significance of Your College Experience

In your lifetime many events, people, places, and things will alter your views, personality, goals, and livelihood. Few decisions, people, or travels will have a greater influence on the rest of your life than your decision to attend college and the years you spend in structured higher learning. College can mean hopes realized, dreams fulfilled, and the breaking down of social and economic walls that may be holding you captive.

Before reading any further, jot down some thoughts about college life, what you value about being in college, and what you expect from your institution.

While in college, I want to achieve . . .

1. _____

2. _____

3. _____

4. _____

I feel college is significant to my life because . . .

1. _____

2. _____

3. _____

4. _____

From my college I expect . . .

1. _____

2. _____

3. _____

4. _____

My college expects from me . . .

1. _____

2. _____

3. _____

4. _____

Noted authors and experts on the first-year student experience John Gardner and Jerome Jewler (1995) suggest that students undergo several life-altering changes and developments during their college years. Some of the changes they cite are

- Self-esteem grows
- Political sophistication increases
- The need for control or power declines
- Autonomy or independence grows
- Appreciation of beauty deepens

Our observations of college students reveal these changes also. If your professor were to make a video of you as first-year students and allow you to view it as seniors, you would be astounded at the changes in you. Beyond changes in appearance you would see development in attitudes, values, judgment, and character. Generally, college tends to teach students to be more gentle, more accepting, more open, and more willing to get involved in their community and to share their resources; often, college creates in students the desire to continue to learn.

No one, not all the researchers in the world, not your authors, not your professors, not even your friends, can put a real value on the experience that college provides or the degree of change you will undergo. The value differs for each student, and, it is private. You may share with others the benefits of your higher education, but fundamentally, the results of these years are quietly consumed by your character, your actions, and your values. Some people will change a little, some people will change a lot. For all, however, change is coming.

What Do You Want?

Thinking about Your Choices

Today, you face many decisions. Some of them will affect the rest of your life. Some changes and decisions will be of your own making; others will be beyond your control. Some will be easily altered; others will hold for the long run.

Before you read further, think about where you are at this very moment and where you want to be in the coming years. Remember the quotation, "If you don't know where you are going, that's probably where you'll end up." The following activity is one of the first cornerstones of this book. It requires you to look at your current status, your peers, your past, and your aspirations and is intended to guide you in evaluating your life, attitudes, and thoughts. Take your time, be honest with yourself, and think in terms of realistic goals.

1. Define success. _____

_____

_____

2. Name one person whom you deem successful. Why is that person successful?

_____

_____

3. List one accomplishment that you want to achieve more than any other in

your life. _____

_____

4. How do you plan to achieve this accomplishment? _____

_____

_____

5. What part will your college experience and education play in helping you reach this accomplishment? _____

_____

_____

6. In what way have you changed the most in the past six months? _____

_____

_____

_____

7. Was this change peaceful? Why or why not? _____

_____

_____

8. Describe the most stressful change you have undergone to date. _____

_____

_____

_____

9. Describe the least stressful change you have undergone to date. _____

_____

_____

10. Describe the most important change in your life to date. _____

_____

_____

11. What do you hope to change in yourself over the next 12 months? _____

_____

_____

12. What will you have to change about yourself to achieve success as you defined it in question? _____

_____

_____

Changes in the Days to Come

One of the first changes you will notice about college is the degree of freedom you are given. There are no tardy notes to be sent to the principal's office, no hall passes, no mandates from the state regarding attendance, and, usually, no parent telling you to get up and get ready for school. You may have only one or two classes in a day. "Great!!" you say, and maybe you're right. This freedom can be wonderful, but it can also be dangerous. Many people do their best when they are busy and have a limited amount of time to accomplish a task. College can give you more freedom than you are used to. You need to learn how to handle it quickly, before the freedom that is intended to liberate you destroys you. Chapter 5 will help you with priority management.

Another change coming your way involves the workload for your courses. The workload is likely to be greater than what you are used to. You may be assigned a significant amount of reading as homework. Although you may have only two classes in one day, the rule of thumb is that for every hour spent in class, a *minimum* of 2 hours should be spent in review and preparation for the next class. Quick math: if you are taking five classes and are in class for 15 hours per week, you need to spend 30 hours studying; this makes a 45-hour week—5 hours more than a normal work week for most people! Not I, you may say, and you may be right. It all depends on how wisely you use your time and how difficult the work is. However tempting, don't make the mistake of putting off assignments for very long. Waiting until the last minute may cause serious problems for you sooner or later, probably sooner. And, think about your schedule before you register to make sure that you have enough time to deal with the demands of the courses you have selected. Talk to friends, hall assistants, and returning students about your schedule; see what they think about it. Although you may have to register for your first semester without benefit of these resources, thereafter be sure to make good use of them.

You have probably already noticed a difference between your college professors and your high school teachers in terms of teaching style and relationship with students. You may have encountered a teaching assistant, usually a graduate student who serves as an instructor in first-year and sophomore-level classes. Unlike teaching assistants, college professors take on many different roles. They are involved in research, community and college service, teaching, and committee work.

A significant change you may face in the days and weeks to come is the amount of diversity in the people around you. You may have come from a high school with a fairly homogeneous student body. If you went to school in a metropolitan area such as New York, Atlanta, Los Angeles, Boston, Chicago, Dallas, or Washington, D.C., you may be used to a diverse student body. Regardless of your background, you will meet students, peers, and classmates whose views, values, customs, language, sexual orientation, race, ethnicity, and origin are 100 percent different from yours. You will encounter people who are atheistic and people who are ultra religious; people who are pro-life and people who are pro-choice; people are against the death penalty and people who support capital punishment; people who abhor interracial relationships and people to whom race does not matter. If you come from a region or from a family in which these positions are not openly expressed, you must prepare yourself for change and realize how much you can learn from diversity. Chapter 3 is dedicated to understanding diversity.

Remember, the most healthy way to deal with change is to realize that it happens daily and to prepare for it.

Premises about Change

The author and speaker Eric Olesen (1993) suggests that a person undergoes three stages when change occurs:

> The real voyage of discovery consists not in seeing new lands, but in seeing with new eyes.
>
> M. Proust

- Letting go

- Making the transition

- Starting over

Letting go means simply agreeing that change is coming. **Making the transition** entails being in the middle of change, dealing with new ideas, new methods, and new information. **Starting over** means accepting that change has occurred. Starting over requires persistence and determination; it brings with it problems, tortures, pain, and yes, beauty. Yet starting over can be easier than letting go. Sometimes, to let go it helps to remember the old saying, "every time a door closes, a window opens."

Several characteristics are common to any change, regardless of its cause.

CHANGE IS NEVER EASY

Even the best changes in our lives, such as earning a promotion, having a baby, getting married, or buying a home, come with a degree of stress and anxiety. To deal effectively with change, we need to realize that even good change is often hard.

CHANGE IS ALMOST ALWAYS MET WITH RESISTANCE

Human beings are creatures of habit. We tend to resist change, especially if the change affects a security that has been enjoyed for a long period of time.

THE PERSON WHO INITIATES CHANGE IS ALMOST ALWAYS UNPOPULAR

The person who initiates change, the change agent, frequently is an outsider or is relatively new to a situation. By suggesting that change could improve a situation, this person threatens the status quo. Olesen (1993) suggests that when change occurs, everyone begins at zero, everyone begins anew. Thus, people who have been secure for years fear losing that security, and the person proposing change often becomes the subject of rumor and innuendo.

CHANGE CREATES UNFAMILIAR GROUND

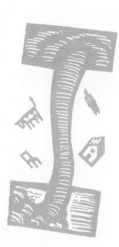

We are more comfortable with what is familiar to us; the unfamiliar can be scary and sometimes dangerous. We may be inclined to shy away from change because it creates unfamiliar ground. It may be helpful to recognize that every new step is basically unfamiliar—for you and everyone around you. Not to take the step only limits your possibilities and weakens your opportunities. It is important to learn how to move out of the comfort zone, where you feel secure and warm. A ship may be safe in the harbor, but that is not what ships are made for.

CHANGE TAKES COURAGE

Often, because of the resistance and negative reactions of others, a change agent will remain quiet. It takes courage to initiate change.

Even if a change will eventually benefit others, you sometimes have to risk unpopularity and ridicule to initiate change.

Physical and Emotional Reactions to Change

By the time you've read this far, you've probably gone through a few changes. Were they exciting? Were they stressful? When you experience change, your body typically goes through a process of physical and emotional change as well. Learning to recognize these symptoms in order to control them can help you control the stress that can accompany change. You may already have experienced some of these emotional and physical changes since arriving at your college. Take a moment now to reflect on your first few days in your new surroundings.

1. How did you feel on entering your first class in college? _____

_____

_____

_____

2. If you are married or have children, how did you feel when you had to leave your family today? _____

_____

_____

3. How did you feel when you received your first syllabus outlining the content of a course? _____

_____

_____

4. If you are living on campus, what physical changes occurred just before you met your new roommate? _____

_____

_____

_____

For most of you, these events caused a degree of stress and anxiety because you were experiencing change. Chapter 10 will help you learn to deal with the stress associated with college and everyday events.

Don't be shocked if your body and spirit begin to feel

- Nervousness
- Stress
- A sense of being on the edge
- Fear
- Fatigue
- Guilt
- Homesickness
- Denial
- Anger
- Depression

These feelings are normal when you go through a powerful change, but they are temporary. If any of these feelings are becoming overwhelming or life threatening, seek counseling, talk to your friends, go to your advisor, or speak with your professors. These people are your support group; use them. Don't wait until it is too late to ask for help. Don't hide your feelings and pretend that nothing is wrong. Change is not easy. One of the most crucial steps in successfully dealing with change is realizing that it can cause problems.

> In human life there is a constant change of fortune; and it is unreasonable to expect an exemption from this common fate.
>
> Plutarch

Preparing for and Dealing with Change

Take a moment to reflect on what changes you might expect to experience this semester. Then list each change in one of the wedges on the change wheel: record the change that you consider most stressful or the biggest change in the largest wedge; put the smallest change or the change that causes the least stress in the smallest wedge. As the semester continues, reflect on this wheel to see if you were correct in your assumptions about the change and stress you face in college.

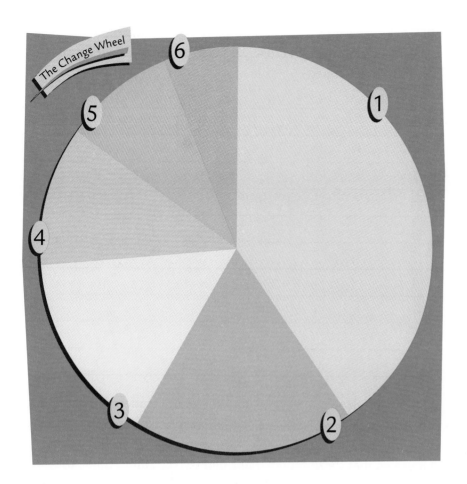

The Change Wheel

Your world is different now that you are in college. People are different, attitudes are different, and classes are different. List some of the most obvious differences between your high school and your present institution.

1. _____

2. _____

3. _____

4. _____

5. _____

Beyond the changes just listed, what changes have taken place in your personal life?

1. _____

2. _____

3. _____

4. _____

5. _____

Take a moment to think about where you want to be in one year, two years, or when you graduate. What changes will have to take place for this to happen?

_____

_____

_____

_____

_____

_____

_____

Successful people in general, and successful students in particular, know how to deal with change and embrace the positive effects that change brings. A study of people who were more than 100 years old revealed that these centenarians had two common traits: they accepted death as a part of life, and they knew how to deal with change.

ATTITUDES THAT HINDER CHANGE

You can develop attitudes that hinder change and stop growth. Such attitudes are dangerous because they rob you of opportunity, happiness, growth, and goals. These attitudes include:

- The "I can't" syndrome
- Apathy, or the "I don't care" syndrome
- Closed mindedness
- Unfounded anxiety
- Fear of taking chances
- Loss of motivation
- The "let someone else deal with it" syndrome

If you can learn to control and watch out for these negative attitudes, you will begin to view change as a wonderful and positive life-long event.

CORNERSTONES for dealing with change

The successful student prepares for change. The cornerstones for dealing with change will help you create a healthy attitude about change. You may wish to refer to these cornerstones on a daily basis in the coming weeks.

GET INVOLVED IN THE CHANGE

Most people let change happen to their lives; they don't try to direct the focus or the outcome of the change. Successful students get involved in the change that is happening in their lives and try to direct it toward a desirable outcome.

LET GO

The successful student knows how to let go of past events, places, and people who are not assisting in creating the desired future outcome.

HOLD ON

Holding on to people, memories, trinkets, and dreams that make you feel good and help you see today and tomorrow more clearly is healthy. The successful student knows when to hold on and when to let go. Both actions may be difficult, but both are necessary for dealing with change.

ASK FOR HELP

One of the most effective ways to deal with change is to ask for help, so don't be afraid or ashamed to do so. Many people will be having experiences similar to yours. Asking for help is the first step in finding a person to whom you can relate and with whom you feel comfortable.

DEVELOP A SENSE OF HUMOR

Laughter is one of the most powerful medicines available. Remember to laugh, smile, lounge around outside, admire the oak trees in the fall or flowers in the spring, eat a pizza, go to the movies. Too often, we forget to nourish our souls; we forget to feed our spirit a daily diet of beauty, and it grows tired and weary. Laughing and refusing to take life too seriously can provide the shot in the arm you need to make it through the week.

FOCUS ON THE OUTCOME

To deal effectively with change you need to look beyond the moment of fright or anxiety, to develop the ability to see the outcome. There has to be rain before there can be a rainbow. Moving beyond immediate gratification and realizing the potential long-term gain is a positive way to approach change.

SEARCH FOR TRUTH

Successful students know that they do not possess all the answers to every question; no one does. If you can look at change as a way of searching for the truth and deeper meaning, change will become less frightening, even though the truth can sometimes be unsettling.

TAKE RISKS

Although it does not come easily, learning to take calculated risks can be a tool for positive and steady growth.

HAVE AN OPEN MIND

Some of the most successful students deal with change by being open-minded, unbiased, and ready to listen to all sides.

VIEW CHANGE AS GROWTH

If your life is peaceful all the time, you are probably not growing or changing. Of course, everyone experiences times when things go according to plan and there is little change or anxiety; this is normal. But, if nothing has changed in your life in the past five years, you are most likely stagnating. Change means growth and as such, it is healthy; without change, there can be no progress.

COMMUNICATE WITH PEOPLE

One of the most effective and healthy ways to deal with change is to talk with others about it. Tell your friends and family what you're going through. Seek out people who may be going through, or may have recently gone through, the same changes.

MAINTAIN PERSPECTIVE

"This, too, shall pass." You may have to rely on this motto for a while to help you realize that change will not always be this stressful or this painful. Think clearly. Think about all the changes you've experienced in the past and how small they seem now compared with what they felt like when you were going through them. Keep things in perspective and deal with them accordingly. Enjoy the ride—"you shall pass this way but once."

The transition from one place to another is never easy, even when it is what you want. Entering college has forced you to assume new roles, develop new friendships, meet new people, work under different circumstances, and perhaps adjust your lifestyle. These changes form the very essence of the college experience; they create wonderful new experiences. Now is the time for you to seek new truths, associate with new and different people, read books that you will never have time to hold in your hands again, develop a solid philosophy of life, explore new religions, go to plays, buy season football tickets, join a club, read a book of poetry, go on a picnic with friends, sing, laugh, cry, write home, and love much. The winds of change are coming—fly!

How Well Do You Understand Yourself?

If you have been using the Internet, you know that URLs change frequently and are sometimes removed. If you cannot locate a particular exercise, try to find one that provides similar information.

The first four chapters in this book are devoted to helping you learn more about yourself. The Keirsey Temperament Sorter is designed to help you discover some new things about you. Using the Internet address (`http://sunsite.unc.edu/jembin/mb.pl`), locate the Keirsey instrument and complete the test. The computer will automatically score the test for you.

By examining your score, what did you learn about yourself? _____

_____

_____

_____

_____

What are your dominant factors? _____

_____

_____

_____

_____

What are your secondary factors? _____

_____

_____

_____

_____

How do you think your self-esteem correlates with your dominant factors? _____

_____

_____

_____

_____

The one minute journal

In a minute or less, jot down one major idea you learned from this chapter.

In the midst of winter, I finally learned that there was in me an invincible summer.

Albert Camus

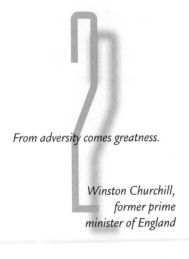

2

Planning Your Dreams: Motivation, Goal Setting, and Self-esteem

This story began about ten years ago, when I met Leeah, a shy, sullen, withdrawn young woman, the daughter of an acquaintance. I had met Leeah's mother, a hotel housekeeper, while conducting training for the hotel staff, and knew that Leeah's mother had high hopes for her daughter. I thus took an interest in Leeah.

Leeah's family lived under difficult circumstances. Her father

had abandoned the family when Leeah was a small child; her mother had supported the seven of them by working as a housecleaner. Leeah's mother was concerned for her daughter's future. Leeah had had few opportunities, little direction, and little encouragement—almost everything was working against her.

I asked Leeah about her plans after graduation from high school. Leeah responded that she would like to go to college but could not afford it. I asked to see Leeah's transcript and learned that she was ranked very high in her graduating class. Leeah had more opportunities to go to college than she could imagine.

I helped Leeah apply for grants and scholarships and gave her a job as a student assistant. It soon became obvious that Leeah was a serious student. She studied at every opportunity; she read voraciously, from classics to current events; she asked questions; and she observed everything. She was like a sponge, literally soaking up knowledge. Gradually, she began to change. She became more friendly and outgoing, her confidence seemed to increase, and she smiled more often. Leeah was becoming a classic example of the powerful difference that education plus motivation, goal setting, and improved self-esteem can make in a person's life.

Leeah matured rapidly and began to take on more responsibility. Although she had been awarded an endowed scholarship, which provided full tuition and room and board, she

She began to realize what she could become.

worked two jobs. She upgraded her wardrobe, bought a car, and became totally independent. She still conferred with me occasionally, but Leeah made most of her own decisions. She was growing quickly and positively, and she was beginning to know who she was and what she wanted. More important, she began to realize what she could become. All her professors quietly marveled at the dramatic changes in her.

When Leeah took my class as a junior, she was introduced to goal setting, motivation strategies, and using adversity as a strength. She listened quietly, asked questions, and quickly designed her own blueprint for success. Her self-esteem was at a high level. Leeah was on her way because she had a clearly defined plan and she was willing to pay the price to reach her goals.

Prior to graduation, Leeah applied to several prestigious graduate schools and was accepted at every one. She graduated with honors and was awarded several scholarships for graduate school. She continued to work two jobs during the summer; she wanted to save money for her expenses so that she would not have to work during the semester and could concentrate on her studies. Leeah was highly motivated, goal directed, and focused on her plans.

Several years later, Leeah stopped by my office. She had earned her CPA credentials and was a full-fledged accountant working for a Big Eight accounting firm. Dressed in a classic suit and carrying a briefcase, Leeah stood up straight, smiled with confidence, and spoke assertively. I was struck with the awesome difference between this Leeah and the one I had met those many years ago.

Today, Leeah owns her own accounting firm, and several CPAs work for her. She is a great example of the power of motivation and goal setting.

You Are on Your Own

The great thing about going to college as a traditional student is that you get to be your own boss. For the first time in your life, you will be free to make your own decisions, choose your own friends, and determine your own destiny. There will be no one to tell you to go to bed, to get out of bed, to wear a jacket, to comb your hair, to clean up your room, or to watch out for strangers. You have the freedom to party all weekend, drink beer for breakfast, and ignore your homework—that's the good news.

On the other hand, you will probably not have teachers who know your parents or live in your neighborhood. Instead, you will have university professors who expect you to take responsibility for your own learning. To many of them, you will be just another face in a big sea of faces. You probably won't know many people when you arrive on campus, and you will meet people who are very different from those you have known. The competition will be tough; many professors will be more demanding and less empathetic than the teachers you may be used to, and their directions and information may not be as specific.

If you are a nontraditional student, you will be able to explore new career choices, learn from traditional students, expand your opportunities, and broaden your personal and professional network—all exciting possibilities. However, you will be juggling schedules, racing back and forth between work and school, readjusting to the demands of completing assignments and writing papers, and, at the same time, helping your family adjust to your new schedule.

Your classmates will hail from all over the country and perhaps from all over the world. People of many races and religions will cohabit your college campus. You will attend classes with people of all ages—10-year-old prodigies, 35-year-old businesspeople, 40-year-old homemakers, and 70-year-old grandmothers, as well as the traditional students, aged 18 to 23. Some of these people will expose you to ideas unlike any you have experienced. You will associate with highly motivated, scholarly students, fraternity and sorority members, big name athletes, and students whose focus is partying and having a good time (for as long as they are able to last before flunking out). Welcome to college life and all the excitement and challenges it will bring you!

As you can see, you will need to be highly motivated to accomplish all the expectations that lie before you. In this chapter you will be given tips for staying motivated, setting goals, and keeping your self-esteem at a satisfactory level. You will soon notice the direct correlation between motivation, self-esteem, and goal setting. The higher your self-esteem, the more motivated you are and the more likely you are to set and accomplish significant goals.

When you finish this chapter, you will be well ahead of the average college student because you will have learned to put direction in your life, to plan for success, and to focus on what you want. After completing this chapter, you will be able to

■ Discuss the importance of motivation in your life

■ Discuss the potential role of adversity in your success

■ Discuss the role of fear and desire in motivation

■ Use visualization of your goals to help you achieve them

■ Differentiate between short-term and long-term goals

■ Write goals, objectives, and action steps for accomplishing your own personal strategic plan

■ Discuss the importance of self-esteem.

■ Evaluate your own self-esteem.

- List strategies for improving self-esteem.

- Display a winning attitude and image.

You should know up front that all first-year students don't go on to a second year. According to a recent study, 32 percent of students attending 2,432 participating institutions did not return for their sophomore year (Higher Education Research Institute, UCLA, 1989). But you should also know that you have the ability to become a sophomore and to graduate from college or you would not have been admitted. If you truly want to graduate from college and at the same time enjoy a full social life, you can do it.

Before looking at the motivation process, take a minute to examine your levels of motivation and self-esteem as they are now.

AT THIS MOMENT...

5 = Strongly Agree

4 = Agree

3 = Don't Know

2 = Disagree

1 = Strongly Disagree

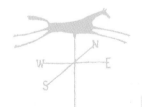

1. I am a highly motivated person at this time.
   1 2 3 4 5

2. I depend on other people to motivate me.   *1 2 3 4 5*

3. I prepare every day for success.   *1 2 3 4 5*

4. I avoid letting my fears stand in my way.   *1 2 3 4 5*

5. I visualize myself succeeding when I try something new.
   1 2 3 4 5

6. I know how to write goals with measurable objectives, deadlines, and action steps.
   1 2 3 4 5

7. I like who I am.
   1 2 3 4 5

8. I feel confident in my ability to do well in college.
   1 2 3 4 5

9. I am able to speak up in class.
   1 2 3 4 5

10. I think positive thoughts about myself and have a positive mental image of myself.
    1 2 3 4 5

A SELF-ASSESSMENT Total your points from these ten questions. Refer to the following rating scale to determine where you stand in relation to motivation, goal setting, and self-esteem.

0–10 *Your motivational level is low. You do not spend a lot of time thinking about your future plans; you probably do not write your goals down or review them daily; you probably have a poor self image.*

11–20 *Your motivational level and self-esteem are somewhat low. You may have goals, but you do not write them down and you do not review them daily. You do not think highly of yourself.*

21–30 Your motivational level and self-esteem are average. You may write down your goals, but you probably do not have them posted and you do not review them daily. Your self-esteem is "up and down."

31–40 Your motivational level, goal-setting skills, and self-esteem are above average. You probably write down your goals, post them, and refer to them frequently. You typically feel good about yourself.

41–50 Your motivational level, goal-setting skills, and self-esteem are excellent. You write down your goals, post them, refer to them daily, establish time lines for their completion, and update them often. You almost always feel confident and OK with yourself.

Now, refer to your journal and respond in writing to your findings. Consider the following questions when writing in your journal:

1. Do you feel that you are a motivated person?

2. What motivates you?

3. Do you have a major cause of insecurity and low self-esteem?

4. What makes you insecure and unsure?

5. On what occasions do you feel most secure and capable?

6. Who makes you feel good about yourself?

Motivation Comes from Within

The first thing you need to know about motivation is that it comes from within—no one else can give it to you. Someone may pump you up or temporarily inspire you, but on a daily basis you must reach down inside and find the will to motivate yourself. Your college experience will make hundreds of unique, life-changing opportunities available to you, but no one will force you to take advantage of these gifts. Keep your eyes open, desire to achieve, and be willing to pay the price; college will open the door for you to make your dreams come true.

Deciding what you really want in life makes it possible to direct your energies toward a specific goal. It is much easier to become motivated if you are passionate about achieving something specific.

> Everything starts as somebody's daydream.
>
> Larry Niven,
> science fiction author

Attitude—The First Step in Getting What You Want

How many people have you met who turned you off immediately with their negative attitudes? They whine about the weather or their parents; they verbally attack people who differ from them; they degrade themselves with negative remarks. Listen for the negative comments people make and the messages they send out about themselves. When people continually feed their brains negative messages, their bodies respond accordingly.

You may feel that you have had enough of attitude. Your parents talked to you about it, your teachers hounded you about it. But it is important! The impact of a bad attitude on your self-esteem is overpowering, and the importance of a good attitude should not be underestimated. Focusing on the positive can bring dramatic changes in your life.

We all know that life sometimes deals bad blows, but your goal should be to be positive much more often than you are negative. Positive attitudes go hand in hand with energy, motivation, and friendliness. People with positive attitudes are more appealing; negative people drive others away.

Listen to yourself for a few days. Are you whining, complaining, griping, and finding fault with everything and everybody around you? Do you blame your roommate for your problems? Is your bad grade the professor's fault? Are your parents responsible for everything bad that ever happened to you? If these kinds of thoughts are coming out of your mouth or are in your head, your first step toward improved self-esteem is to clean up your act.

To be successful at anything, you have to develop a winning attitude, you have to eliminate negative thinking. Begin today: tell yourself only positive things about yourself; build on those positives; focus on the good things; work constantly to improve.

Thought for every morning: This is going to be a great day for me!

Winners get up early with an attitude of "I can't wait for this day to start so I can have another good day." O.K., O.K.—so you may not get up early, but you can get up with a positive attitude. Tell yourself things that will put you in the right frame of mind to succeed. When you are talking to yourself—and everybody does—feed your brain positive thoughts. Think of your brain as a powerful computer; you program it with your words, and your body carries out the program.

Pay attention to the messages you send out to others as well. What kinds of remarks do you make about you and about others when you are with your friends? Do you sound positive or negative? Do you hear yourself saying positive things such as

Oliver is such a great guy!

My parents are really cool.

I'm making great progress on my exercise program.

I had a long talk with Dr. Smythe, and he really does care about his students.

My golf game is coming around.

Jane is teaching me to dance, and I'm loving it.

List some positive statements you say to yourself. _____
_____
_____
_____

Now list some negative statements you say to yourself. _____
_____
_____
_____

You have spent time preparing for college—you have gotten your clothes ready, bought supplies, adjusted to roommates. Now you need to spend an equal amount of time preparing your mental attitude to succeed. You will have a great advantage over most other entering students, indeed, over most other people, if you have a winning attitude. Start developing it today! Use the following steps today and every day.

PREPARING FOR SUCCESS

1. Prepare for success the evening before—organize your clothes and books and make a list of things you need to do the next day. (You'll read more about this in Chapter 5.)

2. Eat properly, get enough rest, and exercise. Winners know that a fit mind requires a fit body.

3. Get up early (at least occasionally), sing in the shower, think about positive outcomes.

4. Talk to yourself using positive "I" statements: "I will have a good day today;" "I will perform well today because I have prepared to do well;" "I will be happy and positive and outgoing."

5. Read motivational books as well as biographies of famous people who overcame adversity to reach their goals. Reading will help keep you motivated while expanding your knowledge!

6. Practice your religion and seek spiritual wellness.

CHOOSE YOUR FRIENDS CAREFULLY

Although your motivation and attitude belong to you and are uniquely yours, they can be greatly influenced by the people with whom you associate. People do tend to become like the people with whom they spend time.

As a new college student, you have a clean slate where friends are concerned. You need to choose your very best friends carefully. Of course you want to spend time with people who have interests in common with yours. That's a given. But you also want your friends to have ambition, good work habits, positive attitudes, and high ethical standards. Seek out people who read good books, watch educational television programs, are goal oriented, and don't mind taking a stand when they believe strongly about something. Find friends who will work out with you, go to the library with you, attend plays and concerts with you. One of the best ways to make the most of your college education is to befriend people who have interests and hobbies that are new to you. Staying focused is much easier if you surround yourself with positive, motivated, goal-oriented people.

> They who have conquered doubt and fear have conquered failure.
> James Allen

Overcoming Doubts and Fears

Fear is a great motivator; it probably motivates more people than anything else. Unfortunately, it motivates most people to hold back, to doubt themselves, to accomplish much less than they could, and to hide the person they really are.

One of the biggest obstacles to reaching your potential may be your own personal fears. If you are afraid, you are not alone; everyone has fears. It is interesting to note that our fears are learned. As a baby, you had two fears: a fear of falling and a fear of loud noises. As you got older, you added to your list of fears. And, if you are like most people, you let your fears dominate parts of your life, saying things to yourself like: "What if I try and fail?" "What if people laugh at me for thinking I can do this?" "What if someone finds out that this is my dream?"

You have two choices where fear is concerned. You can let fear dominate your life, or you can focus on those things you really want to accomplish, put your fears behind you, and go for it. The people most successful in their fields will tell you that they are afraid, but that they overcome their fear because their desire to achieve is greater. Barbra Streisand, recording artist and stage performer, becomes physically nauseated with stage fright when she performs, yet she faces these fears and retains her position as one of the most popular entertainers of our time.

Name one of the smallest fears you have now. What can you do to overcome it?

_____

_____

_____

_____

_____

_____

What is your greatest fear? Why do you think you have this fear? _____

_____

_____

_____

_____

_____

_____

What steps do you think you can take to overcome this fear? _____

_____

_____

_____

_____

_____

_____

MOVING OUT OF YOUR COMFORT ZONE

Successful people face their fears because their motivation and ambition force them out of their comfort zones. Your comfort zone is where you know you are good, you feel confident, and you don't have to stretch your talents far to be successful. If you stay in your comfort zone, you will never reach your potential and you will deny yourself the opportunity of knowing how it feels to overcome your fears.

Deciding to go to college probably caused you some level of discomfort and raised many fears: "What if I can't make good grades?" "What if I flunk out?" "What if I can't make the team?" "What if I can't keep up with the kids just out of high school?" "What if I can't do my job, go to school, and manage a family at the same time?" The mere fact that you are here is a step outside your comfort zone—a very important step that can change your life dramatically.

Everyone has a comfort zone. When you are doing something that you do well, and you feel comfortable and confident, you are in your comfort zone. When you are nervous and afraid, you are stepping outside your comfort zone. When you realize you are outside your comfort zone, you should feel good about yourself because you are learning and growing and improving. You cannot progress unless you step outside your comfort zone.

The circle shown represents your comfort zone. Think of several activities in which you feel confident and comfortable and write them in the circle.

Comfort Zone

Now look at the illustration that shows the same comfort zone circle with three larger circles around it. The larger circles represent taking small steps to move out of your comfort zone.

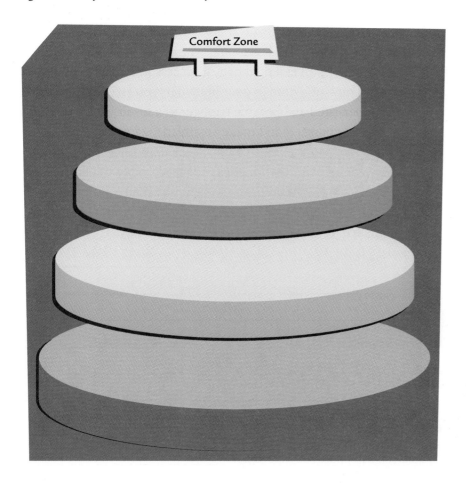

In each of the three larger circles write something that you would like to do, to experience, to be, to take a risk on—something that would take you out of your comfort zone. Work on taking the first step outside your comfort zone by tomorrow. When you are at ease with that one, move to the next circle. Say to yourself, "A little better every day."

Incorporate this practice into the habits that you want to form. Plan to take one step outside your comfort zone every day. Soon your comfort zone will be greatly expanded, and you will become more confident and able to move on to the next steps more quickly.

DEALING WITH ADVERSITY AND FAILURE

To be motivated, you have to learn to deal with failure. Have you ever given up on something too quickly, or gotten discouraged and quit? Can you think of a time when you were unfair to yourself because you didn't stay with something long enough? Did you ever stop doing something you wanted to do because somebody laughed at you or teased you? Overcoming failure makes victory much more rewarding. Motivated people know that losing is a part of winning: the difference between being a winner and being a loser is the ability to try again.

If you reflect on your life, you may well discover that you gained your greatest strengths through adversity. Difficult situations make you tougher and more capable of developing your potential. Overcoming adversity is an essential part of success in college and in life.

Think of a time in your life when you faced difficulties but persisted and became stronger as a result. Perhaps you failed a course, didn't make an athletic team, lost a school election, had a serious illness, broke up with a long-term boyfriend or girlfriend, or experienced your parents' divorce. If you are a nontraditional student you may have been fired from a job or passed over for a promotion, suffered through a divorce, or experienced a death in the family.

Describe your experience of adversity. _____

_____

_____

_____

_____

_____

_____

What did you learn from this experience? _____

_____

_____

_____

_____

_____

_____

How can you use this experience as a reminder that you can overcome adversity,

learn to grow from it, and become a better person as a result of it? _____

_____

_____

_____

_____

_____

_____

If you study the lives of the people we consider our greatest heroes—presidents, executives, movie stars, generals, athletes—you will discover that they all share the ability to persist in the face of adversity. Before he was elected president, Abraham Lincoln dropped out of grade school, went bankrupt while operating a store, lost a bid for a seat in his state legislature, started and failed at another business, twice ran for the House and lost, twice ran for the Senate and lost, and lost a bid for the vice presidency. After he was elected president and during the Civil War, Lincoln was disliked by many Americans. He endured an unhappy marriage and the death of his son. He delivered a speech that today is admired as a classic but was widely ignored at the time. Still, he persisted and is now one of our most revered presidents. Few people are aware of Lincoln's failures, but the world knows of his successes.

Dolly Parton, world-famous entertainer, was raised with 12 brothers and sisters in a two-room mountain shack. Her family was extremely poor. They had no screens on their windows; chickens ran in and out of their house; and Dolly and her sisters made their own makeup from Merthiolate and baking flour. At her high school graduation, seniors were asked to stand and share their plans. When Parton announced that she was going to Nashville to become a songwriter, the audience broke up laughing. The next day she boarded a bus for Nashville, where she struggled to survive until Porter Wagoner discovered her. The secret to Dolly Parton's success was that she had a dream and she never took her eyes off this dream, she persisted even when people laughed at her, she paid the price, and she overcame adversity. Dolly Parton has talent; yet many talented people are never successful because they fail to persist in the face of adversity.

The Goal-Setting Process

Goal setting itself is relatively easy. Many people make goals, but fail to make the commitment to accomplish those goals. Instead of defining their goals in concrete, measurable terms, they think of them occasionally and have vague, unclear ideas about how to attain them. The first step toward reaching a goal is the commitment to pay the price to achieve it. Opportunities abound everywhere; commitment is a scarce commodity.

When you are ready to make a commitment to achieve your goals, write them down, along with steps for accomplishing deadlines that

When I was 11 years old, my mother died. Although my father was there to raise me, I had to assume many adult responsibilities while still attending elementary school. As I grew up, there were several careers that I thought about pursuing; however, they became what seemed to be unreachable dreams to me. I attended college after graduating from high school, but I was not motivated enough to continue. I never set any type of goals for myself. I quit during my second year of college.

I began to think about what I really wanted out of life after leaving college, and how I could make a difference with my life. I never knew the importance of establishing goals until I re-enrolled in college a few years later. I then decided that college was a good place to start fulfilling my educational goals.

Goals are dreams that you put into action. I realized that in order to accomplish what I wanted in life, I must set goals and work hard to accomplish them. Also, I realized that I must have an idea about the time frame in which I wish to accomplish my ambitions. I started by setting short-term and long-term goals and making sure that they were achievable. I realized that setting unrealistic goals would not help me achieve my dreams, but would lead only to excessive frustration.

I decided to start out with short-term goals and when I accomplish them, I will progress to my long-term goals. I believe if you have the patience and discipline for setting and accomplishing short-term goals, you will have a great chance at accomplishing your long-term goals. Setting goals has made me improve in every aspect of my life; from personal situations to study habits. Setting goals has helped me make better decisions regarding my career. I just keep reminding myself that I am not a failure until I stop trying . . . then, and only then, will I fail.

must be honored. These goals are your targets. Now you are ready to act, to begin accomplishing your goals, and you need to do so without delay. Be prepared to fail, because you surely will fail some of the time, but you must be equally committed to getting up and trying again. Your commitment to success must be so strong that quitting would never even occur to you.

When you have accomplished your goals, you need to begin the process again. Successful people never get to a target and sit down; they are always *becoming*. They reach one goal and begin dreaming, planning, preparing for the next accomplishment.

A Goal Is Anything You Can Have, Be, or Do

Before you work on your goals, think about goals in these terms: you can *have* a boat; you can *be* a member of the student government, or you can *play* a musical instrument. Use the following questions to help you decide what goals to set.

■ DO, BE, OR HAVE EXERCISE

What do I want to do? _____

_____

_____

What do I want to be? _____

_____

_____

What do I want to have? _____

_____

_____

> To thine own self
> be true.
> Shakespeare

CHARACTERISTICS OF ATTAINABLE GOALS

It is usually easier to set goals than to achieve them. To be able to set attainable goals, you need to know their characteristics. Attainable goals must be

- **Reasonable.** Your goals need to be based on your abilities, desires, and talents. If you made terrible grades in English composition and hate to sit at a computer, you shouldn't set a goal to become a writer. On the other hand, if you are a star athlete and love to work with young people, your goal might be to become a coach.

- **Believable.** To achieve a goal, you must really believe it is within your capacity to do so. You may want a sailboat very badly, but the cost may be prohibitive. If you want it, but don't believe you can get it, you are probably fooling yourself—at least at this stage of the game.

- **Measurable.** A goal needs to be concrete and mesurable in some way. If you set a vague goal, such as "I want to be happy," you cannot know if you've attained your goal, because you have no way of measuring it.

- **Adaptable.** Your goals may need to be adapted to changing circumstances in your life. You may begin with a goal and find that you have to change direction for one reason or another. Maybe you don't like this goal once you learn more about it or perhaps some insurmountable obstacle arises. You might have to adjust your expectations and the goal itself in order to achieve it.

- **Controllable.** Your goals should be within your own control; they should not depend on the whims and opinions of anyone else. For example, if your goal is to learn to play golf well enough to score 90, you need to control your practice and the times you play; you do not want to practice based on the needs of your roommate, who may have strengths and weaknesses different from yours.

▪ **Desirable.** To attain a difficult goal, *you* must want it very badly. You cannot make yourself work for something just because someone else wants it. If you have always dreamed about becoming a teacher of young children set this as your goal; it will be extremely difficult for you to stay on course to become a medical researcher because your parents want you to follow in their footsteps.

Look at your responses in the Do, Be, or Have Exercise. Measure them against the characteristics of attainable goals. Do you think the goals you discussed are within your reach? Can you control events that could prevent you from attaining them? Do you really believe you can do what you want to do? Can you measure your success? Can these goals be adjusted if necessary? Do you really want to do, be, or have the things you listed?

HOW TO WRITE GOALS

Webster's New Collegiate Dictionary defines a goal as "the end toward which effort is directed." The process of goal setting involves deciding what you want and working to get it. Goals can be short term or long term. Short-term goals can usually be accomplished within six months or a year, although they could be accomplished in a much shorter time. "Within six months I will save enough money to spend a week skiing in Vail" is a short-term goal; "Within six years, I will become a certified public accountant (CPA)" is a long-term goal.

When you write goals you need to include a goal statement, action steps, and target dates. The goal statement should be specific and measurable, that is, it should entail some tangible evidence of its achievement. An example of a goal statement is "I will lose ten pounds in six weeks." You can make goal statements from intangibles if you can devise a way to measure the desired outcome. For example, "I will develop a more positive attitude by the end of six weeks as evidenced by at least three people's commenting on my improved attitude and by my dealing positively with at least three negative situations weekly."

After you write the goal statement, you'll need to create specific action steps that explain exactly what you are going to do to reach your goal. Then decide on a target date for reaching your goal.

The final step in writing goals is to write a narrative about what your goal accomplishments will mean to you. If your goals don't offer you significant rewards, you are not likely to stick to your plan. An example format for a goal statement, with action steps, target date, and narrative follows.

Goal Statement:

Action Steps

1. _____

2. _____

3. _____

Target Date:

Narrative Statement:

_____

_____

_____

_____

Now you are ready to begin the exciting adventure known only to goal setters. To help you get started, we'll discuss some common areas for which you might want to set goals. After reading this section, however, you might want to venture off in a different direction. That's perfectly all right, since these are *your* goals.

■ CATEGORIES FOR GOALS

Personal or Self-Improvement. Set a goal that relates to your personal life. For example, you might want to work on punctuality.

Goal: I will be on time and prepared for all my classes this semester.

Academic. You might set a goal of reaching a certain grade point average. A word of caution: don't set an average of 4.0 as your goal if you have always been a B student; strive first for a B+. Remember the "a little better every day" philosophy.

Goal: I will earn at least a B+ on my first English exam.

Family. You might want to do something nice for your parents or for a younger sibling.

Goal: I will go home for my brother's birthday and will spend the weekend doing whatever he wants to do.

Career. You could decide on a major or choose some electives that will allow you to explore new areas of interest.

Goal: I will take an elective in sports management next semester to determine if this major appeals to me.

Financial. Now is a good time to focus on managing your money, even if you don't have a great deal of it. Set a goal that will help you to establish good financial management practices.

Goal: I will save $400 by Christmas so I can buy my family gifts.

Community Service. Set a goal to become involved in community service. Serving other people can be as rewarding for you as it is for those you help.

Goal: I will volunteer ten hours of my time each week to the Madison Hospital in the area of childrens' physical therapy.

Social. You might want to work on certain social skills, such as restaurant etiquette or dancing, or you might want to limit your social life to certain activities.

Goal: I will take a course in dancing to improve my social skills.

Health. Set goals that will help you to relieve stress and stay in top condition. You might set goals that involve exercise, proper diet, or enough rest.

Goal: I will limit my fat gram intake to 36 grams per day.

Spiritual. Set goals to keep you spiritually fit. Anything that makes you feel alive and well can be part of your spiritual goal, such as walking on the beach or watching a touching movie.

Goal: I will participate in at least three activities each week that are spiritually rewarding and renewing for me.

Sometimes a few weeks or months after setting a goal, it becomes apparent that you are not moving in the right direction to achieve that goal. For example, suppose you came to college on a football scholarship, but after practicing for a while you realize that you don't have the time both to play football and to pursue the rigorous curriculum that will enable you to become a doctor. You can always change your goal. If you change just because accomplishing the goal is difficult, you are defeating yourself. But if something happens to prevent you from ever achieving your goal, or you realize it isn't right for you, or you decide to move in a new direction that is more appealing or important to you, it is appropriate to change your goals.

On the following pages, you will be given the opportunity to set a goal to begin working on right away. This goal should be a short-term goal. By working on short-term goals first, you will be able to feel the excitement of accomplishing a goal rather quickly. Think carefully about the most important things you could do to improve yourself and to make you feel better about yourself.

Use the Personal Strategic Success Plan form to write a goal statement with action steps, target date, and narrative statement for a goal that can be accomplished in a month. Then begin working on a plan to accomplish the most important goals you need to reach this semester. At the same time you are working on your most important semester goals, focus on completing the short-term, one-month goal. Reward yourself when you complete this goal. You may reproduce this sheet as often as you like.

■ PERSONAL STRATEGIC SUCCESS PLAN This is going to be the best year I have ever experienced. I am going to college, where I will succeed because I am prepared to succeed. I have a head start on most people because I have an excellent attitude, I am willing to work hard, and I have a plan for what I want to accomplish. Every day I will get a little better. I will think positive thoughts, act decisively, push myself out of my comfort zone, and take care of my body and my mind. *Nothing will stop me from accomplishing my goals!*

Once you have mastered the steps in goal setting and motivation outlined in this chapter, you are on the way to building the best person you are capable of becoming. Use these ideas as you move through college and later in your career. Remember that goal setters usually accomplish the most.

After you have finished writing your goals, use the following evaluation plan to determine if your goals are appropriate.

> **Passion will carry you through a lot; disappointment, pain, the worst of times and the best of times.**
> Eva Marie Saint, Academy Award– and Emmy Award–winning actress

Goal Statement:

Action Steps

1. _____
2. _____
3. _____
4. _____

Target Date:

Narrative Statement:

_____
_____
_____
_____
_____
_____
_____
_____
_____
_____
_____
_____
_____
_____
_____
_____
_____
_____
_____
_____
_____
_____
_____
_____

I hereby make this promise to myself.

Date _____ Signature _____

EVALUATION PLAN FOR YOUR GOALS

Do I really want to achieve this goal enough to pay the price and to stick with it?

What is the personal payoff to me if I achieve this goal?

Who will notice if I achieve this goal? Does that matter to me?

How realistic is this goal? Am I way over my head for this stage of my development?

Do I need to reduce my expectations so I won't be disillusioned in the beginning and increase the difficulty of my goal only after when I have reached the first steps?

Can I control all the factors necessary to achieve this goal?

Is this goal specific and measurable?

Does this goal contribute to my overall development? Is this goal allowing me to spend my time in the way that is best for me right now?

How will I feel when I reach this goal?

Will my parents and friends be proud that I accomplished this goal?

Will the achievement of this goal increase my self-esteem?

The Impact of Self-Esteem on Your Motivation

Some people are not as motivated as they might be because they suffer from poor self-esteem. Self-esteem is how you feel about yourself—the value you place on who you are as a person—and it impacts everything you do. Your grades, relationships, extra-curricular activities, and motivation can all be impacted by your self-esteem.

You might think of self-esteem as a photograph of yourself that you keep locked in your mind. It is a cumulative product developed through many experiences and through relationships with many people.

People who demonstrate a high degree of self-esteem and confidence usually have five characteristics.

These characteristics are considered key to a person's ability to approach life with confidence, maintain self-direction, and achieve outstanding accomplishments. As a high school senior or on the job, you might have felt pretty good about yourself, but since you have entered a new environment, you may find that your self-esteem has been lowered. It is natural to be nervous or to feel threatened as you move into a new environment. If your self-esteem is healthy, you will soon feel comfortable again.

All of us have had experiences that have negatively affected our self-esteem and kept us from being as successful and happy as we could be. Can you think of experiences in your past that have had a negative impact on your self-esteem?

Before reading any further, familiarize yourself with these important things to remember about self.

- If you change your feelings about your self, your behavior will change. Learning to love your self will most likely result in better grades, improved relationships, and more direction and focus in your life.

- Your self needs routine, consistency, and patterns; therefore, introducing change to your self may bring some resistance. (Change is the hardest thing for human beings to face, even when they want it and when they know that in the long run, it will be best.)

Influences on Self-Esteem

The concept of the child within has been a part of our culture for more than 2,000 years. Psychotherapists have used different names for this concept: Donald Winnicott called it the "true self," Carl Jung used the "Divine Child," and Emmett Fox used the "Wonder Child;" many others refer to it as simply the inner child.

The child within is the very best part of us. It is our joy, enthusiasm, energy, spontaneity; it determines whether we are funfilled and happy, as well as fulfilled and productive. Troubled, dysfunctional families damage the inner child, resulting in anxiety, fear, emptiness, confusion, and low self-esteem. No matter what your past, however, you can learn to improve your self-esteem and along with it, your happiness and success.

Many young girls believe that girls can't do math as well as boys; young men who show emotion may be ridiculed for not "being a man;" some boys believe that girls are more academically oriented than are boys. These and similar notions, perpetuated by society, can contribute to the development of poor self-esteem and a damaged inner child.

Many people, especially women, are unhappy with their appearance, and these feelings often engender low self-esteem. The disorders bulimia and anorexia may arise when thinness is inextricably linked to a person's feeling good about herself—these disorders are found primarily in women. College students carry the extra baggage of a societal value that links self-esteem and appearance, again, particularly for women. Sandra Haber, a New York City psychiatrist, specializes in eating disorders.

Many people are obsessed with their outer shell and believe that if they can be thin enough or wear the right clothes or have big muscles, they will somehow miraculously be loved by others.

Haber believes that what we see in the mirror is what we take into all our roles. In other words, how we see ourselves equates to our self-esteem.

Many people are obsessed with their outer shell and believe that if they can be thin enough or wear the right clothes or have big muscles, they will somehow miraculously be loved by others. Recently there has been an increase in the number of young boys taking steroids to pump themselves up, even though they know it can be dangerous to their health. Paying attention to physical appearance is important and can improve your feelings about yourself, but emphasis on appearance without attention to mental and emotional well-being will rarely bring about lasting change.

Alcoholism, drug dependency, abusive relationships, and promiscuous sexual behavior are other symptoms of low self-esteem. No one is born with low self-esteem. Many of the root causes of low self-esteem begin in childhood and are often in the form of "messages" given to us by parents, teachers, peers, and others. Since many of these thoughts relate to poor self-esteem originated many years ago, you need to realize that correcting these problems may take time. The result is worth the effort, however, if you learn to love and value yourself.

■ BEHAVIORS ASSOCIATED WITH POOR SELF-ESTEEM Some of the most frequently observed behaviors associated with poor self-esteem are listed here. Place a check by the characteristics you recognize in yourself.

_____ *Am critical of myself and others*

_____ *Have guilty feelings*

_____ *Set unrealistic goals*

_____ *Have many physical complaints*

_____ *Hold extreme views of life*

_____ *Have little belief in my capabilities*

_____ *Am destructive*

_____ *Abuse substances*

_____ *Put myself down*

_____ *Am self-destructive*

_____ *Have difficulty facing reality*

_____ *Worry unreasonably*

_____ *Feel that I must always be dressed perfectly*

_____ *Place too much importance on brand-name clothing*

_____ *Always arrive late*

_____ *Always arrive early*

_____ *Have difficulty establishing intimacy*

_____ *Am preoccupied with what others may think of me*

_____ *Cannot adequately face the demands of life*

Now look over your responses and list the three items that you think have the most negative impact on your self-esteem.

1. _____

2. _____

3. _____

Later you will refer to this list and work on improving these areas.

Improving Your Self-Esteem

WHY SHOULD YOU DO IT?

You may be wondering what the point of all this is, why should you worry about self-esteem when you already have concerns about grades, work, laundry, relationships, and a million other things? Who has time for all this extra stuff? Maybe you think you can wait to worry about your self-esteem when you finish college. The reason you need to be concerned *now* is that your grades, work, social life—everything—are tied up with your self-esteem.

Several outstanding psychiatrists and professors stress the importance of addressing self-esteem in the educational process, believing that self-esteem goes hand-in-hand with academics. Carl Rogers

No one expects you to be perfect or to know everything.

(1972), a noted psychiatrist who has developed many psychological theories and ideas about self-esteem, wrote, "Sometimes I feel our education has as one of its major goals the bringing up of individuals to live in isolation cages." Leo Buscaglia (1982), a well-known professor who has taught for years on the subjects of love and relationships, asks, "How many classes did you ever have in your entire educational career that taught you about you?"

Your relationships with others—friends, parents, children, professors, bosses, spouses—depend on how well you have developed your own self-esteem. You are not an isolated human being. Every day you must relate to others, and your self-esteem will influence the kinds of relationships you build. You will continue to meet new people and face new challenges with the people you know as you grow and mature, and these challenges are likely to increase in complexity. Unless you are planning to live a life alone in the woods, you will rely on your ability to relate positively to all kinds of people. The basis for those relationships lies within you, in your self-esteem.

WAYS TO INCREASE YOUR SELF-ESTEEM

■ **TAKE CONTROL OF YOU OWN LIFE** If you let other people rule your life, you will always have poor self-esteem. You will feel helpless and out of control as long as someone else has the power over your life. Part of growing up is taking control of your life and making your own decisions. Get involved in the decisions that shape your life. Seize control—don't let life happen to you!

■ **ADOPT THE IDEA THAT YOU ARE RESPONSIBLE FOR YOU** The day you take responsibility for yourself and what happens to you is the day you start to develop your self-esteem. When you can admit your mistakes and celebrate your successes knowing you did it your way, you will learn to love yourself much better.

■ **REFUSE TO ALLOW FRIENDS AND FAMILY TO TEAR YOU DOWN** You may have family or friends who belittle you, criticize your decisions, and refuse to let you make your own decisions. Combat their negativity by admitting your mistakes and shortcomings to yourself and by making up your mind that you are going to overcome them. By doing this, you are taking their negative power away from them.

■ **CONTROL WHAT YOU SAY TO YOURSELF** "Self-talk" is so important to your self-esteem and to your ability to motivate yourself positively. Your brain is like a powerful computer and it plays messages to you continually. If these self-talk messages are negative, they will have a detrimental impact on your self-esteem and on your ability to live up to your potential. Make a habit of saying positive things to yourself: "I will do well on this test because I am prepared." "I am a good and decent person, and I do deserve to do well." "I will kick the ball straight."

■ TAKE CAREFULLY ASSESSED RISKS OFTEN Many people find risk taking very hard to do, but it is one of the very best ways to raise your self-esteem level. If you are going to grow to your fullest potential, you will have to learn to take some calculated risks. While you should never take fool-hardy risks that might endanger your life, you must constantly be willing to push yourself out of your comfort zone.

■ DON'T COMPARE YOURSELF TO OTHER PEOPLE You may never be able to "beat" some people at certain things. But it really does not matter. You only have to beat yourself to get better. If you constantly tell yourself that you "are not as handsome as Bill," or "as smart as Mary," or "as athletic as Jack," your inner voice will begin to believe these statements, and your body will act accordingly. One of the best ways to improve self-esteem and to accomplish goals is simply to get a little better everyday without thinking about what other people are doing. If you are always practicing at improving yourself, sooner or later you will become a person you can admire—and so will others!

Using Motivation and Self-Esteem to Accomplish Goals

You have now studied some of the basic principles of motivation, and you understand the impact that self-esteem can have on your ability to achieve your plans and dreams. At this point, you are ready to begin the actual goal-setting process.

CORNERSTONES

for motivation, goal setting, and self-esteem

- Know what you want and focus your motivation on achieving it.

- Don't give into defeat; use failure as a stepping stone to succeed next time.

- Step outside your comfort zone every day.

- Use the power of positive mental images; love yourself.

- Turn loose negative thoughts.

- Broaden your circle of friends choosing some people who are different from you.

- Picture yourself happy, successful, and achieving your goals.

Planning and Goal Setting

If you have been using the Internet, you know that URLs change frequently and are sometimes removed. If you cannot locate a particular exercise, try to find one that provides similar information.

All first-year students come to college hoping to be successful, but some arrive on campus with few ideas of exactly what they want to achieve. Still fewer have defined exactly what success is to them. This exercise is designed to help you focus on what you want to achieve, do, or be. The more focused and goal oriented you are, the more successful you will become. Access the URL (`http://www.ozcmail.com.au/~berghous/goals ct.html`). Read the article on planning and goal setting and then respond to the following questions.

What are some reasons that cause people to fail to set goals? _____

_____

_____

What are some of the "positives" mentioned in the article that might help you become more adept at setting goals? _____

_____

_____

Why is it important that goals be your very own and that they not be influenced by others? _____

_____

_____

Why must goals be written? _____

_____

_____

Name several other "musts" to be considered when setting goals. _____

_____

_____

Access the URL (http://www.aboutcollege.com/goals.htm) which is an article about goal setting. Read the article and respond to the following questions.

What do you picture yourself doing five years from now? _____

_____

_____

_____

Who could you talk to to get advice on how to accomplish at least one of your goals? _____

_____

_____

_____

What questions would you ask this person? _____

_____

_____

_____

Some of your goals should be personal and some should be professional. List at least two in each category:

Personal: _____

_____

_____

_____

Professional: _____

_____

_____

_____

What obstacles are keeping you from accomplishing your goals? _____

_____

_____

_____

The one minute journal

Write about one specific piece of information that you read in this chapter that you think will motivate you.

3

The meaning of life is felt through

relationships . . .

Relationships with others and with

one's own self.

From what it is at birth to whom

we become as a child . . .

The meaning of life flows through

relationships . . .

Learning from nature, the sages,

our peers,

From our emerging selves in a state

of becoming.

Jonas Salk, scientist

Understanding Differences: A Celebration of Diversity

The professor called him Jimmie, but the class would later learn that his name was Jhi' Ming. He was a small, quiet man who sat in the front row of the communication class. During the fifth week of class, four team leaders were asked to choose members to form a group that would work together to solve a problem. The first leader chose Shawanda, the second leader chose Phillip, the

third leader chose Clifford, and the fourth leader chose Carolyn. The selection process continued until everyone had been chosen except Jimmie. The first leader, Nanette, was forced to include Jimmie in her group by the process of elimination. There were no audible sounds of dismay, but everyone in the class knew that Jimmie had not been chosen because he was "different". Jimmie was considered different because he was older than the others, because he was married, because he had children, and because he was Vietnamese.

The groups began working right away. Nanette asked for advice on solving her group's problem. Several times, Jimmie suggested solutions, but his opinions were ignored and others were sought. Jimmie finally stopped contributing to the conversation and sat quietly with his group until time was called.

After class, Nanette told another group leader that she was disappointed that she had to "get stuck with that oddball!" They laughed and continued down the hall to another class. Fortunately, Jimmie did not hear the conversation as he had already left.

Little did Nanette, the other members of her group, or their classmates know what they were to learn from Jimmie during the remaining weeks of the semester. This shy, quiet man had a remarkable history, which would change the lives of every student who had the privilege of being in his class. This man called

Nanette began to realize what a wealth of information, history, and honor each of us carries in our souls.

Jimmie, whose opinions were shut out by his group, would send shock waves through the hearts of 24 students during his presentation the next week. Those students would never again call him an "oddball."

"My name is Jhi' Ming Yen," he began. "Today, I will share with you the history of my life and the triumph of my family." The class was somewhat uninterested at first, but within a minute, Jhi' Ming's story had begun to affect every person in the class. "When I was 15, I saw my mother die in front of my eyes. She, my father, my sister, and I were running toward the American embassy in Saigon when she was shot in the back by a sniper's bullet. She was carrying my eight-year-old sister when she fell to her death. My father, sister, and I were able to make it aboard one of the last evacuation helicopters before my country fell." The class was completely silent.

"When we finally arrived in the United States, I found work in New York City as a dishwasher. My father cleaned kitchens in hotels— menial work for a man who had served in the medical profession in Vietnam for over 15 years. My father's degree meant nothing in this country. We had to begin our lives all over again . . . 'from scratch,' as you would say."

His story unfolded like a book of horrors and triumphs as the class listened, for the first time, to the quiet man who sat in the front row. He continued, describing what had happened in the years since he left his country, his mother, and the only life and world he knew. Jhi' Ming was no longer a stranger. When the class was over, Nanette and her classmates finally understood how important it is to

give people who are different a chance. They began to realize what a wealth of information, history, and honor each of us carries in our souls. As others shared their lives and histories, the class began to see that people of a different culture, age, marital status, sexual orientation, ethnicity, race, religion, and educational level can add monumental dimensions to another's life. They began to learn how to celebrate diversity, because they allowed Jhi' Ming to share the priceless gift of his life's story. Equally important, perhaps, they learned how Jhi' Ming had adjusted to American culture; he and his family worked hard, earned respect, and made it in a new world.

You Are a Culture of One

During our formative years, each of us develops a unique set of values, beliefs, and customs. We are virtually programmed, based on who raises us, our race, our nationality, where we live, where we go to school, our religion or lack of religion, our friends, our relatives, and our experiences and opportunities. Like fingerprints, no two people with their beliefs, customs, and experiences are exactly alike. This amazing phenomenon is what makes human beings interesting and makes the differences we see in people from cultures other than our own especially interesting as well as personally educational.

Culture is learned. People are born into a culture, but their culture is not a physical trait, such as eye color or hair texture. You probably developed, or absorbed, most of your personal culture from your family. The process is almost like osmosis in plants, it is as though culture seeps gradually through your skin. Many of the beliefs and values you embrace have been passed from one generation to another.

In college, you are likely to find your values, beliefs, and actions changing as you meet new people and become involved in new situations and as your horizons broaden. Quite simply, your college experience enhances your understanding, and your cultural beliefs change as a result. This change is known as **cultural adjustment**. You can, and should, expect to have your beliefs greatly tested—and perhaps adjusted—before you graduate.

Cultural adjustment doesn't mean that you must abandon your family, church, basic values, and friends. It may mean, however, that you need to reevaluate why you feel the way you do about certain situations and certain groups. You may have been taught that people belonging to a certain group are bad. As you learn and grow, you may find that they are not bad at all, just different from you, and, like Nanette and her classmates, you will probably discover that this different culture is one to be celebrated.

In this chapter you will be given an opportunity, through a series of scenarios, to put yourself in other people's shoes and thereby gain a better understanding of how someone different from you may feel. After studying this chapter you will be able to

- Discuss different types of prejudices, including racial, religious, sexual, gender, regional, and international

- Develop communication skills for relating to people from different cultures and backgrounds

- Identify your own biases, attitudes, and expectations

- Learn to examine critically your own thinking and actions relative to people from different cultures

- Plan ways in which you can eliminate your personal prejudices and biases

- Discuss strategies for interacting more effectively with people from a variety of cultures

Take a moment now to assess your current feelings relative to people who are different from you.

5 = Strongly Agree

4 = Agree

3 = Don't Know

2 = Disagree

1 = Strongly Disagree

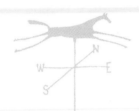

1. Many of my friends have backgrounds different from mine.   *1 2 3 4 5*

2. I readily accept people from different regions.   *1 2 3 4 5*

3. I am interested in knowing people whose nationality is different from mine.   *1 2 3 4 5*

4. I am open to relationships with people who are of a different race from me.   *1 2 3 4 5*

5. I can accept people who are homosexual or bisexual.   *1 2 3 4 5*

6. I have been taught things by my parents or others that may contribute to my personal biases.   *1 2 3 4 5*

7. I am accepting of people who belong to religions that promote beliefs very different from my own.   *1 2 3 4 5*

8. I would be comfortable dating someone from another nationality, race, or religion.   *1 2 3 4 5*

9. I am accepting of the attitudes, values, and beliefs of people of generations other than mine.   *1 2 3 4 5*

10. I am comfortable around people who are physically, emotionally, or mentally challenged.   *1 2 3 4 5*

A SELF-ASSESSMENT Total your points from these ten questions. Refer to the following rating scale to determine where you stand in relation to dealing with cultural diversity.

0–10   You have a great deal of difficulty relating to and accepting people from different cultures, nationalities, races, religions, sexual orientations, and age groups.

11–20   You have some difficulty relating to and accepting people who have different beliefs and backgrounds from yours.

21–30   You have learned to accept some cultural differences, but you still have some difficulty fully accepting all people.

31–40   You are more accepting of cultural differences than is the average person.

41–50   You have very few biases or problems relating to people of different cultures and beliefs.

Now, refer to your journal and respond in writing to your findings. Consider the following questions when writing in your journal.

1. Why is it important to understand someone from another culture?

2. Discuss one prejudice you have toward a particular group of people. Why do you have these beliefs?

3. What steps do you think you can take to reduce your biases?

The Components of Culture

Sometimes we can tell that people are from a different culture or ethnic group because of the way they look and dress or by the way they speak—dress and speech are two visible signs of culture. Other components of culture are not so visible. Sociologist David Popenoe (1993) identifies five components of culture.

- Symbols

- Language

- Values

- Norms

- Sanctions

Symbols are items that stand for something, such as the American flag. Most Americans respect the flag and know that it stands for honor, duty, patriotism, service, and freedom. People of other nationalities might not understand that the stars and stripes on the American flag are significant symbols in American culture. The key to relating to people from any culture is understanding. Some common symbols and what they stand for are as follows:

purple signifies royalty in some cultures

a *pineapple* is a sign of welcome and hospitality in the Southern United States

red is associated with anger in some cultures

a *hexagonal sign* indicates Stop! in several countries

Name a symbol from your culture: _____

What does this symbol mean? _____

Language is another important component of culture; the meaning of a word can vary across cultures. For example, if you were to ask for a biscuit in England, you would get a cookie. How many different words can you think of for that nonalcoholic, carbonated beverage many of us like to drink? Pop? Soda? Soft drink? Coke?

The African American culture in the United States has given some words meanings that are specific to that culture. For example, a "shade and fade" haircut is typical of language used by African American college students. Other cultures within the United States have done the same.

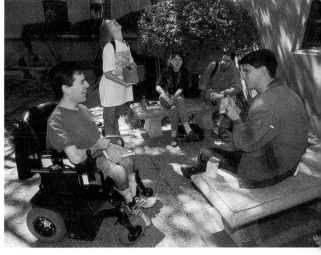

What is a phrase specific to your culture? _____

_____

What does it mean? _____

_____

Values are typically based on family traditions and religious beliefs. What is wrong in one society may be acceptable in another. Most young people in the United States would be unwilling to allow their parents to choose their future spouse, yet in many countries this practice is still common. Some religious services are joyous celebrations; others are formal and solemn. The African American AME church is usually filled with soulful, joyous singing, while the Primitive Baptist Church may include songs not accompanied by musical instruments and may be more solemn—there is no one proper way to conduct a religious ceremony. Like so much else, what is correct depends on the culture.

Name a value of the culture in which you were raised: _____

_____

Why is this value important to you? _____

_____

Norms relate directly to the values of a culture or society—they are how we expect people to act based on those values. In an elegant restaurant, for example, you expect people to conduct themselves with more dignity than you might expect in a fast-food restaurant.

What is a norm in your culture? _____

_____

Why do you think it is a norm? Why is it important? _____

_____

Sanctions are the ways in which a society enforces its norms. When a society adopts a set of norms that are upheld as valuable, it typically seeks a way to enforce these norms through formal laws. In every society there are people who do not abide by the rules, people who break the law. A person in the United States who breaks the law may be sent to jail or may be required to perform community service. In some cultures punishment is much more severe. For example, the punishment for stealing in some Middle Eastern cultures may be to sever the thief's hand. In the United States this punishment would not be acceptable, but elsewhere it is.

What is a sanction in your culture? _____

_____

Why do you think it is a sanction? _____

_____

_____

If you have a desire to understand and appreciate others, you can learn to celebrate diversity and gain valuable lessons from almost everyone you meet.

The Power of an Open Mind

To experience other people and to receive the benefits of knowing someone, you need to enter all relationships with an open mind. If you have a derogatory mind-set toward a race, an ethnic group, a sexual orientation, or a religion, for example, you have internal barriers that can keep you from getting to know who a person really is.

Everyone you meet is a game player to a certain extent. Most people do not allow you to see who they are until they know they can trust you. We protect ourselves and our egos by holding back, covering up, and otherwise shielding ourselves from possible hurt and pain until we know a person will accept us for who we are. Regardless of background, all people want to be accepted for themselves; they want to be able to act naturally and to be comfortable just being themselves.

Learning to interact with people from different cultures is a matter of keeping an open mind and looking at each person as an individual, not as a race, a class, or a religion. We cannot help but be influenced by what we have been taught and what we have experienced, but we can overcome prejudices and biases if we view people as individuals. If you intend to grow as an educated person and as a human being, you will need to expand your capacity to accept and understand people from different cultures within and outside your country.

MY CULTURE OF ONE

Take some time now to identify exactly who you are as a culture of one.

Describe the place(s) where you grew up—the people, the size of the city or town, the schools you attended. _____

_____

_____
_____
_____

Discuss some of the basic beliefs you learned from your family. _____

_____
_____
_____
_____

Do you think some of the beliefs you learned from your family might not be right for you today? Why or why not?

_____
_____
_____
_____
_____

Discuss some of the basic beliefs you learned from your teachers.

_____
_____
_____
_____

Name some ways in which your background is reflected in your culture of one, for example, what you wear, your hairstyle, some of the slang phrases you use.

_____
_____
_____
_____
_____

_____
_____
_____
_____

Discuss how you may have been influenced by extracurricular activities, sports, friends, or travel. _____
_____
_____
_____
_____
_____

Discuss how religious teachings or the absence of religious training has influenced your beliefs. _____
_____
_____
_____
_____

If you are in a relationship, describe how your partner has influenced your beliefs, actions, or values. _____
_____
_____
_____

If you have children, discuss how your values, ideas, and associations have changed since you became a parent.

_____
_____
_____
_____
_____
_____

You Are the Center
of Your Own Universe

Make use of your responses to the "Culture of One Exercise" together with other pieces of information from your personal background to complete the next exercise. The figure inside the box represents you as you are today. The boxes the figure is juggling represent all aspects of your cultural background that have shaped your beliefs, customs, and habits. In each box, list one source of your personal cultural development. On the lines below, write the basic beliefs, rules, or values you learned from that source. For example, your religious background (source) may have prohibited attending movies (rule). Looking very carefully at your personal background, try now to identify those unique beliefs and experiences that make you who you are. (See the examples provided.)

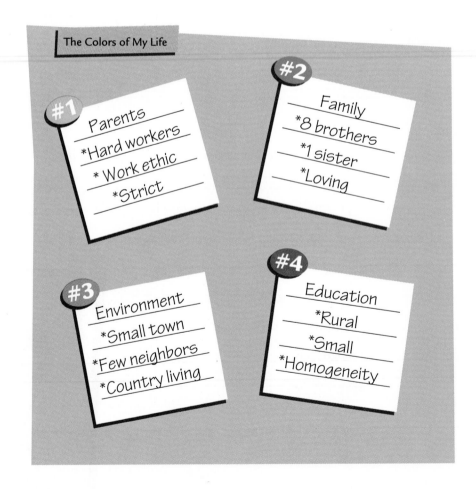

The Colors of My Life

#1
Parents
*Hard workers
* Work ethic
*Strict

#2
Family
*8 brothers
*1 sister
*Loving

#3
Environment
*Small town
*Few neighbors
*Country living

#4
Education
*Rural
*Small
*Homogeneity

The Colors of My Life

#1

#2

#3

#4

#5

#6

Changing Demographics
of the United States

The demographics of the United States are radically different from what they were 50 years ago. Projections point to an increasingly diverse mixture of people with whom you will work and interact; therefore it is increasingly important for you to learn to understand, work effectively with, and accept that you live in a global community with people from a variety of cultures. According to Carol Kleiman, author of *The 100 Best Jobs for the 90's and Beyond*, "Only fifteen percent of the net new entrants to the workforce will be white men, as the nation's demographics shift and present-day minorities and women become the majority of entry-level workers" (1992).

Perhaps the best opportunity for you to experience multiculturalism will be at college, particularly if you are attending a large or metropolitan university. When you graduate you will have a great advantage if you have become cross-culturally oriented and learned to communicate effectively with people who embrace values, beliefs, and customs that are different from yours.

Researchers Gardenswartz and Rowe (1993) suggest that one cultural mindset determines our behavior and attitudes, from when to smile and with whom to make eye contact, to how to deal with conflict and talk to a supervisor. For example, a teenager's not looking an adult in the eye during a conversation may be considered disrespectful by Anglos, but is a sign of

respect for Hispanics. One of the great problems we all face in dealing with cultural diversity is that we typically interpret other people's behavior through our own cultural mindset. Americans may find it strange that in some cultures parents arrange their children's marriages. People from Asian cultures may have difficulty understanding the relative lack of respect Americans show toward elders compared with their culture, in which older people are revered. You can greatly enhance your education this term if you make up your mind to look beyond your own cultural mindset when you encounter people from other cultures.

Who Are You?

In *Managing Diversity*, Gardenswartz and Rowe (1993) refer to "individuals as being like the proverbial onion with layer upon layer of cultural teaching." They suggest that cultural identity is shaped by the following factors:

- **Ethnicity**—the ethnic group with which a person identifies and the person's native language

- **Race**—the racial group or groups with which a person identifies

- **Religion**—the organized denomination or sect to which a person subscribes or rejects

- **Education**—the level and type of learning a person receives

- **Profession/field of work**—the type of work a person is trained to do

- **Organizations**—groups or associations to which a person belongs or has belonged, such as the military, a scouting group, a labor union, or a fraternal organization

- **Parents**—the messages, verbal and nonverbal, given by a person's parents about ethnicity, religion, values, cultural identity, etc.

In addition to these powerful cultural influences, gender, family, peers, and place of birth also significantly determine a person's cultural identity.

The Golden Rule

for Celebrating Diversity

At one time or another, most of us have been exposed to the Golden Rule: Do unto others as you would have them do unto you. As you work to improve and expand your knowledge of cultural diversity, it may help you to look at this rule from a different angle. In considering the following scenarios, first by yourself and then with a group, see if you can apply a new version of the Golden Rule: **Do unto others as they would have you do unto them.**

Robyn Williams
The California State University
at Fresno
Fresno, California

When I was younger, I considered myself to be an open minded person. I knew that the color of one's skin, one's socio-economic status nor one's age mattered. The problem was that I had attended an affluent, predominantly white high school where I never really had to deal with any issues of race or age or background.

While in college, I took a job as a tutor in the English Writing Center. Students from across campus would come to the center to receive assistance with grammar, punctuation, and the overall writing process. As a tutor, I worked with students in groups of three or four several times a week. The majority of students enrolled in the class were ESL (English as a Second Language) students. The students I worked with ran the gamut in terms of ethnicity. I tutored Asian students, Loation students, African American students, and Hispanic students. This proved to be one of the most important and the most rewarding experiences of my life.

Many students stand out in my mind, but one student always comes to the forefront. Vang was from Laos and had only been in the United States two years. When he came to the group, he was very shy and did not interact with the group. His English was very broken and he was difficult to understand at times. Vang was never prepared for the group tutoring session. He never prepared a writing sample to share and when I asked the group to write during the session, he would only doodle. I assumed that he did not really want to be there and I began to focus my attention on others in the group who seemed to want my help. Shortly after this, Vang stopped coming to the group sessions.

A few weeks later I saw Vang on campus and stopped to ask him why he had quit the group. He became teary-eyed and explained that his English was not very good and that he was ashamed and embarrassed by his ability. He felt that HE was wasting MY time! I was stunned; I had no idea that he felt this way. We talked for a while and he agreed to return to the group with a writing sample.

I must say that I had never read anything so moving. His grammar was poor and his sentence structure weak, but as he described the quality of his life in Laos and his journey to the United States, I began to doubt that I was not prejudice. I was ashamed that I had judged Vang before I knew him. I was ashamed that I had labeled a human being based on a few encounters.

I learned from Vang that people who are different from us can teach us so much about the world, human nature, honor, and hope. I realized that there is no textbook in the world that can give you the insight into a human being like interaction can. My experiences with Vang and others in the center opened my eyes as well as my heart. I know that I am a better person today. I am richly rewarded for having people of diverse backgrounds in my life. I encourage you to seek out diversity in your classes and during events on campus. You are not really living until you embrace all that the world and its people have to offer.

I THINK I WOULD...AN EXERCISE IN CULTURAL UNDERSTANDING

Respond to each scenario in the space provided. Discuss how the situation makes you feel, how you would feel if you were the person in the cultural minority depicted, and what you might do or say to improve this situation for everyone involved.

Your class may be asked by the instructor to discuss your responses to these scenarios in an open discussion. If so, be aware that these scenarios contain information sensitive to some of your classmates, perhaps to you. While the purpose of the discussion will be to help everyone understand how their classmates feel, each person in the class should be mindful of others' feelings. Later in Chapter 4, you will study critical thinking and you will learn that "thinking" and "saying" are two entirely different concepts. Think before you speak. Speak your mind openly, but carefully, to avoid damaging others' self-esteem. Remember, we all take in "messages" about ourselves from others.

You may find that some of your beliefs change slightly—or maybe even dramatically—as you work on these exercises. Growth that allows you to open up your mind, to move beyond biases and prejudices, and to seek to understand people who are different from you is positive growth.

■ SCENARIO #1 You and Jack, a friend from high school, are attending the same college. Jack has a physical disability that requires him to use a wheelchair. He was an outstanding basketball player and swimmer prior to a diving accident, which left him a paraplegic. Jack is an honor roll student. He is an avid basketball fan, attends all the games, and plays on a wheelchair team. He has a great sense of humor. He long ago dealt with his personal situation and now he even jokes about it. Jack is one of your favorite people.

Since you and Jack have been in class together, you have been noticing that people tend to treat him differently from others. Sometimes people talk loudly when talking to Jack, as if he couldn't hear. Because getting to and from classes is difficult, Jack has someone to help him maneuver around campus. One day you overhear a student talking to the person who is helping Jack as if Jack weren't there. "What happened to him?" "Can he use his arms?" Although Jack is handsome, friendly, and personable, he is usually left out of the many social activities in which other classmates participate. You know that your classmates would like and admire Jack if they got to know him.

How do you think Jack feels when people treat him as though he doesn't exist?

_____

_____

_____

_____

Why do you think some people have difficulty relating to people who have physical disabilities? _____

_____

_____

> You have to move to another level of thinking, which is true of me and everybody else. Everybody has to learn to think differently, think bigger, to be open to possibilities.
> **Oprah Winfrey,**
> **actress and television**
> **personality**

_____

_____

_____

What could you do to help Jack become accepted just like any other student?

_____

_____

_____

_____

What could you say to classmates that might help them understand how to relate to Jack better and might make them and him feel more comfortable?

_____

_____

_____

_____

■ SCENARIO #2 Douglas met Andy on the first day of class. Douglas struck up a conversation with Andy because he saw a tennis racket in Andy's gym bag—a welcome sight. Douglas had not found anyone to play tennis with since his arrival on campus. The two decided to get together later in the afternoon to play a game. When the game was over, each knew that he had found a friend. They discovered that they lived in the same residence hall, had the same professor for English, only at different times, and both loved to play tennis. As the semester progressed, Douglas and Andy became very close friends; they studied history together, went to hall parties together, ate together when their schedules permitted, and double-dated once or twice.

Douglas and Andy enjoyed many of the same sports and movies and had tastes similar in music. Douglas felt that he had met a true soul mate, and Andy could not have been happier to have Douglas to talk to and hang around with. Andy knew, however, that things could soon change. He had made a serious decision; before the Christmas break he would tell Douglas that he was gay.

Exams ended on Wednesday. Andy decided to break the news to Douglas on Tuesday night. They talked and laughed sitting on a bench outside the athletic center; then the conversation grew still, and Andy chose his words carefully. He told Douglas that he was gay and that he had been involved with someone at home for almost a year.

If you were Douglas, what would your reaction have been? _____

_____

Was Andy right to risk their friendship by telling Douglas about his sexual orientation? _____

_____

_____

_____

Should Andy have told Douglas sooner? _____

_____

_____

_____

If Douglas were to walk away from the friendship, how do you think Andy would feel? _____

_____

_____

_____

_____

Imagine that Douglas, a heterosexual, accepted Andy's orientation, but that Andy went on to say that he was interested in having a relationship with Douglas. How do you think Douglas would have reacted? _____

_____

_____

_____

Does being gay carry a cultural or social stigma? Why or why not? _____

_____

_____

_____

_____

■ SCENARIO #3 Jerry, an 18-year-old black student, was walking to his residence hall one evening after a fraternity meeting. A pickup truck slowed to match his pace as he walked along the side of the road. One of the two men in the truck leaned out the window and called him a "n----" and spat in his direction. As the men drove off, Jerry saw a Rebel flag displayed at the back of the truck.

On reaching his residence hall, Jerry noticed the same truck, now empty, parked outside the hall. As he neared the front door, Jerry heard racial slurs being yelled at him from a third story window directly above the entrance to the dorm. Clearly the students were very drunk. As Jerry unlocked the door, the slurs were mixed with threats to urinate on him. Jerry entered the residence hall just as drops of liquid fell around him.

How would you feel if you were Jerry? _____

_____

_____

_____

_____

What action, if any, do you think Jerry should take? _____

_____

_____

_____

_____

Do you think racial discrimination is a problem on college campuses? _____

_____

_____

_____

_____

■ SCENARIO #4 Tonya was a first-year student at a major research university. She had an excellent academic background. She had always loved science and math and was seriously considering a major that would allow her to incorporate her love of these subjects into a career. In her second semester at the university she enrolled in a calculus class taught by Dr. Ralph Bartlett. This class was especially important to Tonya for two reasons. First, Dr. Bartlett was the department chair for the program she was considering pursuing, and second, the course was her first college math course, so she wanted to start off strong.

On the first day of class Dr. Bartlett made some disparaging jokes about women in the field of science. Although these comments made Tonya uncomfortable, she thought perhaps she was being oversensitive. As the semester progressed, so did Dr. Bartlett's derogatory asides about women. Nonetheless, Tonya loved the course; she was earning A's and she felt that she had found her niche. She decided to major in this area. Tonya made an appointment to discuss possible career opportunities with Dr. Bartlett. Shortly into the appointment, Dr. Bartlett made it clear to Tonya that he didn't think she could cut it and suggested that she look for another program.

How would you feel if you were in Tonya's shoes? _____

_____

_____

_____

_____

What action should Tonya take in regard to Dr. Bartlett? _____

_____

_____

_____

_____

How would you feel if you were a male in Tonya's class? _____

_____

_____

_____

_____

Do you think women face discrimination in higher education? In the workforce?

_____

_____

_____

_____

■ SCENARIO #5 Gregg is in an orientation class for new students. He loves the class and most of the students in it. He is particularly close to Jessie. Gregg and Jessie were both raised in small towns, were active in their high school student councils, and love sports. They also have strong religious convictions, although they act on them differently.

Gregg holds firmly to his own beliefs, but he also believes in free choice and people's right to choose their own religion. Jessie is extremely conservative as well as vocal in his approach to religion, and he readily condemns views that differ from his. Although Gregg believes that Jessie has a right to express his feelings and share his views with others, he also believes that Jessie should be more tolerant of others' beliefs.

Gregg has noticed that students avoid talking with Jessie in class and that they share less and less during class discussion. This concerns Gregg because he really likes Jessie, but he doesn't want the class to lose its openness. One day during a discussion on abortion, Jessie openly condemned a student when she shared that she had had an abortion. After class Gregg heard several students say how much they disliked Jessie's attitude.

Would you be willing to share your views in class if Jessie were one of your classmates? _____

_____

_____

_____

If you were Gregg, how would you deal with Jessie? _____

_____

_____

_____

How tolerant are you of people's differing religious views? _____

_____

_____

_____

Can people be too religious? _____

_____

_____

_____

Do some religions carry a social stigma? _____

_____

_____

_____

CORNERSTONES for celebrating diversity

- Accept the fact that each person is a culture unto himself or herself.

- Be willing to change some of your attitudes, beliefs, and values in order to grow.

- Recognize that some of your personal values and beliefs may need cultural adjustments.

- Spend more time on inclusivity than on exclusivity.

- Learn to appreciate that different is not necessarily bad or wrong.

- Develop relationships with people from a variety of backgrounds, religions, races, and nationalities.

- Make an effort to relate to people with disabilities as just people.

- Listen to people whose sexual orientation differs from yours and try to understand them.

- Be open to relationships with people from different socioeconomic backgrounds and understand that their value systems may be very different from yours.

- Strive to rid yourself of filters that may skew your thinking against a person or a group of people.

- Read about various cultures and explore ways to understand more.

- Try to accept people for who they are.

Understanding Others

If you have been using the Internet, you know that URLs change frequently and are sometimes removed. If you cannot locate a particular exercise, try to find one that provides similar information.

Have you ever thought about how difficult it is for first-year students who are different from you to fit in? Sometimes we think we are the only ones who feel lost or out of step with what is going on. The truth is, most first-year students feel a little lost. Read the article at the address (`http://www.aboutcollege.com/goals.htm`) and put yourself in the place of the international students who are discussing their feelings in this article.

What courtesies do Jordanian and Indian students show their professors? _____

_____

_____

_____

How do you think international students feel in the casual environment of the American classroom? If you are an international student, discuss the differences in your culture compared to the American setting. _____

_____

_____

_____

What are the attitudes of these students toward the drinking habits of some American college students?

_____

_____

_____

How might you make an international student feel more welcome on your campus? _____

_____

_____

_____

The one minute journal

i n a minute or less, discuss one major lesson you learned
from this chapter.

> *People everywhere enjoy believing*
>
> *things that they know are not true.*
>
> *It spares them the ordeal of think-*
>
> *ing for themselves and taking*
>
> *responsibility for what they know.*
>
> *Brooks Atkinson*

Think before You Leap: Using Critical Thinking Skills in College and Life

POINT: America is in decline! There is no sense of community, no compassion for others. Road rage takes lives every hour. Violent crime among teens is up 141%! Pick up a newspaper and turn to the editorial page. Almost every word written is negative. Politicians are taking bribes, babies are left for dead by teenage mothers and fathers, auto theft is up, and pornography on the Internet is corrupting our youth.

How can you decide which point to believe?

COUNTERPOINT:
America, the land of waving wheat, purple mountains' majesty, and shining seas. America, the land of plenty. America is back! Violent crime among adults is down 26%. The economy is better than it has been in over 20 years. The stock market is booming. Innercity families are reclaiming their neighborhoods. Urban cities are cleaning up, and tourism is at an all-time high. Medical advances have helped us prolong life and relieve suffering.

Which viewpoint is correct? Does America need to "get back on track," or is America on track? How can you decide which point to believe? How much thought, critical thought, have you given the issue? As you move through your daily routine, how often do you stop to consider the fate of your country?

If you had one chance to change a social or economic policy in this nation, what would it be? Would you create communities; would you eliminate prejudice? Would you bring back the "Summer of Love?" Would you create a new social ethic geared toward kindness and compassion? Would you introduce sex or moral education into the school system? Would you create a policy giving all people equal human rights? Would you eliminate the IRS? What is your wish? Have you ever considered it? Does America need fixing? Are you part of the problem?

Take a moment to evaluate the question in your own mind. What are *you* thinking right now? More importantly, why are you thinking the way you are right now? What is causing you to believe, feel, or think one way or the other? What are the facts and/or opinions that have led you to your conclusion? At this moment, are you basing your thoughts about this issue on emotions or facts, fallacies or truths, data or opinions, interviews or hearsay, reason or misjudgement, fear or empathy?

Understanding why and how we formulate thoughts and ideas is the main objective of this chapter. This chapter is about believing and

disbelieving, seeking, uncovering, debunking myths, proving the impossible, possible. It is about proof, logic, evidence, and developing ideas and opinions based on hard-core facts or credible research. This chapter is about seeking truth and expanding your mind to limits unimaginable. This chapter is about the fundamental aspect of becoming an educated citizen; it is about human thought and reasoning. After completing this chapter, you should be able to

- Define critical thinking

- Describe the characteristics of critical thinkers

- Discuss the value of critical thinking

- Define emotional restraint

- Conduct objective research

- Analyze problems, ideas, and information

- Solve problems

- Differentiate fact from opinion

- Identify fallacies and errors in thinking

- Correct fallacies and errors in thinking

- Recognize fallacious persuasive terminology

- Identify faulty tactics in persuasion and argumentation

Take some time now to evaluate your knowledge and understanding of critical thinking.

AT THIS MOMENT...

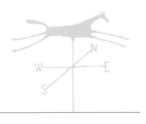

5 = Strongly Agree

4 = Agree

3 = Don't Know

2 = Disagree

1 = Strongly Disagree

1. I can identify a fallacy.
   1 2 3 4 5

2. I know how to identify facts. *1 2 3 4 5*

3. I know how to identify opinions. *1 2 3 4 5*

4. I know how to research a problem. *1 2 3 4 5*

5. I can separate emotion from reason.
   1 2 3 4 5

6. I can identify the characteristics of critical thinkers.
   1 2 3 4 5

7. I can identify the elements of persuasion.
   1 2 3 4 5

8. I can recognize unprovable statements.
   1 2 3 4 5

9. I can recognize fallacious persuasive statements.
   1 2 3 4 5

10. I can analyze information.
    1 2 3 4 5

A SELF-ASSESSMENT Total your points from the ten questions.
Refer to the following rating scale to determine where you
stand in relation to your higher order thinking skills.

0–10   *Your critical thinking skills are rusty. You do not give enough
analysis to problems or issues. You may not be able to determine
fact from opinion.*

11–20   *Sometimes, you use your analytical skills to help solve problems or
deal with issues, but not very often.*

21–30   *Your thinking skills are average. Most of the time you do not rush
to judgement. You tend to be somewhat open-minded and fair in
your decisions. You know how to analyze information.*

31–40   *You think about things in detail. You try to look at most angles
before you make a decision. You are fair and you are not afraid to
try new solutions.*

41–50   *Your critical thinking skills are exceptional. You are open-minded,
fair, and know how to find the answers to problems or critical
issues. You are not judgmental. You have keen analyzing skills.*

Now, refer to your journal and respond in writing to your findings.
Consider the following questions when writing in your journal.

1. Why is it important to a college student to be able to think as an
   independent person?

2. What are the ramifications of not thinking independently?

3. What is one situation in which you did use good reasoning and
   thinking to solve a problem or address an issue?

A Working Definition of

Critical Thinking

There are almost as many definitions of critical thinking as
there are people who try to define it. According to *The
American Heritage Dictionary, critical* is defined as "careful and
exact evaluation and judgement." *Thinking* is defined as "to reason
about or reflect on; to ponder." *Critical thinking,* then, might be defined

as evaluating and judging your reasoning and reflections. This definition is not, however, a complete description. Critical thinking can also mean thinking deeper, being skeptical, questioning strongly held beliefs, or taking no information or opinion for granted. It is also important to note that critical thinking is not innate, it is a learned skill that every student can acquire and polish.

For the purpose of this chapter, we will use the working definition of critical thinking as defined by Diane Helpern in her book, *Thought and Knowledge, An Introduction to Critical Thinking* (1996). She defines critical thinking as "thinking that is purposeful, reasoned, and goal directed—the kind of thinking involved in solving problems, formulating inferences, calculating likelihoods, and making decisions . . . . "

The Importance of
Critical Thinking

Have you ever made a decision that turned out to be a mistake? Have you ever said to yourself, "If only I could go back . . . ?" Have you ever regretted actions you took toward a person or situation? Have you ever planned an event or function that went off flawlessly? Have you ever had to make a hard, painful decision that turned out to be "the best decision of your life?" If the answer to any of these questions is yes, you might be able to trace the consequences back to your thought process at the time of the decision. Let's face it, sometimes good and bad things happen out of luck. More often than not, however, the events in our lives are driven by the thought processes involved when we made the initial decision.

Critical thinking can serve us in many areas as students and citizens in society. As a student, critical thinking can help you focus on issues; gather relevant, accurate information; remember facts; organize thoughts logically; analyze questions and problems; and manage your priorities. It can assist in your problem-solving skills and help you control your emotions so that rational judgements can be made. It can help you produce new knowledge through research and analysis and help you determine the factual accuracy of printed and spoken words. It can help you in detecting bias and in determining the relevance of arguments and persuasion.

As a citizen, critical thinking can help you get along with others. It can help you realize cause and effect in the world. It can assist you in financial planning, stress reduction, and health issues, and help you make rational, informed decisions in a variety of cultural and civic duties, such as voting, volunteering, or contributing money.

Critical thinking is a skill that is not only valuable in the academic arena, but also invaluable in relationships, neighborhood planning, environmental concerns, and life-long goal setting, to name a few. It can help you and your family solve problems together. It can help you make decisions that permanently affect the lives of your family members, and it can help you choose alternatives that are best for you, your family, and your friends.

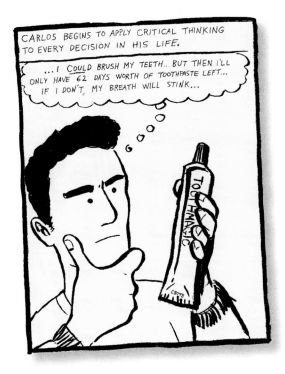

CARLOS BEGINS TO APPLY CRITICAL THINKING TO EVERY DECISION IN HIS LIFE.

...I COULD BRUSH MY TEETH... BUT THEN I'LL ONLY HAVE 62 DAYS WORTH OF TOOTHPASTE LEFT... IF I DON'T, MY BREATH WILL STINK...

■ AN INSIDER'S VIEW

Carla Chapman
The University of Nebraska
at Kearney
Kearney, Nebraska

From the day I was born, making decisions seemed like a simple process to me. If I saw something that I needed or wanted, I went for it with blind motivation. It took many years before I realized that decision making and thinking was anything but simple. More importantly, I realized that making a decision without critically thinking was dangerous, foolish, and many times, embarrassing.

My first experience with "acting before thinking" came early in my life. My brother and I were playing in the mud where we made mud-pies. We would pretend to eat them. One day, we discovered that one of the pies had a rather large worm in it. Never having had a worm in a pie before, we both fought over it. Before we knew what had happened, we had torn the pie and the worm into two pieces. To prove to my brother that I had won the battle, I promptly ate my half. Immediately, I realized that this was not a well-thought-out decision.

Throughout my life, I have struggled for other "worms." I always thought I needed control, that I needed to win. At the age of 34, I accepted the fact that I needed to change the way I approached decision making and thinking. I felt that one way to do this was to return to college. It was not an easy decision.

My decision came because I needed to learn how to make healthy decisions based on thinking, not emotions. I have an extremely adventurous side. I am spontaneous and sometimes act before thinking. However, returning to college taught me how to think and critically analyze a situation. My first decision after deciding to attend college was to decide on a major. By the time I enrolled in my first classes, I had almost memorized the catalog. I talked to students, interviewed faculty, and took every assessment and skill test available to me.

After all of this work, and though I made my decision based on critical evaluation, I did not accept anything at face value. I did not make a rash judgement. This new decision-making process of research, evaluation, and assessment took longer and was much harder, but the rewards of using critical thinking skills were well worth the effort. My plans are to pursue a masters and doctoral degree. This would not have been possible if I had not learned how to think and evaluate critically.

A Plan for Critical Thinking

As you begin to build and expand your critical-thinking skills, we should consider the steps involved. Critical-thinking skill development involves

- Emotional restraint

- Thinking on a higher level

- Research

- Analysis

- Questioning

- Problem solving

- Determining fact from opinion

- Identifying fallacies

- Seeking truth in argument and persuasion

The remainder of this chapter will detail, through explanation, exploration, and exercises, how to build a critical-thinking plan for your academic and personal success.

> **What we need is not the will to believe, but the will to find out.**
> **Bertrand Russell**

 STEP ONE: EMOTIONAL RESTRAINT

Did James Earl Ray really kill Martin Luther King, Jr.? Is there life beyond earth? Did a member of Tupak's entourage participate in his murder? Should the drinking age be lowered to 18? Should 16-year-olds be allowed to drive a car? What emotions are you feeling right now? Did you immediately formulate an answer in your mind? Are your emotions driving your thinking process?

Emotions play a vital role in our lives. They help us feel compassion, help others, and reach out in times of need, and they help us relate to others. Emotions, on the other hand, can cause some problems in your critical-thinking process. You *do not* have to eliminate emotions from your thoughts, but it is crucial that you know when your emotions are clouding an issue.

Consider the following topics:

- Should abortion remain legal?

- Can the theory of evolution and creationism coexist?

- Should tobacco companies be held liable for their products?

- Should students in today's college curriculum be *required* to take classes in English literature, studying Shakespeare, Milton, and Johnson?

As you read through the statements, did you immediately form an opinion? Did old arguments surface? Did you feel your emotions coming into play as you thought about the statements? If you had an immediate answer, it is more than likely that you allowed some past judgements, opinions, and emotions to enter the decision-making process, *unless* you have just done a comprehensive, unbiased study of one of these issues. As you discussed these in class or with your friends, how did you feel? Did you get angry? Did you find yourself groping for words? Did you find it hard to explain why you held the opinion that you voiced? If so, these are warning signs that you are allowing your emotions to drive your decisions. If we allow our emotions to run rampant (not using restraint) and fail to use research, logic, and evidence (expansive thinking), we will not be able to critically examine the issues nor have a logical discussion regarding the statements.

If you feel that your emotions caused you to be less than objective, you might consider the following tips when you are faced with an emotional decision:

- Listen to all sides of the argument or statement before you make a decision or form an opinion.

- Make a conscious effort to identify which emotions are causing you to lose objectivity.

- Do not let your emotions withdraw you or turn you off from the situation.

- Don't let yourself become engaged in "I'm right, you're wrong" situations.

- Work to understand *why* the other person(s) feel their side is valid.

- Physiological reactions to emotions, such as increased heart rate and blood pressure and an increase in adrenaline flow, should be recognized as an emotional checklist. If you begin to experience these reactions, relax, take a deep breath, and concentrate on being open-minded.

- Control your negative self-talk or inner voice toward the other person(s) or situation.

- Determine if your emotions are irrational.

In the space provided below, develop a step-by-step plan to evaluate one of the statements listed above. You do not have to *answer* the question; your task is to devise a plan to critically address the statement without emotional interference. **Example:** *Does violent TV or movies cause violent crime?* Before you answer yes or no, your first step might be to define violent TV/movies. A second step might be to define violent crime. A third step might be to research the association between the two. A fourth step might be to objectively evaluate the research, asking the following questions: (1) From where does the research originate: the TV or movie industry, a parental guidance group, or a completely detached agency? (2) How old is the research? (3) How long was the research conducted? This type of questioning does not allow your emotions to rule the outcome.

Select one of the topics from those listed on pages 88 and 89, or develop your own statement, and devise a plan for critical analysis.

STATEMENT _____

_____

Step 1. _____

_____

Step 2. _____

_____

Step 3. _____

_____

Step 4. _____

_____

Step 5. _____

_____

> A great many people think they are thinking, when they are merely rearranging their prejudices.
> **William James**

STEP TWO: THINKING ON A HIGHER LEVEL

Critical thinking involves looking at an issue from many different angles. It encourages you to dig deeper than you have before; get below the surface, struggle, experiment, and expand. It asks you to look at something from an entirely different angle so that you might develop new insights and understand more about the problem, situation, or question. Thinking on a higher level involves looking at something that you may have never seen before or something that you may have seen many times, and trying to think about it more critically than before.

As you begin to look "with different eyes," take a moment and complete the activities below. They are provided to encourage you to look at simple, common situations in a new light. Remember, these exercises do not measure intelligence.

Review the following example of a "brain teaser" and solve the remaining teasers. You will need to break down a few barriers in thought and look at them from a new angle to get them all.

Brain Teasers

Examples:	4 W on a C	4 Wheels on a Car
	13 O C	13 Original Colonies

1. *SW and the 7 D*   _____

2. *I H a D by MLK*   _____

3. *2 P's in a P*   _____

4. *HDD (TMRUTC)*   _____

5. *3 S to a T*   _____

6. *100 P in a D*   _____

7. *T no PLH*   _____

8. *4 Q in a G*   _____

9. *I a SWAA*   _____

10. *50 S in TU*   _____

How did you do? Was it hard to look at the situation backwards? Most of us are not used to that. As you continue to build your critical-thinking skills, look at the design below. You will find nine dots. Your mission is to connect all nine dots with four straight lines without removing your pencil or pen from the paper. Do not retrace your lines. Can you do it?

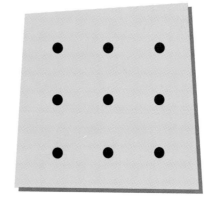

U.S. Penny

Finally, as you begin to think beyond the obvious, examine the penny to the left. You will see the front and back sides of the penny. Pretend that the world has ended and all traces of civilization are gone. Someone from another planet, who speaks our language, has come to earth and the *only* thing left from our civilization is one penny. Below, list the things that could be assumed about our civilization from this one small penny. You should find at least ten.

1. _____

2. _____

3. _____

4. _____

5. _____

6. _____

7. _____

8. _____

9. _____

10. _____

While these activities may seem somewhat trivial, they are provided to help you begin to think about and consider information from a different angle. This is a major step in becoming a critical thinker: looking beyond the obvious, thinking outside the box, examining details, and exploring possibilities.

STEP THREE: CONDUCTING RESEARCH

One of the most important aspects of becoming an educated citizen is the ability to learn how to learn. It is important that you know how to seek and find answers to questions, bibliographical information, historical data, government actions, updates on technology, and advances in society. Many students run to the library or log onto the World Wide Web and take the first pieces of information. They do not know how to begin their research and they do not know how to distinguish scholarly research from popular press writing. This section will give you some basic information about research to assist you in building your critical-thinking skills. Keep these basic steps in mind:

1. **Consider your topic.** One of the first things that you need to consider when you begin your research is your topic. If you haven't decided on a topic or narrowed your existing topic, you will probably have a hard time deciding on what information to gather. For instance, if you wanted to do a five- to seven-page paper on rape,

> The success of any argument, short or long, depends in large part on the quantity and quality of the support behind it.
> Annette Rottenberg

you would find volumes and volumes of books, magazine and journal articles, and Internet resources available. The topic is too broad. Decide on a specific area of rape, such as date rape or the profile of a rapist. You might want to narrow your topic to men who are raped or how to prevent rape. Formulating a question or a strong thesis will drive your research. A well-stated thesis can save you many hours in the long run.

2. **Have at least three or more sources** supporting your claim or thesis when conducting your research. If you have only one research article supporting your view, you may not have gotten the entire picture.

3. **Use a variety of resources.** Some of the most beneficial sources can be found in encyclopedias such as

Britannica Encyclopedia of Art, Encyclopedia of World Literature, Encyclopedia of Education, Encyclopedia of Physics

You can also use resources such as indexes. Indexes will refer you to timely material in a variety of places. Some of the most commonly used indexes are

The Reader's Guide to Periodical Literature, The New York Times Index, Applied Science and Technology Index, Education Index, Humanities Index

Abstracts are also another area where you can read about the main issues in a book or article before you take it home. Abstracts can save you valuable time. Some abstracts are

Chemical Abstracts, Psychological Abstracts, Women's Studies Abstracts, Book Review Digest, Congressional Abstracts

4. **Validity.** Know the validity of the sources and research that you use to write your papers or speeches, solve problems, analyze questions, and draw conclusions. The credibility of your sources can mean the difference between having a valid argument or thesis and having unsubstantiated opinions. With the Internet becoming an ever-increasing and popular source for information, it is of ultimate importance that you know the validity of your Internet resources. To critically analyze information sources, use the following guidelines as set forth by Ormondroyd, Engle, and Cosgrave from Cornell University Libraries.

■ Who is the author and what are his or her credentials, educational background, past writings, or experience. Has your instructor mentioned the author? Is he or she cited in other works? Is the author associated with any organizations or institutes?

■ When was the source published? If it is a web page, the date is usually found on the last page or the home page. Is the source current or out of date for your topic?

■ What edition is the source? Second and third editions suggest that the source has been updated to reflect changes and new knowledge.

■ Who is the publisher? If the source is published by a university press, it is likely to be a scholarly publication.

■ What is the title of the source? This will help you determine if the source is popular, sensational, or scholarly.

Popular journals are resources such as *Time, Newsweek, Vogue, Ebony,* and *Reader's Digest.* They seldom cite their sources.

Sensational resources are often inflammatory and written on an elementary level. They usually have flashy headlines and they cater to popular superstitions. Examples are *The Globe, The National Enquirer,* or *The Star.*

Scholarly resources are defined as having a solid research base. They are substantial. They always cite their sources and are usually written by scholars in their fields. Usually, they report on original research.

■ What is the intended audience of your source? Is the information too simple, too advanced, or too technical for your needs?

■ Is the source objective, opinionated, or is it propaganda? Objective sources look at all angles and report on each one honestly. Sources of opinion give unfounded information. Propaganda is information that spreads the same message over and over until it is believed by the masses.

■ Does the source cover the thesis or question substantially, or does it just gloss over the material? Usually, the more in-depth the source, the more substantial it is going to be to your research.

5. **Use caution.** When using the Internet for resources, use extreme caution. Anyone can create a home page or enter information onto the Internet. This can be good, but it can also create a situation in which you have little control over the validity of your resources. Laura Cohen of the University of Albany Libraries suggests, "Internet sites change over time according to the commitment and

inclination of the creator. Some sites demonstrate an expert's knowledge, while others are amateur efforts. Some may be updated daily, while others may be outdated."

To conduct research on the Internet, you can do several things: (1) join a listserv or Usenet newsgroup; (2) go directly to a site if you have the address; (3) browse the Internet using one of the search engines, such as Infoseek, Yahoo, or AOL; or (4) navigate through a subject directory. When using the Internet, you will need to learn how to narrow your topic search. Again, if your subject is rape, it may be too broad. You may have to narrow that search to date rape, or you could use the words, "college—date—rape" if you wanted to see data pertaining only to rape on college campuses.

To evaluate Internet resources, Laura Cohen suggests

- Consider the intended audience of the Internet piece.

- Many items on the Internet are peripheral or useless.

- Check to see if the piece has an author listed (with his or her address).

- To check the validity of the author; trace back the URL to determine from whence the document originates.

- Don't take the information presented at face value; conduct additional research using a variety of sources.

- Web sites are rarely monitored or reviewed like scholarly journals and books. Therefore, look for point of view, bias, currency, and comprehensiveness.

STEP FOUR: ANALYZING INFORMATION

Critical thinking goes further than thinking on a different or higher level or using emotional restraint; it also involves analyzing information. To analyze, you break a topic, statement, or problem into parts to understand the nature of the whole. It is a simple, yet crucial step in critical thinking. An easy way to analyze is to create a chart of the information using a right- and left-hand column.

Nothing in life is to be feared, it is to be understood.
Marie Curie

EXAMPLE: WHY IS PROPER NUTRITION IMPORTANT TO HUMANS?

Physical health	Prevents heart disease, high blood pressure, and high cholesterol, and helps control weight.
Dental health	Helps prevent tooth decay; some foods inhibit decay, such as cheese, peanut butter,

	and protein. Proper nutrition helps prevent gum disease.
Mental health	Self-esteem may increase. You are able to exercise more, thus helping relieve stress and some types of depression.

As you can see, a question properly analyzed prohibits us from just answering the above question with "It's good for you." An analysis forces you to ask *why* it is good or bad, right or wrong, proper or improper.

Now, it's your turn. Analyze the following question. *How can an undeclared student take steps to decide on a career?* Hint: The answer can be found in this edition of *Cornerstone*.

COLUMN A   *COLUMN B*

_____   _____

                                    _____

_____   _____

                                    _____

                                    _____

_____   _____

                                    _____

_____   _____

                                    _____

_____   _____

                                    _____

                                    _____

_____   _____

                                    _____

                                    _____

This method can also be used to formulate new information on a subject. If you read a chapter or article, hear a conversation, or are faced with a problem, you can analyze the situation by creating questions that need to be answered in column A and providing the answer in column B. You may have to use more than one source of information to answer the questions you posed in the A column.

You might also use the *"What If Method"* to break down or critically analyze a situation, question, or problem. This method encourages you to take the situation, question, or information and use the following nine terms in your A column and, through research, answer the questions in your B column. "What if . . ." you looked at the situation:

Laterally	Examining the good, bad, and interesting of it
Universally	Seeing the big picture
Microscopically	Seeing only one small piece or side
Myopically	Shortsighted planning or thinking
As our best friend	Cared for it deeply
As our worst enemy	Did not care for it at all
In pieces	Took it apart and examined it in detail
Environmentally	Its effect on the earth
Mystically	Examining the spiritual or religious implications

Analyze the following statement using the "What If Method": *The United States should move toward a single-party political system, abolishing the Democratic, Republican, and Independent parties.*

COLUMN A   COLUMN B

Laterally   _____

                     _____

Universally   _____

                     _____

Microscopically   _____

                     _____

Myopically _____

_____

As Our Best Friend _____

_____

As Our Worst Enemy _____

_____

In Pieces _____

_____

Environmentally _____

_____

Mystically _____

_____

Using the information provided in your B column, write a brief statement detailing the findings of your analysis.

_____

_____

_____

_____

_____

STEP FIVE: QUESTIONING ASSUMPTIONS AND COMMON TRUTHS

You've asked questions all of your life. As a child, you asked your parents, "What's that?" a million times. You probably asked them, "Why do I have to do this?" In later years, you've asked questions of your friends, teachers, strangers, store clerks, and significant others. Questioning is not new to you, but it may be a new technique for exploring, developing, and acquiring new knowledge. Curiosity may have killed the cat, but it was a smart cat when it died. Your curiosity is one of the most important traits you possess. It helps you grow and learn, and it may sometimes cause you to be uncomfortable. That's OK. This section is provided to assist you in learning how to ask questions to promote knowledge, solve problems, foster strong relationships, and critically analyze difficult situations.

Let's start with a simple questioning exercise. If you could meet *anyone* on earth and ask them five questions, who would you meet, why would you meet them, and what questions would you ask?

I'd like to meet _____

_____

Because _____

_____

I'd ask the person

1. _____

2. _____

3. _____

4. _____

5. _____

Asking questions can be fun in many situations. They help us gain insight where we may have limited knowledge. They can also challenge us to look at issues from many different angles. Answering properly posed questions can help us expand our knowledge base.

If you were about to embark on writing a college paper dealing with the AIDS epidemic in the United States, what questions would you want to have answered at the end of the paper? Take awhile and think about the issue. Write down at least five questions that you will share with the class. At the end of the class' brainstorming session, you will have a better idea of the types of questions needed to fully explore this topic.

My five questions are

1. _____

2. _____

3. _____

4. _____

5. _____

Questioning also involves going beyond the obvious. Examine the advertisement on the next page. The car dealership has provided some information, but it is not enough to make an educated decision. What other questions would you ask to make sure that you are getting a good deal?

1. _____

2. _____

3. _____

4. _____

5. _____

STEP SIX: PROBLEM SOLVING

You face problems every day; some are larger and more difficult than others. Some students have transportation problems. Some have child care problems. Some students have academic problems and some have interpersonal problems. Many people don't know how to solve problems at school, home, or work. They simply let the problem go unaddressed until it is too late to reach an amiable conclusion. There are many ways to address and solve problems. In this section, we will discuss how to identify and narrow the problem, research and develop alternatives, evaluate alternatives, and solve the problem.

It is important to remember that every problem does have a solution, but the solution may not be what we wanted. It is also imperative to remember the words of Mary Hatwood Futrell, President of the

NEA. She states that "finding the right answer is important, of course. But more important is developing the ability to see that problems have multiple solutions, that getting from X to Y demands basic skills and mental agility, imagination, persistence, patience."

■ IDENTIFYING AND NARROWING THE PROBLEM Put your problem in writing. When doing this, be sure to jot down all aspects of the problem, such as why is it a problem, who does it affect, and what type of problem is it? Examine the following situation: You have just failed two tests this week and you are dreadfully behind on an English paper. Now, that's a problem . . . or is it? If you examine and reflect on the problem, you begin to realize that because of your nighttime job, you always get to class late, you are tired and irritable when you get there, and you never have time to study. So, the real problem is not that you have failed tests and are behind; the problem is that your job is interfering with your college work. Now that you have identified and narrowed the problem, you can begin to work toward a solution.

■ DEVELOP ALTERNATIVES A valuable method of gathering ideas, formulating questioning, and solving problems is brainstorming. To brainstorm, you let your ideas flow without any fear of ridicule. A brainstorming session allows all thoughts to be heard. You can brainstorm any matter almost anywhere. You may want to set some guidelines for your sessions to make them more productive.

- Identify the topic, problem, or statement to be discussed

- Set a time limit for the entire brainstorming session

- Write all ideas down on a board or flip chart

- Let everyone speak

- Don't criticize anyone for their remarks

- Concentrate on the issue; let all of your ideas flow

- Suspend judgement until all ideas are produced or the time is up

- If you're using the session to generate questions rather than solutions, each participant should pose questions rather than statements

Using the problem identified above (my nighttime job is causing me to not have enough time for sleep or study), jot down the first few alternatives that come to mind. Don't worry about content, clarity, or quality. Just let your mind flow. Verbalize these ideas when the class brainstorms this problem.

IDEAS _____

_____

_____

■ EVALUATING THE ALTERNATIVES Some of your ideas or the ideas of your classmates may not be logical in solving the problem. After careful study and deliberation, without emotional interference, analyze the ideas and determine if they are appropriate or inappropriate for the solution. To analyze, create an A and a B column. Write the idea in column A and a comment in column B. Example:

A	B
Quit the job	Very hard to do, I need the money for tuition and car
Cut my hours at work	Will ask my boss
Find a new job	Hard to do because of the job market—will look into it
Get a student loan	Go by financial aid office tomorrow
Quit school	No—it is my only chance for a promotion

With your comments in column B, you can now begin to eliminate some of the alternatives that are inappropriate at this time.

■ SOLVE THE PROBLEM Now that you have a few strong alternatives, you have some work to do. You will need to talk to your boss, go to the financial aid office, and possibly begin to search for a new job that allows you to work better hours. After you have researched each alternative, you will be able to make a decision based on solid information and facts.

Pretend that your best friend, Nathan, has just come to you with a problem. He tells you that his parents are really coming down hard on him *for going to college.* It is a strange problem. They believe that Nathan should be working full time and that he is just wasting his time and money, since he did not do well in high school. They have threatened to take away his car and kick him out of the house if he does not find a full-time job. Nathan is doing well and does not want to leave college.

In the space provided below, formulate questions to help Nathan solve this problem.

_____

_____

_____

STEP SEVEN: DISTINGUISHING FACT FROM OPINION

One of the most important aspects of critical thinking is the ability to distinguish fact from opinion. *In many situations—real life, TV, radio, friendly conversations, and the professional arena—opinions surface more than facts.* Reread the previous sentence. This is an example of an opinion cloaked as a fact. There is no research supporting this opinion. It sounds as if it could be true, but without evidence and proof, it is just an opinion. A fact is something that can be proved; something that can be objectively verified. An opinion is a statement that is held to be true, but one that has no objective proof. Statements that cannot be proved should always be treated as opinion. Statements that offer valid proof and verification from credible, reliable sources can be treated as factual.

Examine the following statements:

Thomas Wolfe was a writer.	FACT	This can be verified by many sources and by the volumes he wrote.
Clara Barton founded the Red Cross.	FACT	This can be verified by reading the history of the Red Cross.
Lincoln was the best president ever.	OPINION	This is only an opinion that can be disputed.
American college students spend more money on pizza than do students from other countries.	OPINION	This is an opinion not based on research or fact.
There are more hotel rooms on the corner of Las Vegas Boulevard and Tropicana Avenue in Las Vegas than are in the entire city of San Francisco.	FACT	This can be verified by using data from the Las Vegas and San Francisco Convention Bureaus.

> One can't believe impossible things.
> Alice, *Through the Looking Glass*

"Gone With the Wind" is one of the best movies ever made.

OPINION

This is an opinion, although widely held to be a fact because many movie critics have heralded it as such.

When trying to distinguish between fact and opinion, you should take the following guidelines into consideration:

If you are in doubt, ask questions and listen for solid proof and documentation to support the statement.

Listen for what is not said in a statement.

Don't be led astray by those you assume are trustworthy and loyal.

Don't be turned off by those you fear or consider untruthful.

Do your own homework on the issue. Read, research, question.

Again, if you are unsure about the credibility of the source or information, treat the statement as opinion.

Using the spaces provided below, write three facts, three opinions, and three opinions cloaked as facts. Feel free to use professors' comments, comments from friends or family, newspapers, TV stories, or radio reports to complete this activity.

FACT _____

FACT _____

FACT _____

OPINION _____

OPINION _____

OPINION _____

OPINION AS FACT _____

OPINION AS FACT _____

OPINION AS FACT _____

> **There is no worse lie than the truth misunderstood.**
> **Unknown**

STEP EIGHT: IDENTIFYING FALLACIES

In 1978, Jim Jones, leader of The People's Temple of San Francisco, convinced his congregation that they should sell their worldly possessions and move to Guyana to establish a new house of worship. He told them that their church would not have freedom in the United States and that they needed to move to another country to be able to have the type of religious freedom they were seeking. He used this argument to convince over 800 people to sell all that they owned and follow him to Guyana, where he systematically dissolved all marriages, had many adulterous affairs, and eventually had a senator and news reporters killed. Knowing that the U.S. government would now descend on the compound, he convinced over 800 people to drink a potion of poison. Some recognized that he had made poor judgements and fallacious assumptions and tried to escape, but they were shot to death by his guards. Some tried to convince Jones that the church could move once again. He would not listen. When all was said and done, over 800 people lay dead as the result of fallacies cloaked as truth.

Examples of other, yet less significant, fallacies are below:

- When I wash my car, it rains; therefore, washing my car makes it rain.

- All horses are animals. A zebra is not a horse; therefore, a zebra is not an animal.

- French people are great painters. Just look at Monet, Manet, and Courbet. Louis is French. He must be a good painter.

- If everyone is driving 85 mph on the interstate, I should do it so that I do not get left behind.

- John did not study for his history test and he made an A. Therefore, the test must be easy, so I do not have to study.

- Suzanna had a few beers and she did not get drunk. I can have a few and not get drunk either.

According to the *American Heritage Dictionary,* a **fallacy** is a false notion. It is a statement that is based on a false or invalid inference. *Fallacy* comes from the Latin word *fallere,* which means "to deceive." A fallacy results in getting an individual or a group of people to believe something, to act a certain way, or to hold certain truths that *seem* true, but are not. A fallacy is the failure to follow the rules of logic, thus resulting in an invalid argument (Bosak, 1976). Barbara Warnick suggests that fallacies are "often hard to recognize because they are both appealing and deceptive" (Warnick and Inch, 1994).

Listed below are 10 statements. Read each one carefully. Place an **F** by the statements that you perceive as **fallacy** and an **L** by the statements you perceive as **logical**. While searching for fallacies, keep these terms, as identified by Barbara Warnick (1994), in mind:

_____ 1. *Ladies and gentlemen of the jury. As you can tell by the witnesses presented here, my client could have never, ever committed these murders. You have heard his mother testify that he was a good child. You have heard his siblings testify that he is a loving, caring man to whom they would entrust their children, and you have heard his wife testify that he has been loyal, faithful, and honest for over 23 years. As you can plainly see, he could never have done this heinous act.*

_____ 2. *You can't trust Joe. Time and time again he has proven that he is untrustworthy. He was convicted of stealing that car. He was caught in a lie about cheating on his wife, and the last time that he told you that he would be here, he stood you up. He can't be trusted.*

_____ 3. *My client could not have stolen that car. As the eye witness stated, the car was stolen at 10:36 P.M. My client has a receipt for dinner at a restaurant all the way across town. The time stamped on the receipt is 10:41 P.M. He also has been clearly identified by the cashier at the restaurant at that time on the night of the theft.*

_____ 4. *My parents told me that I should never consider changing political parties. Therefore, I do not plan to do so.*

_____ 5. I studied only 30 minutes for my algebra test and I got an A. Therefore, I don't have to study more than 30 minutes for my history test.

_____ 6. AIDS is a disease that affects people from all walks of life, not just one segment of the population. One way to avoid AIDS is to practice abstinence.

_____ 7. The last major change in my life was so threatening and unpleasant, all change must be just like that.

_____ 8. I read an article in a magazine that crime in America was on the decrease. It must be true.

_____ 9. The American Journal of Medicine states that one glass of red wine a day is good for me. If I drink three or four glasses, I'll be really healthy.

_____10. Stress causes anger, denial, fear, feelings of hopelessness, and mental anguish. Therefore, I should take steps to reduce stress in my life.

STEP NINE: SEEKING TRUTH IN ARGUMENTS AND PERSUASION

Whether or not you realize it, arguments and persuasive efforts are around you daily—hourly, for that matter. They are in newspaper and TV ads, editorials, news commentaries, talk shows, TV magazine shows, political statements, and religious services. It seems at times that almost everyone is trying to persuade us through argument or advice. This section is included to assist you in recognizing faulty arguments and implausible or deceptive persuasion.

First, let's start with a list of terms used to describe faulty arguments and deceptive persuasion. As you read through the list, try to identify a situation in which you have heard someone mask their argument in these terms.

> There is nothing so powerful as truth, and often nothing so strange.
>
> Daniel Webster

FALLACIOUS PERSUASIVE TERMINOLOGY

Ad baculum	Ad baculum is an argument that tries to persuade based on force. Threats of alienation, disapproval, or even violence may accompany this type of argument.
Ad hominem	Ad hominem is when someone initiates a *personal* attack on a person rather than

(continued)

listening to and rationally debating his or her ideas. This is also referred to as slander.

Ad populum	An ad populum argument is based on the opinions of the majority of people. It assumes that because the majority says X is right, then Y is not. It uses little logic.
Ad verecundiam	This argument uses quotes and phrases from people in authority or popular people to support one's own views.
Bandwagon	The bandwagon approach tries to convince you to do something just because everyone else is doing it. It is also referred to as "peer pressure."
Scare tactic	A scare tactic is used as a desperate measure to put fear in your life. If you don't do X, then Y is going to happen to you.
Straw argument	The straw argument attacks the opponent's argument to make one's own argument stronger. It does not necessarily make argument A stronger; it simply discounts argument B.
Appeal to tradition	This argument looks only at the past and suggests that we have always done it "this way" and we should continue to do it "this way."
Plain folks	This type of persuasion is used to make you feel that X or Y is just like you. Usually, they are not; they are only using this appeal to connect with your sense of space and time.
Patriotism	This form of persuasion asks you to ignore reason and logic and support what is right for state A or city B or nation C.
Glittering generalities	This type of persuasion or argumentation is an appeal to generalities (Bosak, 1976). It suggests that a person or candidate or professional is for *all* the *right* things: justice, low taxes, no inflation, rebates, full employment, low crime, free tuition, progress, privacy, and truth.

Below, you will find statements intended to persuade you or argue for a cause. Beside each statement, identify which type of faulty persuasion is used.

AB	Ad baculum
AH	Ad hominem
AP	Ad populum
AV	Ad verecundiam
BW	Bandwagon
ST	Scare tactic
SA	Straw argument
AT	Appeal to tradition
PF	Plain folks
PM	Patriotism
GG	Glittering generalities

_____ 1. *This country has never faltered in the face of adversity. Our strong, united military has seen us through many troubled times, and it will see us through our current situation. This is your country; support your military.*

_____ 2. *If I am elected to office, I will personally lobby for lower taxes, a new comprehensive crime bill, a $2500 tax cut on every new home, better education, and I will personally work to lower the unemployment rate.*

_____ 3. *This is the best college in the region. All of your friends will be attending this fall. You don't want to be left out; you should join us, too.*

_____ 4. *If you really listen to Governor Wise's proposal on health care, you will see that there is no way that we can have a national system. You will not be able to select your doctor, you will not be able to go to the hospital of your choice, and you will not be able to get immediate attention. His proposal is not as comprehensive as our proposal.*

_____ 5. *My father went to Honors College, I went to Honors College, and you will go to Honors College. It is the way things have been for the people in this family. There is no need to break with tradition now.*

_____ 6. The witness' testimony is useless. He is an alcoholic; he is dishonest and corrupt. To make matters worse, he was a member of the Leftist Party.

_____ 7. The gentleman on the witness stand is your neighbor, he is your friend, he is just like you. Sure, he may have more money and drive a Mercedes, but his heart never left the Elm Community.

_____ 8. John F. Kennedy once said, "Ask not what your country can do for you; ask what you can do for your country." This is the time to act my fellow citizens. You can give $200 to our cause and you will be fulfilling the wish of President Kennedy.

_____ 9. Out of the 7000 people polled, 72 percent believed that there is life beyond our planet. Therefore, there must be life beyond Earth.

_____ 10. Without this new medication, you will die.

_____ 11. I don't care what anyone says. If you don't come around to our way of thinking, you'd better start watching your back.

As you begin to develop your critical-thinking skills, you will begin to recognize the illogical nature of thoughts, the falsehoods of statements, the deception in some advertisements, and the irrational fears raised to persuade. You will also begin to understand the depths to which you should delve to achieve objectivity, the thought and care that should be given to your own decisions and statements, and the methods by which you can build logical, truthful arguments.

Critical-Thinking Project

Choose one topic on which you would get interested in building an argument. It should be something to which you have already given considerable thought. As you research this topic and build your case, keep in mind that your analysis, evaluation, critique, and findings should use research from varied sources and should explore different angles. Also keep in mind the credibility, reliability, and validity of your sources. Your argument should be free of opinions and fallacies.

Sample topics for your consideration:

Is euthanasia ethical?

Is technology ruining our world?

Is genetic engineering ethical?

Is America in decline?

Should the paparazzi be regulated?

Should all people be allowed free speech?

Is our constitution outdated?

Should sex education be taught in public schools?

Is the U.S. criminal justice system fair to all citizens?

Is poverty in America a serious problem?

Should the United States have gun control?

When does life begin?

Do animals have rights?

State the argument or problem. _____

_____

_____

_____

Why have you chose this situation? _____

_____

_____

_____

What are the major issues surrounding this situation? _____

_____

_____

_____

How could this well-designed argument or solution help society? _____

_____

_____

_____

How could this argument or solution harm society? _____

_____

_____

_____

What are your opponents saying about the issue? _____

_____

_____

_____

What are two facts *supporting* your side? _____

_____

_____

_____

What fallacies have been used to persuade people to think "the other way?"

_____

_____

_____

What are the global ramifications of your situation? (Lateral, Universal,
Microscopic, Myopic, Best Friend, Worst Enemy, Pieces, Environment, and
Mystic) _____

_____

_____

_____

What is the most surprising thing that you discovered? Why? _____

_____

_____

_____

What research sources did you use to gather your information? _____

_____

_____

_____

 for critical thinking

- Strive for objectivity in thought, action, and decision making.

- Use the What If Methods when evaluating difficult and controversial issues.

- Reserve judgement until all the facts are known.

- Seek truth, even if the answers are painful and unpopular.

- Use only credible and reliable sources for research.

- Ask questions.

- Do not assume—research.

- Avoid rigid, concrete thought; strive for flexibility in thinking.

- Use emotional restraint.

- Work hard to identify fact from opinion.

- Avoid generalizations.

Critical Thinking and Decision Making

If you have been using the Internet, you know that URLs change frequently and are sometimes removed. If you cannot locate a particular exercise, try to find one that provides similar information.

F. Scott Fitzgerald made this important statement: "Either you think or else others have to think for you and take power from you, pervert and discipline your natural tastes, civilize and sterilize you." Critical thinking is quite simply making your own decisions after weighing carefully all the choices.

As beginning college students, you will probably be faced with making decisions that you may have never had the freedom to make before. Decisions like: "Do I study or party?" "Do I drink excessively merely to keep up with the others who make mindless decisions, or do I set my own limitations?" "Do I major in engineering because my dad wants me to, or do I follow my own heart?" "Do I extend my normal circle of friends to include international students from whom I can learn so much?" "Do I automatically judge gay students and put them in a category, or do I get to know them as individuals and then make my decisions about their friendships?"

A major reason to go to college is to learn to think and make your own decisions. Critical thinking is a skill that will be useful to you forever as you try to formulate your own ideas and discover truth. Access this URL (`http://www.znet.com/norman1/ct/indexX2.htm`), which offers you an entire course in critical thinking. As you can see, you can actually enroll in the course if you desire. For purposes of this exercise, however, you are to read Week One's information. Read everything and take the test. How did you do?

Name one major thing you learned from reading this information on critical thinking. _____

_____

Reread the section on Media Culture. Why is critical media literacy important to you as a citizen? _____

_____

_____

_____

Why are critical thinkers sometimes portrayed as cynics? _____

_____

_____

The one minute journal

in a minute or less, jot down one lesson you learned from this chapter.

So Much to Do, So Little Time to Do It: Priority Management

Yolandra was in my class several years ago. She impressed me as the most organized person I had ever known. She always had her calendar with her; she took meticulous notes and transcribed them every day; and she never missed a deadline. In her notebook, she had carefully written goals and objectives for every class. She had a regular schedule, which she

followed exactly, that detailed on which day she would do laundry, on which day she would shop for groceries, and at what time she would exercise. Yolandra adhered to a carefully organized schedule so she would have plenty of time for studying, reviewing her notes, and meeting with professors. Although she was not naturally outstanding academically, through these efforts Yolandra was able to keep her grades among the highest in the class.

Her organization and adherence to her priorities also enabled Yolandra to serve on the student council, to be active in a sorority, and to work 15 hours a week. I have never known a student to be more disciplined about her work. One of the best things about her self-management style was that she always took time to have fun and to be with her friends. Yolandra noted in her calendar "Sacred Day." These were days that were reserved for her to have fun, to renew her spirit, to do nothing—days on which work would not be allowed to interfere with life. Yolandra had learned some of the most important time-management and organizational strategies at a very young age: make a plan, stick to the plan, work hard, play hard, and reward yourself when you have performed well.

One of the best things about her self-management style was that she always took time to have fun and to be with her friends.

THE CROSS-CAMPUS "I'VE-GOT-TO-MAKE-MY-8 A.M.-CLASS-FOR-ONCE" DASH.

You may think, "That's great for Yolandra, but it wouldn't work for me." And you may be right. The important thing to consider as you read this chapter *is* how to design a plan that is right for you, a plan based on your schedule, your interests, and your most productive times of day. You'll want to consider how to manage your time and set priorities based on you and your individual needs. This chapter offers some pointers for getting things accomplished; some of them will work for you and some of them won't, but when you have finished the chapter, you should have a better handle on how to get the job done and still have time for yourself.

If you can't follow a schedule as rigid as Yolandra's, that's fine. Design a schedule you can follow. You might have heard the old saying, "All work and no play makes Jack a dull boy." This statement is true, but so is "All play and no work will make Jack flunk out of school." The trick is to find a happy medium.

What Is Time ?

> For what is time? Who is able easily and briefly to explain it? . . . Surely we understand it well enough when we speak of it. . . . What then is time? If nobody asks me, I know; but if I were desirous to explain it to someone . . . plainly I know not.
>
> St. Augustine

Have you ever tried to define time? It's almost like trying to catch a sunbeam or stretching to put your arms around a rainbow. Time is elusive and flexible and also restrictive and binding. Most of us have the idea that time is external to our bodies. We make plans to manage time as though it were a concrete object that could be placed in a box and manipulated at will.

After completing this chapter, you will be able to

- Assess your current status of organization

- Differentiate between "doing" time and "being" time

- Design a plan for accomplishing your daily, weekly, and monthly goals

- Organize your schedule to include all components of a balanced life

- Understand the importance of scheduling the most taxing items on your list for your personal peak performance time

- Say "no" if saying "yes" would cause you to be stressed, unhappy, and unable to focus on your own goals and interests

- Include in your plan some time for rest, relaxation, and doing nothing

- Learn to take fun breaks

- Put into practice the cornerstones for using effective organization and time management

Managing Time So You'll Have More Fun

As you focus on managing and organizing your time and using it wisely, remember that you are not learning to manage your time just so you can accomplish more work. The real reward of time and priority management is that it allows you to have more *fun*. Most of us prefer play to work. So if you approach the concept of time management with the idea that you will be gaining play time—time to relax, go to the movies, play with your children, be with a special person, laugh with friends, exercise, or just do nothing—you are much more likely to stick to your plan. Before studying organization and priority management practices, take a minute to assess the techniques you are using now.

1. I lead a balanced life with a reasonable amount of time devoted to play.
   1 2 3 4 5

2. I usually plan my days and weeks carefully.
   1 2 3 4 5

3. My daily plans are related to my short-term and long-term goals. 1 2 3 4 5

4. I know how to prioritize tasks for best results.
   1 2 3 4 5

5. I plan projects carefully before plunging in.
   1 2 3 4 5

6. I have a specific place for supplies and items I use frequently. 1 2 3 4 5

7. I feel that I have control over events in my life.
   1 2 3 4 5

8. I have a clear understanding of my value system.
   1 2 3 4 5

9. I am able to say no when a request does not fit with my personal objectives.
   1 2 3 4 5

10. I use a personal calendar that allows me to manage all my school, personal, and work time. 1 2 3 4 5

5=Strongly Agree

4=Agree

3=Don't Know

2=Disagree

1=Strongly Disagree

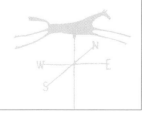

A SELF-ASSESSMENT Total your points from these ten questions. Now, refer to the following rating scale to see where you stand in relation to priority management.

0–10   *Your priority-management skills are very weak. You use little planning and feel little control over the events in your life. You are usually late with assignments, and time rules your life.*

11–20   *Your priority-management skills are weak. You try to get things accomplished on time, but you usually do not plan in advance, and you spend a great deal of time catching up.*

21–30   *Your priority-management skills are average. You have some success getting things done. You plan some of your day, but you may not stick to your schedule.*

31–40   *Your priority-management skills are very good. You develop a daily and weekly plan and follow it closely. Your assignments are usually turned in on time, and you have some free time for fun activities.*

41–50   *Your priority-management skills are excellent. You are a planner, and you get things done that need to be done. You set goals and work in a timely fashion to accomplish them. You use a calendar and update it daily.*

1. Are you a good priority manager?

2. What is the biggest problem with priority management?

3. What can you do to improve your skills in this area?

> Ordinary people think merely how they will *spend* their time; people of intellect try to *use* it.
> Arthur Schopenhauer,
> Aphorisms on the Wisdom of Life

Working Hard and Playing Hard

Developing and perfecting priority-management skills are critical to your success as a college student. You have probably wondered how some people get so much done, how some people always seem to have it together, stay calm and collected, and are able to set goals and accomplish them. At the same time, you are aware of others who are always late with assignments and are unable to complete projects and live up to commitments.

Although college students' abilities may vary greatly, most have the intellectual ability to succeed; the difference between success and

Going to college in the United States has always been a dream of mine. The week before I left home, I had so many doubts and fears. I did not know what was going to happen to me. I did not know what type of people I was going to meet. I did not know if I would like it. I only knew that I had to start at ground zero.

I have managed to survive because I took the time to meet new people and make friends. I know that college is an academic place, but it is also a place to meet new and interesting people. So, I made the decision early that I would create a schedule that allowed me the opportunity to meet and socialize with a new world of colorful people as well as time to study.

I see so many people who socialize all the time. They will tell you their life story in an instant. They neglect their academic work for social times. I have seen people fail because they did not know how to manage their time properly. Being new to the United States, I needed to meet people, but I also needed to succeed academically. I had to learn how to manage my priorities so that I could have time to do both.

Making the decision to have time for friends was very helpful to me. Had I not done this, I would be very lonely in the United States. So, I had to make it work. Using my quality time for study and friends has given me a wonderful experience in college. I know the value of managing priorities so that we have time in life to do what we enjoy.

failure is often the person's ability to organize and manage time and to set priorities. Have you ever thought about the statement "Life is a series of choices"? You can't do everything, so you have to make choices! Making choices is what priority and time management are all about.

This chapter presents guidelines to help you focus on managing your time so that you can devote a sufficient part of your day to your work and studies but still be able to have fun and develop the top line.

THE DIFFERENCE BETWEEN BEING AND DOING

Do you know the importance of being as well as doing? If you are a doing person, you focus on what you accomplish, how many awards you win, how much money you make, how many offices you hold. In other words, you are focused on a destination. If you allow some time for being, you will experience the journey that life is meant to be. You will take time to walk on the beach, to work out in the gym, to enjoy a play or a football game. The measure of your life should be much more than numerical facts and figures. Can you think of people who spend all their time doing and very little time being?

Discuss ways in which you have spent your time doing since you arrived

on campus. _____

_____

_____

_____

Discuss ways in which you have spent your time being since you began your college career. _____

_____

_____

_____

At this point of your development, are you spending too much time either doing or being?

You know that you will experience many hectic days when you won't have balance, quiet, and being time, but the goal is to have it as often as you can. Balance doesn't mean that you should play as much as you work; the demands of today's schedules usually don't allow for that. Balance does mean that a reasonable portion of every day should be devoted to that elusive top line—quality and joy. Some days you may feel like a juggler as you look for ways to live as well as to work.

■ FOCUSING ON QUALITY AND JOY Focus on this idea: you are building you. So don't take a haphazard approach. Consider your choices carefully, but leave time for spontaneity.

If part of your overall organizational plan is to include joy and quality of life, you need to identify what these two concepts mean to you in concrete terms. Later you will use your responses here to help you design your own unique priority-management plan.

WHAT BRINGS ME JOY?

_____

_____

_____

_____

_____

WHY?

_____

_____

_____

_____

_____

WHO BRINGS ME JOY?

_____

_____

_____

_____

WHY?

_____

_____

_____

_____

As you think about quality of life, relate to it as *enjoying this day.* Some college students, especially non-traditional students, can be so focused on getting that piece of paper that they don't take time to taste what college is and should be about. Savor the college experience, squeeze every drop from it, start a foundation on which you will continue to build all your life—a foundation that includes joy and quality of life, as well as work and accomplishments.

Now look over the checklist of activities or experiences that might have a part in a plan that includes quality of life. Since quality of life is a personal matter, some of the things on this list may not appeal to you. Place a check by each item you might like to do or experience. Then add others to your personal list of things that are important to your quality of life now or that you think you might like to experience.

■ QUALITY OF LIFE EXPERIENCES CHECKLIST

____ Watching a sunset

____ Walking on the beach

____ Reading a book

____ Listening to music

____ Skiing in the mountains

____ Dancing

____ Doing volunteer work in the community

____ Going bird-watching

____ Going to the zoo

_____ Attending football games

_____ Ice-skating

_____ Painting

_____ Doing aerobics

_____ In-line skating

_____ Talking to a friend

_____ Writing a letter

_____ Chatting on the Internet

_____ Working out in the gym

_____ Playing basketball or
other sport

_____ Learning a computer game

_____ Preparing a gourmet meal

_____ Taking a spontaneous trip

Others: _____

_____

_____

_____

_____

_____

_____

Later, you will use this list to help you design your own personal priority-management plan.

JUGGLING MULTIPLE PRIORITIES

Sometimes you need to be in several places at once, but of course you can't be. These situations can be extremely frustrating unless you learn to set priorities. Practice dealing with such a situation by working on the following problems.

■ DECISIONS, DECISIONS You are walking out of your room and the telephone rings. A friend with a problem is calling, and you can tell that this conversation needs to be a long one—your friend has relationship problems. You have only 12 minutes until your student council meeting starts, and it is important that you arrive on time.

Explain how you would handle this situation in such a way that you could make your meeting and still be helpful to your friend. _____

_____

_____

_____

_____

_____

_____

You have been assigned a group project with a deadline of October 15. At every meeting, the group seems to spend all its time on "What if we did this?" and never reaches a decision. The deadline is approaching rapidly, and no one is completing the assignment.

How could you demonstrate your leadership abilities and priority-management skills? _____

_____

_____

_____

_____

You have been in your room working on your computer for four hours without a break. You have been using the Internet to research information for a paper. Your eyes are tired, you are hungry, and your back is beginning to ache. You had hoped to finish this paper by noon, but because some of the references were difficult to locate, you now realize that you will have to work at least two more hours. You obviously need a break.

Explain what you would do on a break to energize you, relieve your stress, and help you come back to this task refreshed. _____

_____

_____

_____

_____

After working for six hours on a beautiful Saturday, you finish your paper at 3 PM. You feel wonderful because the paper is finished and the deadline is still a week away. You have been working on this paper gradually, instead of throwing it together at the last minute. You feel that you have done your very best work, and you will be proud to turn the paper in to your professor.

How would you reward yourself for the discipline you have used to finish this project? _____

_____

_____

_____

_____

_____

_____

_____

YOUR BODY'S CYCLES

Priority management and the ability to concentrate are closely linked. Since many people are able to concentrate on visual or auditory stimuli for only about 20 to 30 minutes before they begin to make errors, cramming for tests rarely works. Some people are able to concentrate effectively for longer periods of time, and some people for shorter periods; you'll need to determine your own ability to concentrate and then to plan for short breaks to avoid making errors.

Other factors affect concentration in different ways.

- **Complexity of material.** May lead to frustration.

- **Time of day.** Effect depends on type of task.

- **Noise.** Improves concentration for some people if it is not too loud.

- **Hunger.** Makes it difficult to concentrate.

- **Environment.** Positive or negative feedback and support or lack of support affect concentration.

- **Pace.** If too fast may result in errors; if too slow may result in boredom.

You have a prime time when you are most capable of performing at your peak.

If you are interested in sports or exercise, you know that your body responds to exercise and physical activity differently at different times of the day. Time of day affects your mind similarly. For instance, you may find that you complete work involving comparison and memory best in the morning; or, if you have gathered all the statistics and information needed to make a decision, you may handle this type of task best in the afternoon. You have a prime time when you are most capable of performing at your peak. For many people, even if they don't like to get up early, the peak performance time is in the morning if they have had enough rest. Other people function best late at night. Of course you want to work on the most important and demanding jobs at your peak working time. To determine your best working time answer the following questions:

1. Are you lethargic in the morning until you have been up for an hour or so?

2. Did you try to schedule your classes this semester after 10 am so you could sleep later?

3. Do you feel a little down around 5 pm but feel ready to go again around 8 pm?

4. Have you tended to pull all-nighters in the past?

5. Do you wake up early and spring right out of bed?

6. Do you have a hard time being productive during the late afternoon hours?

7. Is it impossible for you to concentrate after 10 PM?

8. Are you one of those rare college students who loves 8 AM classes?

If you answered yes to questions 1 through 4, or to most of them, you are a night person; if you answered yes to questions 5 through 8, or to most of them, you are a morning person. Being a morning person does not mean that you can never get anything done at night, but it does mean that your most productive time is morning. If you are a morning person, you should tackle difficult, complex problems early in the morning when you are at your peak. If you are a night person you should wait a few hours after getting up in the morning before you tackle difficult tasks.

MAXIMIZING YOUR TALENTS

The first step toward productivity is to organize so that your talents, skills, and work habits are used to their fullest potential. You know the saying "A place for everything and everything in its place." A certain amount of "everything in its place" is critical to productivity, but execution of this concept may be different for the highly organized person from what it is for the person who works among stacks of projects. Some suggestions for organizing according to your best working style follow. These suggestions are guidelines, which you can adjust to fit your personal needs.

TIPS FOR HIGHLY ORGANIZED PEOPLE

- Select a place on your desk or a desk drawer to keep your stapler, scissors, tape, pens, pencils, paper clips, and so on. Always return these items to their proper place.

- Purchase a book bag, and organize your materials by class. Take with you only those materials that you will need until you can return to your room or home to pick up different materials.

- Use a separate notebook for each class.

- Purchase a small filing cabinet (or a cardboard file box) and some file folders, and file your materials by class. *Save all old tests.*

TIPS FOR LESS-STRUCTURED ORGANIZERS

- Designate one desk drawer where you will always put your basic supplies, such as tape, scissors, and stapler.

- Keep your materials for each class in separate clear plastic stacking boxes or colored cardboard filing boxes. Stack them so you can see them. A small filing cabinet may also be helpful. Save old tests for reviewing for finals.

- As soon as you finish working or return from class put things away in the appropriate box.

- Buy different colored file folders so that each class or project has its own color.

> The more time we spend . . . on planning . . . a project, the less total time is required for it. Don't let today's busy work crowd planning time out of your schedule.
> —Edwin C. Bliss, *Getting Things Done*

Planning—The Secret to Priority Management

"I don't have time to plan." "I don't like to be fenced in and tied to a rigid schedule." "I have so many duties that planning never works." *No more excuses!* To manage your time successfully, you need to spend some time planning. Follow the steps for effective planning for one week. Then see how your productivity at the end of the week compares to your productivity before you used these ideas. Some of these ideas will work for you, and others won't.

STEPS FOR EFFECTIVE PLANNING

■ PLANNING AND ORGANIZING FOR SCHOOL Use the priorities chart to make a list of your highest priorities for this semester.

■ Focus on a few key things that you value the most

■ Include both long-range and short-range tasks

■ Focus on some items that are fun, relaxing, and growth oriented

Sometimes it helps to put all your tasks in a grid so that you can see them all at once. Many students like to lay out an entire week—or several weeks—and then set their priorities accordingly. You might want to use a chart like the "Master Schedule" to map out a plan for meeting all your responsibilities.

Next, use the chart called "Everything I Know I Need to Do Now." Check your list of priorities to be sure not to overlook any.

■ Include long-range projects, such as term papers

■ Include any special events that you really want to attend and that may be rewarding to you

■ Exclude anything that other people want you to do, but that you don't really have time for and that are not important to you and your goals and objectives

Learning to say no is important. Before you say yes to another committee or social activity, ask yourself, "Is this something I really want to do? Will it help me achieve my goals, or will it stress me out and divert my time and thinking away from what I really want to accomplish this semester?" If you are unsure, say, "Let me think about this overnight, and I will give you an answer tomorrow." Don't let other people make their priorities yours. You have your own set of priorities.

If you are a visual thinker who needs to see things to remember to do them, try one of the following approaches. Put your list on colorful Post-it notes so that you can move items around on a poster board or stick them on a typing stand and place it on your desk among the clutter. You might consider three columns of notes—school, work, fun. Alternatively, you might transfer your list to a poster and use colored markers to highlight priorities. Or, you might function best with a neat list in a notebook or on a section of your daily calendar. Visualizing your work may help you to stay focused.

	Monday	Tuesday	Wednesday	Thursday	Friday	Saturday	Sunday
6:00 A.M.		Study for Exam					
6:30 A.M.	Gym		Gym		Gym		
7:00 A.M.							
7:30 A.M.							
8:00 A.M.		Math		Math			Library
8:30 A.M.		↓					
9:00 A.M.		↓					
9:30 A.M.	Biology		Biology		Biology		↓
10:00 A.M.		Eng Exam		Eng			↓
10:30 A.M.							
11:00 A.M.		↓					
11:30 A.M.		Library			Essay		
12:00 P.M.		↓					
12:30 P.M.		↓					
1:00 P.M.		↓					
1:30 P.M.		LUNCH ←					→
2:00 P.M.		Review Biol.			Study		Library
2:30 P.M.		↓					↓
3:00 P.M.		↓					↓
3:30 P.M.		↓					↓
4:00 P.M.		Lab Test		Lab			↓
4:30 P.M.							↓
5:00 P.M.							↓
5:30 P.M.		WORK		WORK	WORK		↓
6:00 P.M.		↓		↓	↓		
6:30 P.M.		↓		↓	↓		
7:00 P.M.		↓		↓	↓		
7:30 P.M.		↓		↓	↓	Go out	
8:00 P.M.		↓		↓	↓	↓	
8:30 P.M.		↓		↓	↓	↓	
9:00 P.M.		Study	Study			↓	
9:30 P.M.		↓	↓			↓	
10:00 P.M.		↓	↓			↓	
10:30 P.M.		↓	↓			↓	
11:00 P.M.						↓	

1. _____
   _____
   _____

2. _____
   _____
   _____

3. _____
   _____
   _____

4. _____
   _____
   _____

5. _____
   _____
   _____

6. _____
   _____
   _____

7. _____
   _____
   _____

8. _____
   _____
   _____

9. _____
   _____
   _____

10. _____
    _____
    _____

Things I Need
to Purchase to Put My Priority-Management Plan in Place

1. _____

   _____

   _____

2. _____

   _____

   _____

3. _____

   _____

   _____

4. _____

   _____

   _____

5. _____

   _____

   _____

6. _____

   _____

   _____

7. _____

   _____

   _____

8. _____

   _____

   _____

9. _____

   _____

   _____

10. _____

   _____

   _____

Now, carefully look over the examples of "Today" lists for traditional and nontraditional students. Then use the blank form to make a list of everything you can reasonably do tomorrow and still take some fun breaks and spend some time being instead of just doing. Schedule no more than 60 to 75 percent of your time; leave time for thinking, planning, and interacting.

▨ Include segments of long-range projects (e.g., going to the library to begin research for a paper or project that isn't due for six weeks)

▨ Build in flexibility, in case a project takes longer than foreseen

When you have completed your Today list, place a 1, 2, or 3 by each item in the priority code column. Place a 1 by those items that absolutely must be done on this day if you are to avoid a major crisis. For example, you absolutely must finish a paper that is due the following day because the professor will not accept late papers. Place a 2 by those items that should be done today if possible because they are important, and further delay of these items could create a stressful situation and become a major problem. For example, you should read the three chapters in your psychology textbook that will be discussed

TODAY		Date	Jan. 25	
List of Priorities		Appointments and Classes		
Priority Code		End-of-Day Checklist		
3	Buy Mom's Gift		8:00	Math Class
3	Wash Car		9:00	History Class
1	Study - French Test	✓	10:15	Student Gv. Mtg.
1	Exchange Work Hours	✓	11:30	Canteen w/ John
2	Run 3 Miles		12:30	Lunch w/ Rolanda
1	Read Ch.14	✓	2:00	Study
2	Write 2/15 Paper		5 - 6	Run w/ Rolanda
Expenses for Today		Phone Numbers Needed Today		
lunch - 2.50 gas - 5.00 notebook - 3.79		Mary - 555 -1234		
Fun Breaks				
Canteen @ 11:30 w/ John Run w/ Rolanda				
Sacred Day to Look Forward to: Ski Trip !! Feb. 18				

TODAY		Date	Jan. 25	
List of Priorities		**Appointments and Classes**		
Priority Code		End-of-Day Checklist		
1	Lynnette's Play	✓	8:00	History Class
1	Meet w/ Boss	✓	9:30	Meet w/ Boss
1	Study for 1/26 Psy Test	✓	10:00	Write Report
2	Grocery Store		11:30	Walk w/ Ann
3	Call Smith @ Party		12:15	Call Tom's Teacher
1	Pick up Children	✓	3:30	Pick up Children
Expenses for Today		**Phone Numbers Needed Today**		
gas - 20.00 chicken - 12.70 groceries - 75.99		Mrs. Todd - 555-1212 Smiths - 555-0013		
Fun Breaks				
Walk w/ Ann Lynnette's Play				
Sacred Day to Look Forward to: Feb. 15 - Weekend in Mtns.				

in class the following day. The professor has indicated that it is important to read these chapters prior to the discussion. *Preparation relieves stress and improves your confidence.* Place a 3 by those items that could be done today if time permits, but that have no major bearing on overall goals and objectives. For example, shopping for a new pair of shoes would rate a 3. If it is not done today, you will not have a major crisis.

Now, put your plan to work. As soon as you have any time that is free from class, work, meals, committees, athletic practice, and so on, focus on accomplishing the first priority item on your list. Work hard to discipline yourself to finish this item in a certain amount of time. When you have finished the first task, move to the next one. As you work, occasionally focus on the fact that you will get a reward when you finish this task.

Reward yourself with short, fun breaks—watch a brief TV program, call a friend to talk for a few minutes (but limit your time), drink some juice, or eat an apple. Then go back to work! Work as long as you continue to be productive and don't feel that you are getting stale and performing inadequately. If you are a nontraditional student with a family, a fun break might be to talk with your children or partner about their day, to play a game, to take a walk together, or to ride bikes. Nontraditional students and their family members feel time pressures keenly. Don't expect to put your life and theirs on hold while you go to school. If you do, you all will begin to build resentments, which can damage your family life.

Write appointments and meetings in a calendar that you keep with you at all times. Own only one calendar. It is a mistake to try to keep a big calendar at home and carry a small one with you. *Always* take your calendar to meetings and classes. You might try placing stickers in strategic spots on your calendar to help you focus on important tasks that you might otherwise overlook, such as fun breaks and sacred days. Fun breaks, sacred days, and rewards give you something to look forward to. They are diversions from work that you enjoy *after* you have earned them!

Determine what style of calendar works best for you. Since you have to carry it everywhere, you'll probably want to select one that is not too heavy or bulky. Until you find a calendar you like, feel free to duplicate the Today sheet or any other forms in this book as often as you like.

		1	**2**	**3**	**4**	**5**	**6**
			Pick up Children			7 pm Lynnette's Play	
	7	**8** 7–9 pm Study	**9**	**10** 7–9 pm Study	**11** Meet w/ Boss	**12**	**13** Football game w/Tom
	14	**15** 7–9 pm Study	**16**	**17** 7–9 pm Study	**18** *Psy test	**19**	**20**
	21	**22** 7–9 pm Study	**23** Pick up Children	**24** 7–9 pm Study	**25**	**26** Ski trip! →	**27**
	28 Ski trip! →	**29** 7–9 pm Study	**30** Pick up Children	**31** 7–9 pm Study			

■ **PLANNING AND ORGANIZING FOR WORK** Some supermen and superwomen work full-time and go to school full-time while they juggle families and other responsibilities. *We don't recommend this schedule unless it is for one semester only, when you are pushing to graduate.* If kept up for a long period, you will burn out from the stress such a pace imposes on your mind and body, and if you have children, they may be adversely affected by your overfull schedule. If you work less and, if necessary, take longer to graduate, you will have more opportunity to savor your college experience.

Use the following questions to help you get organized:

What are your most important responsibilities at work? _____

_____

_____

_____

_____

Be sure to plan carefully to accomplish these tasks. Your job and your reputation at work depend on their accomplishment, and this job may be the one that gets you your dream job later on.

What measures do your employers use to evaluate your work? _____

_____

_____

_____

All bosses have pet things they want done—always get these done on time! If you are given a formal evaluation, read it carefully to be sure that you are performing well in all categories.

Must you keep strict hours or can you use flexible scheduling? _____

_____

_____

_____

If your talents are in great demand, such as graphic arts skills or computer skills, if you can teach a sport or activity, such as swimming, or if you have an academic strength and can tutor, you may be able to set your own hours to a greater extent than if you have to meet an employer's schedule.

Thinking Long Range

Learning to think and plan carefully on a daily and weekly basis are extraordinary tools that will help you improve your grades, find time to have more fun, and relieve the stress caused by poor planning. It is even more helpful to enter these daily and weekly plans into a long-range overview. To best accomplish long-range planning, you need a calendar that covers at least a quarter or semester. Bookstores usually carry academic planners that cover a year. If it works better for you, you can make your own long-range calendar and post it in your study area so it is easily accessible. A poster board marked up with colored markers, each color having a different significance, might work for you. There are many ways of accomplishing long-range planning. The main thing is to "just do it!"

On this long-range calendar, you can enter the dates of exams, when papers are due, your roommate's birthday, dates of cancelled classes, group meetings, holidays, ski trips, vacations, and other crucial dates you need to remember.

If you are a part-time student or a non-traditional student, some of your entries might be similar to these: work for Joe this weekend, Mr.

Simmon's visit from home office, sales report due, Mary's dance recital, Joe's baseball game, long weekend with family, church retreat, or paint the trim on house.

You might also want to use your long-range calendar as a "tickler file." This simply means that if you have a paper due on October 22, you might want to make a reminder note on September 15 so you can begin research and not get caught in one of those gruesome "spend-every-waking-minute-in-the-library weekends."

Your long-range calendar should also remind you of doctor and dental appointments, a registration appointment with your advisor, and study group meetings. You might want to keep up with expenses by inserting the money you spend each day and by noting the reasons. If you are having budgeting problems, this information might provide insight as to how you can better allocate your money.

Use this long-range calendar as a motivator as well as a planner. As you look at November and see all the work laid out before you, you can also look at basketball games, ski trip, visit with friends at another university, and Thanksgiving Holidays. See the sample Long-Range Planner for an idea of how such a calendar might look. Then use the blank "Long-Range Planner" to make your own long-range plan for two months.

Week	Sunday	Monday	Tuesday	Wednesday	Thursday	Friday	Saturday
Jan. 5			Start on paper—due Jan. 18			Jock's visit	
Jan. 12		Math Quiz			Oral Presen- tation		
Jan. 19	Mom's B'day		Group mtg. 8 a.m. @ Bill's		English Composition due		
Jan. 26		History Test		Basketball —Kentucky		Weekend at Mary's parents ← →	
Feb. 2			Dr. Logan out of town —no class!				
Feb. 9		Basketball game— Georgia				Ski Trip ← →	

Week	Sunday	Monday	Tuesday	Wednesday	Thursday	Friday	Saturday

CORNERSTONES

for priority management
at work

- Organize your materials at work as they are organized at home.
  If you have a desk in both places, keep your supplies in the same
  place in both desks. Simplify your life by following similar patterns at work and at home.

- If you are a visual thinker and need to see different assignments,
  be considerate of others who may work close to you. Keep your
  work area as orderly as you can and still have it work for you.
  Clear plastic boxes, colored file folders, and colored file boxes will
  work as well for you on the job as they do at home.

■ Write directions down! Nothing is so irritating to busy bosses as having to give directions multiple times. Keep a notebook for repetitive tasks, use a software program, or do whatever helps you to remember.

■ Some jobs, for example, working the night desk at a hotel, are ideal for students because they allow time for study. If you have such a job, use the time after you have finished your work responsibilities to read chapters or study for exams. Never let your work responsibilities slide because you are studying on the job. Employers always notice.

■ Build relationships with fellow employees. Go out of your way to be polite, personable, and thoughtful. Remember people's birthdays with cards; compliment people; congratulate employees who are promoted or recognized in other ways. Don't engage in too much idle chatter. You are being paid to work. Other employees may resent you if you create disturbances with behavior that is out of place at the office. Don't waste time on gossip. Avoid negative people—they drain your energy.

■ When you are given projects that require working with others, plan carefully to do your work well and on time. Never hold up other employees' work because you have failed to get your job done. If necessary, come in early or stay late to get your job done. It will make a positive impression on your employer.

■ Keep a Rolodex file of important phone numbers and addresses that you use frequently. Cut off nonproductive telephone calls. Never use the telephone at work for social chats. Employers hate this habit!

■ Perform difficult, unpleasant tasks as soon as you can so you don't have them hanging over your head.

■ When you plan your work schedule, allow for unexpected problems that might interfere with the schedule. Plan what you can realistically accomplish so that you won't get frustrated.

Use these tips to help generate ideas for managing your time better, performing more effectively, and reducing stress at work. List your ideas in the space provided.

_____

_____

_____

■ PLANNING AND ORGANIZING AT HOME Some people organize effectively at work and school and allow things to fall apart at home. Whether you are a traditional student living in a residence hall or a nontraditional student living in a house with your family, your home should be pleasant and safe. It should be a place where you can study, relax, laugh, invite your friends, and find solitude. The following ideas about home organization will help you maximize your time.

for priority management at home

For Traditional Students:

■ Organize as effectively at home as you do at work.

■ If you have roommates, divide the chores. Insist on everyone doing his or her share. If your roommate is a slob and is driving you crazy, get a new roommate at the first opportunity.

■ Break bad habits, such as leaving dishes in the sink or letting laundry pile up. Plan a rotation schedule for major household chores and stick to it—do laundry on Mondays and Thursdays; clean bathrooms on Saturdays; iron on Wednesdays; and so on. Your parents will be much happier to see you if you don't expect them to do five weeks' worth of mildewed laundry when you are home for the weekend.

- Organize your closet and your dresser drawers. Get rid of clothes you don't wear.

- Put a sign by your telephone that reads "TIME" to remind yourself not to waste it on the phone.

- If you can't study in your room because of drop-in visitors or loud roommates, go to the library.

- Pay bills twice monthly. Pay them on time so you don't ruin your credit rating.

- If you drive to class or work, fill up your tank ahead of time so you won't be late.

For Nontraditional Students:

If you are a nontraditional student and have children, teach them to be organized so they don't waste your time searching for their shoes, books, and assignments. Teach family members responsibility! You can't work, go to school, and hold everybody's hand all the time. Give each of your children a drawer in a filing cabinet. Show them how to organize their work. You will be preparing them to be successful.

- If you are a perfectionist and want everything in your home to be perfect, get over it! You have many more important things to do than to spend your valuable time cleaning floors until you could have dinner on them.

- Get rid of the clutter in your garage, basement, or closets. Perhaps you can persuade your children to sell some of their old toys and other items that are cluttering up their rooms if you tell them they can keep the money. The idea is to reduce most of the clutter in your home.

- Establish a time for study hall in your home. Children do their homework, and you do yours. Any other adults in the house should have duties of a similar nature during this time so that the house is quiet.

- If you have a family, insist that all of you organize clothes for school or work for several days.

- Put a message board in a convenient place for everyone to use.

- If your children are old enough to drive, have them run errands at the cleaner's, post office, and grocery store.

- Carpool with other parents in your neighborhood.

- Delegate, delegate, delegate! You are not superwoman or super-man. Tell your family you need help. Children can feed pets, make their beds, fold clothes, vacuum, sweep, iron, and cut the grass if they are old enough.

- Schedule at least one hour alone with each of your children each week. Make this a happy, special time—a fun break!

- Plan special times with your spouse or partner if you have one so that he or she does not get fed up with your going to school. Nontraditional students must have support from their families in order to perform well at school.

- Tell your family and friends when you have to study; ask them to respect you by not calling or dropping by at this time.

- Post a family calendar where everyone can see it. Put all special events on it—for example, Janie's Recital, Mike's Baseball Game, Jasmine's Company Party. Plan to be able to attend special functions as much as possible. Be sure to put these dates on your personal calendar.

- Put sacred days on this calendar so that your entire family has something to look forward to.

- Take time to smell the roses.

Building a Priority-Management Plan

IF YOU NEED TO BE HIGHLY ORGANIZED

(If structure is not your strong suit, go to the next section.) Traditional time-management principles will probably work best for you because you are more likely to be organized, time conscious, and disciplined. For you, time management will consist largely of controlling the events in your life—getting to them on time, being prepared, being in control, working within a carefully designed system, starting and ending on time, and filing things in the right place.

You can never gain total control of all the events in your life—and perhaps it is good that you can't. One main goal for you is to control selectively as much as you can and to learn to relax and enjoy being during a segment of free time. Another goal is to learn to deal with frustration when you can't control events, other people, or circumstances so that you can avoid over stress.

Look through the chapter and make a list of major points that relate to you and

your work style. _____

_____

_____

_____

_____

_____

Use these key points and the forms provided in this chapter to design a time-management plan that suits your needs. Be sure to build in fun and relaxation time and strive for balance!

Refer to the exercise you completed earlier in this chapter on who and what brings you joy. Include in your management plan a few of the things that you enjoy most.

Now review the Quality of Life Experiences checklist that you completed. If you plan carefully and discipline yourself, how many of these items can you work into your plan as fun breaks, rewards, or sacred days?

IF YOU LIKE LESS STRUCTURE

You know by now that there is really nothing wrong with the way you do things. You may need to tighten up your time-management style, but you can still manage your time and avoid having your life geared to a rigid format that is uncomfortable and unnatural for you.

Make a list of the key points you learned in this chapter that will help you

design a time-management plan. Look back through the chapter and find major

ideas you want to remember. _____

_____

_____

_____

_____

_____

Now use the ideas in this chapter to design a plan for one week. Be sure to build in some techniques that require you to meet deadlines and to bring some degree of organization to your supplies and belongings.

Refer to the list you made earlier in this chapter of people and things that bring you joy. How many of these favorite people and experiences can you work into your schedule as fun breaks, rewards, or sacred days?

Remember to work first—and then reward yourself!

Your priority-management and organizational system should be individualized and tailored to your own unique work style. The main consideration in creating a plan should be: "Does it work for me?" If your grades are good, you feel good, your work performance is above average, your social life is active, your home is reasonably clean and orderly, your personal appearance is as good as you can make it, and you have some time to have fun and relax, you have a good system. Stick to it, and work to improve it!

 **CORNERSTONES** of priority management and organization

- Understand the importance of "balance" in your life.

- Realize that you are preparing to work in a new and different work environment.

- Know the difference in "being" and "doing."

- Focus on quality and joy.

- Be able to list *who* and *what* bring you joy.

- Include fun breaks, rewards, and sacred days.

- Learn to organize in a manner that maximizes your abilities.

- Devise strategies for managing your time effectively at school, work, and home.

- Keep a calendar and use other planning guides to keep you on track.

Getting Things Done

If you have been using the Internet, you know that URLs change frequently and are sometimes removed. If you cannot locate a particular exercise, try to find one that provides similar information.

Managing time and setting priorities are two of the most important skills you have to master as a college student. You will always have more to do than you can do and more choices than you can possibly accept. Setting wise priorities demonstrates growth as you mature as a college student. Following the rule, "Work first, play second" will improve your GPA. Reward yourself when you have been disciplined and follow your planned schedule. To locate suggestions for managing time, find this URL (`http://www.dartmouth.edu/admin/acskills/time_tips.html`). After reading the list Suggestions for Managing Time, on a separate sheet of paper make a tentative weekly schedule. Keep this list with you and try to follow it during the coming week. Put numbers which identify the order of priority and importance by each item. Then read the article, "10 Tips for Improving Time Management." Print this list and post it in the area where you work and study to remind you to use your time wisely.

IF YOU REALLY WANT TO TICK OFF YOUR PROFESSORS

Many college professors have been teaching for a long time and they have heard some of the same questions and statements much too often. As you read this list, you might use the statements to help you plan wisely. For example, if you are not able to attend a class, you are not excused from the material you missed or the assignment that might be due. So it isn't fair? You are in college now, and you might as well begin learning that life isn't fair. The professor is not your mother and will be insulted if you ask these questions: "Did I miss anything?" or "I didn't know we had a test because I cut class. Do I have to take it now?"

One of your first priorities in every class should be to locate a "buddy" with whom you can study, trade notes, get information that you may have missed, etc. Try to find someone who appears to be a responsible student, a good note taker, and perhaps someone you would like to get to know. Get your buddy's phone number so you can call quickly.

Access this URL (`http://monster.educ.Kent.edu/docwhiz/poprof.html`) and study "Doc Whiz's 40 Ways to P.O. the Prof," and be sure you don't use any of them.

The one minute journal

I n a minute or less, jot down what you learned in this chapter.

_____

_____

_____

_____

_____

_____

_____

_____

_____

_____

_____

_____

_____

_____

_____

_____

_____

_____

_____

_____

I Heard You! I Heard You! What Did You Say?: The Art of Active Listening

LaTonya had been through a rough evening. She had received a phone call from home to say that her grandmother was very ill and had been taken to the hospital. As she sat in math class the next morning, her mind was flooded with images of home. She had lived with her grandmother most of her life. In her mind's eye, she saw a house filled with people and

she could smell the bread baking in the oven. She saw her grandmother calling her down to eat before the arrival of the school bus. Her daydream was so vivid that for a moment, LaTonya could feel the gentle kiss of her grandmother on her forehead.

LaTonya was filled with anxiety wondering whether her grandmother would be all right. Her mind was a million miles away when a deep voice rang through her daydream. "Do you agree with the solution to this problem, Ms. Griffin?"

LaTonya knew the voice was speaking to her, but it took her a few seconds to focus on it. Again the instructor asked, "Do you agree with the solution to this problem, Ms. Griffin?" LaTonya had no idea whether she agreed or not. She had not heard the problem or the solution. She looked at the instructor and out of embarrassment and intimidation, she answered, "Yes, I do."

The situation took a turn for the worse. "Why do you think this is the proper way to solve this problem, Ms. Griffin?" LaTonya sat, bewildered, at her desk. She looked down at her notes for help, but she had written only the date and the topic for the day on her

A deep voice rang through her daydream.

notepad. The tension grew as the entire class waited for her answer. "I don't know, Dr. Huggins, I don't know."

How many times has this happened to you? We have all probably been in a similar situation recently. It isn't uncommon. Sometimes a person's mind wanders because of anxiety, dullness, or lack of interest; sometimes, because of simple mathematics. What does that mean? Well, most people speak at a rate of 125 words per minute, and most listeners can listen at almost 700 words per minute (Beebe and Beebe, 1994). This simple mathematical fact means that it is easy for people to lose concentration and fail to listen actively. If we toss in

personal anxiety or problems such as what LaTonya faced, or a boring speaker who causes you to lose interest, the problem of actively listening is compounded.

One of the practical traits most common to successful students is the ability to listen actively. Listening actively means knowing how to listen, what to listen for, how to evaluate the information you hear, and where to store the information you gain. This chapter is intended to help you to become an active listener. After completing this chapter, you will be able to

- Differentiate between listening and hearing

- Define active listening

- List the benefits of active listening

- Identify active and passive listening characteristics

- Identify key phrases and words for effective note taking

- Identify obstacles to active listening

- Listen visually

- Describe and use the cornerstones for effective listening

Take some time now to assess what types of listening skills you possess.

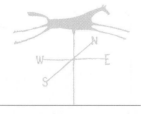

A SELF-ASSESSMENT Total your points from these ten questions. Refer to the following rating scale to determine where you stand in relation to your active listening skills.

0–10 *You have a great deal of difficulty focusing on the message and listening actively.*

11–20 *Your ability to focus and your listening skills are below average.*

21–30 *Your ability to focus and listen actively is average.*

31–40 *Your ability to focus and listen actively is above average.*

41–50 *You have excellent listening skills. You are able to focus on the message and weed out distractions.*

Now, refer to your journal and respond in writing to your findings. Consider the following questions when writing in your journal.

1. Do you agree or disagree with the results of the assessment? Why?

2. Do you know an excellent active listener? What qualities does that person have?

3. What do you feel you need to do to become a more active listener?

The Importance of Listening

Listening is one of the most important and useful skills human beings possess. For all animals, listening is a survival skill needed for hunting and obtaining food; for humans, listening is necessary for establishing relationships, growth, survival, knowledge, entertainment, and even health. It is one of our most widely used tools. How much time do you think you spend listening every day? Research suggests that we spend almost 70 percent of our waking time communicating, and 53 percent of that time is spent in listening situations (Adler, Rosenfeld, and Towne, 1989). Effective listening skills can mean the difference between success or failure, A's or F's, relationships or loneliness.

For students, good listening skills are critical. Over the next two to four years you will be given a lot of information in lectures. Cultivating

and improving your active listening skills will help you to understand the lecture material, take accurate notes, participate in class discussions, and communicate with your peers.

The Difference Between Listening and Hearing

We usually do not think much about listening until a misunderstanding occurs. You've no doubt been misunderstood or misunderstood someone yourself. Misunderstandings arise because we tend to view listening as an automatic response when it is instead a *learned, voluntary* activity, like driving a car, painting a picture, or playing the piano. Having ears does not make you a good *listener.* After all, having hands does not mean you are capable of painting the Mona Lisa. You *may* be able to paint the Mona Lisa, but only with practice and guidance. Listening, too, takes practice and guidance. Becoming an active listener requires practice, time, mistakes, guidance, and active participation.

Hearing, however, is not learned; it is *automatic* and *involuntary*. If you are within range of a sound you will probably hear it although you may not be listening to it. Hearing a sound does not guarantee that you know what it is, or what made it. Listening actively, though, means making a conscious effort to focus in on the sound and to determine what it is.

Listening is a four-step cycle, represented by the mnemonic ROAR.

R—Receiving the information

O—Organizing the sounds heard and focusing on them

A—Assigning meaning

R—Reacting

Receiving means that you were within the range of the sound when it was made. Receiving a sound is not the same as listening. To become an active listener, when receiving information make an effort to

1. Tune out distractions other than the conversation at hand.

2. Avoid interrupting the speaker.

3. Pay close attention to nonverbal communication, such as gestures, facial expressions, and movements.

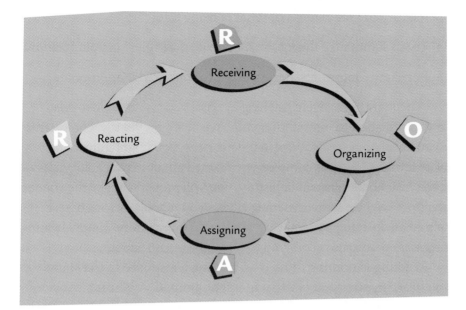

4. Concentrate on what is being said at the moment, not on what will be said next.

5. Listen for what is not said. Were important facts omitted?

Organizing and Focusing means choosing to listen actively to the sound, to pay attention to its origin, direction, and intention. To become an active listener, when organizing and focusing on information make an effort to

1. Sit up straight or stand near the person speaking, so that you involve your entire body.

2. Make eye contact with the speaker; listen with your eyes and ears.

3. Try to create a visual picture of what is being said.

Assigning refers to mentally assigning a name or meaning to what you have been listening to. Sometimes you may have to pay special attention to sounds in order to assign the correct name or meaning to them. Have you ever been sitting inside and heard a crash? You might have had to hear it again before you could identify the sound as dishes falling, books dropping, or static on the radio. Your brain tries to create a relationship between what you hear and what you have heard before; it tries to associate one piece of information with another. Once the association is made, you will be able to identify the new sound by remembering the old sound.

To become an active listener, when assigning meaning to information make an effort to

1. Relate the information to something that you already know.

2. Ask questions to ensure that there are no misunderstandings.

3. Identify the main ideas of what is being said.

4. Try to summarize the information into small "files" in your memory.

5. Repeat the information to yourself (or out loud if appropriate).

When you are actively listening in class, you will be able to relate new information to information you have heard previously. For instance, if you hear about *Oedipus Rex* in theater class, you might immediately relate it to the Oedipus complex you learned about in psychology class. If you hear about Einstein in history, you will probably make the connection from science. Active listening allows you to make associations that help create learning patterns for your long-term memory. Simply hearing information does not allow you to make these associations.

Reacting is nothing more than making a response to the sound you hear. If you hear a crash, you might jump; if you hear a baby cry, you might pick the baby up; if you hear a voice, you might turn to see who is speaking. Reacting can be a barrier to active listening. Tuning out because you are bored or do not agree with the speaker's point of view is a way of reacting to information.

To become an active listener, when reacting to information make an effort to

1. Leave your emotions behind; do not prejudge.

2. Avoid overreacting.

3. Avoid jumping to conclusions.

4. Ask yourself, "How can this information help me?"

Practical Definitions of Listening

According to Ronald Adler (Adler, Rosenfeld, and Towne, 1989), the drawing of the Chinese verb meaning "to listen" provides the most comprehensive and practical definition of listening. To the Chinese, listening involves the ears, the eyes, undivided attention, and the heart. Do you make it a habit to listen with more than your ears? The Chinese view listening as a whole-body experience. People from Western cultures seem to have lost the ability to involve their whole body in the listening process. We tend to use only our ears and sometimes, we don't even use them—remember LaTonya at the beginning of the chapter.

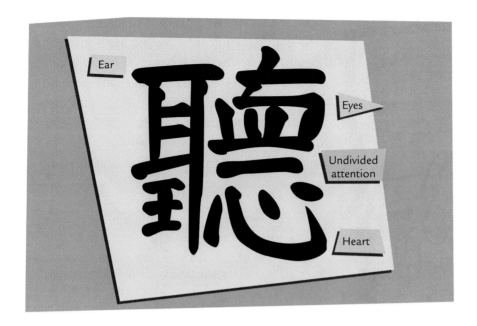

The American Heritage Dictionary defines listening as follows: "To make an effort to hear something; to pay attention; to give heed." This standard definition is not very concrete nor does it offer much direction. Listening needs to be personalized and internalized. To understand listening as a whole-body experience, we can define it on three levels:

1. Listening with a purpose

2. Listening objectively

3. Listening constructively

Listening with a purpose suggests a need to recognize different types of listening situations—for example, class, worship, entertainment, and relationships. People do not listen the same way in every situation.

Listening objectively means listening with an open mind. You will give yourself few greater gifts than the gift of knowing how to listen without bias and prejudice. This is perhaps the most difficult aspect of listening. If you have been cut off in mid-conversation or -sentence by someone who disagreed with you or if someone has left the room while you were giving your opinion of a situation, you have had the experience of talking to people who do not know how to listen objectively.

Listening constructively means listening with the attitude of, "How can this be helpful to my life

or my education?" This type of listening involves evaluating the information you are hearing and determining whether it has meaning to your life. Sound easy? It is more difficult than it sounds because, again, we all tend to shut out information that we do not see as immediately helpful or useful. To listen constructively, you need to know how to listen and store information for later dates.

■ AN INSIDER'S VIEW

Prince Wilson
The Community College
of Southern Nevada
Las Vegas, Nevada

I have come to know that listening is one of the most important things that a person can learn to do. I thought I was a good listener until a professor proved me wrong one day.

The history class had never been my favorite class, but it was interesting most of the time. One day, however, I was daydreaming and not really paying attention to the lecture or the professor. I could only think about getting out of class and getting home. There were some personal things I needed to take care of.

Near the end of class, the professor turned off the overhead and that was my cue to pack up and get ready to go. I began to pack my book bag. I knew that he was still talking, but I was not really listening. I heard him say something about a paper being due. I knew that we had a paper due and I had started on it already; no need to listen to that anymore.

Class met again on Tuesday. Near the end of class, the professor told us that he would now take our papers. I was shocked. It could not be due now. There was no way. When did this happen? I asked the person next to me if this was a mistake. She said no, he had told us about this on the Thursday before . . . at the end of class.

I went to the professor and told him that I had not heard the instructions. He told me that I needed to learn how to listen for instructions. I asked if I could bring him the paper later and he told me no. The deadline had passed.

Because I chose not to listen, I failed my paper. I did not do as well in the class as possible because I failed to take the time to actively

have come to know that listening is one of the most important things that a person can learn to do.

listen to all that was said by the professor. This situation in which I did not listen taught me a valuable lesson. Hearing and listening are two entirely different things.

Obstacles to Listening

Several major obstacles stand in the way of your becoming an effective listener. To begin building active listening skills, you first have to remove some barriers.

OBSTACLE ONE: PREJUDGING

Prejudging means that you automatically shut out what is being said; it is one of the biggest obstacles to active listening. You may prejudge because of the content, because of the person communicating, or because of your environment, culture, social status, or attitude.

■ DO YOU PREJUDGE INFORMATION OR ITS SOURCE? Answer yes or no to the following questions.

1. I tune out when something is boring.　　　　　　　　Yes　　No

2. I tune out when I do not agree with the information.　Yes　　No

3. I argue mentally with the speaker about information.　Yes　　No

4. I do not listen to people I do not like.　　　　　　　Yes　　No

5. I make decisions about information before I
   understand all of its implications or consequences.　Yes　　No

If you answered yes to two or more of these questions, you tend to prejudge in a listening situation.

TIPS FOR OVERCOMING PREJUDGING

1. Listen for information that may be valuable to you as a student. Some material may not be pleasant to hear but may be useful to you later on.

2. Listen to the message, not the messenger. If you do not like the speaker, try to go beyond personality and listen to what is being said, without regard to the person saying it. Conversely, you may like the speaker so much that you automatically accept the material or answers without listening objectively to what is being said.

3. Try to remove cultural, racial, gender, social, and environmental barriers. Just because a person is different from you or holds a different

point of view does not make that person wrong; and just because a person is like you and holds a similar point of view does not make that person right. Sometimes you have to cross cultural and environmental barriers to learn new material and see with brighter eyes.

OBSTACLE TWO: TALKING

Not even the best listener in the world can listen while he or she is talking. The next time you are in conversation with a friend, try speaking while your friend is speaking—then see if you know what your friend said. To become an effective listener, you need to learn the power of silence. Silence gives you the opportunity to think about what is being said before you have to respond.

■ ARE YOU A TALKER RATHER THAN A LISTENER? ANSWER YES OR NO TO THE FOLLOWING QUESTIONS.

1. I often interrupt the speaker so that I can say
   what I want.   Yes   No

2. I am thinking of my next statement while others
   are talking.   Yes   No

3. My mind wanders when others talk.   Yes   No

4. I answer my own questions.   Yes   No

5. I answer questions that are asked of other people.   Yes   No

If you answered yes to two or more questions, you tend to talk too much in a listening situation.

TIPS FOR OVERCOMING THE URGE TO TALK TOO MUCH

1. Force yourself to be silent at parties, family gatherings, and friendly get-togethers. We're not saying you should be unsociable, but force yourself to be silent for ten minutes. You'll be surprised at what you hear. You may also be surprised how hard it is to do this. Test yourself.

2. Ask someone a question and then allow that person to answer the question. Too often we ask questions and answer them ourselves. Force yourself to wait until the person has formulated a response. If you ask questions and wait for answers, you will force yourself to listen.

OBSTACLE THREE: BRINGING YOUR EMOTIONS TO THE TABLE

Emotions can form a strong barrier to active listening. Worries, problems, fears, and anger can keep you from listening to the greatest advantage. Have you ever sat in a lecture, and before you knew what was happening your mind was a million miles away because you were angry or worried about something, like LaTonya in the opening story? If you have, you know what it's like to bring your emotions to the table.

■ DO YOU BRING YOUR EMOTIONS TO THE LISTENING SITUATION? Answer yes or no to the following questions.

1. I get angry before I hear the whole story.   Yes   No

2. I look for underlying or hidden messages in information.   Yes   No

3. Sometimes I begin listening on a negative note.   Yes   No

4. I base my opinions of information on what others are saying or doing.   Yes   No

5. I readily accept information as correct from people whom I like or respect.   Yes   No

If you answered yes to two or more of these questions, you tend to bring your emotions to a listening situation.

TIPS FOR OVERCOMING EMOTIONS

1. Know how you feel before you begin the listening experience. Take stock of your emotions and feelings ahead of time.

2. Focus on the message and determine how you can use the information.

3. Try to create a positive image about the message you are about to hear.

Listening for Key Words, Phrases, and Hints

Learning how to listen for key words, phrases, and hints can help you to become an active listener and a more effective note taker. For example, if your English professor begins a lecture saying, "There are ten basic elements to writing poetry," jot down the number 10 under the heading "Poetry" or number your notebook page 1 through 10, leaving space for your notes. If at the end of class you have only listed six elements to writing poetry, you know that you missed a part of the lecture. At this point, you need to ask the professor some questions.

Some key phrases and words that may help you to become an active listener are

in addition	another way	above all
most important	such as	specifically
you'll see this again	therefore	finally
for example	to illustrate	as stated earlier
in contrast	in comparison	nevertheless
the characteristics of	the main issue is	moreover
on the other hand	as a result of	because

Picking up on transition words will help you filter out less important information, and thus listen more carefully to what is most important. There are other indicators of important information, too. You will want to listen carefully when the professor

Writes something on the board

Uses an overhead

Draws on a flip chart

Uses computer-aided graphics

Speaks in a louder tone or changes vocal patterns

Uses gestures more than usual

Once you have learned how to listen actively, you will reap several key benefits as a student, as an employee, and as a citizen.

TOP 10 REASONS FOR ACTIVELY LISTENING

1. You will be exposed to more information and knowledge about the world, your peers, and yourself.

2. You will be able to help others if you listen to their problems and fears, and you will gain a greater sense of empathy.

3. You will avoid problems at school or work that result from not listening.

4. You will be able to participate in life more fully, because you will have a keener sense of what is going on in the world around you.

5. You will gain friends and healthy relationships, because people are drawn to those to whom they can talk and whom they feel listen sincerely.

6. You will be able to ask more questions and to gain a deeper understanding about subjects that interest you or ideas you wish to explore.

7. You will be a more effective leader. People follow people whom they feel listen to their ideas and give their views a chance.

8. You will be able to understand more about different cultures from around the world.

9. You will be able to make more logical decisions regarding pressing and difficult issues in your life and studies.

10. You will feel better about yourself because you will know in your heart and mind that you gave the situation your best.

Test Your Listening Skills

Your professor will assist you with the following activities to test your active listening skills in a variety of listening situations. You will need to use several types of listening skills to participate.

Close your book, listen to the instructor's story, and then follow the instructor's directions.

_____ 1. A thief approached the cabdriver at a traffic light.

_____ 2. The thief demanded money.

_____ 3. The thief was a man.

_____ 4. The cabdriver's window was down all the way when the thief approached the cab.

_____ 5. The cabdriver gave the thief the money.

_____ 6. Someone sped away with the money.

_____ 7. The money was on the dash of the cab.

_____ 8. The amount of money was never mentioned.

_____ 9. The story mentions only two people, the cabdriver and the thief.

_____ 10. The following statements are true:

   Someone demanded money; the money was snatched up; a person sped away.

	Listener	Additions	Deletions
1.			
2.			
3.			
4.			
5.			

Activity #4
Visual Listening

Listen to your peers and draw the design that they verbally create.

Activity #5
Whispers

Write down what the person next to you whispers in your ear.

_____
_____
_____
_____
_____
_____
_____
_____

Activity #6
I Can Name That Tune

After listening, answer the questions your instructor asks.

1. _____
2. _____
3. _____
4. _____
5. _____

6. _____
7. _____
8. _____
9. _____
10. _____

CORNERSTONES for active listening

- Make the decision to listen. Listening is voluntary.

- Approach listening with an open mind.

- Leave your emotions at the door.

- Focus on the material at hand. How can it help you?

- Listen for key words and phrases.

- Listen for *how* something is said.

- Listen for what is *not* said.

- Stop talking.

- Eliminate as many distractions as possible.

- Listen for major ideas and details.

- Take notes; this makes you actively involved in listening.

- Paraphrase the speaker's words.

- Relate the information to something you already know.

- Encourage the speaker with your body language and facial expressions.

- Don't give up too soon; listen to the whole story.

- Avoid jumping to conclusions.

How Do You Get More Out of Every Class?

If you have been using the Internet, you know that URLs change frequently and are sometimes removed. If you cannot locate a particular exercise, try to find one that provides similar information.

The average college student spends about 14 hours per week sitting in class with opportunities to listen. Most students, however, hear rather than listen. For tips on how to improve your in-class listening abilities, access this URL (`http://www.d.umn.edu/student/loon/acad/strat/ss_listening.html`).

List at least four tips you learned from this article that might help you improve your listening ability:

_____

_____

_____

_____

_____

_____

Many students attend class but appear not to get as much from each class as they should. By carefully preparing for class and by improving your listening skills, you can retain much more of the professor's lecture. One of the best ways to boost your GPA is to prepare carefully *before* class. Another way to improve your grades is to become an active listener. Access the URL (`http://www.sheridanc.onca/career/study/listen/.htm`) and read the article. Then respond to the following questions.

Name two important reasons to read the assignment before class: _____

_____

_____

_____

_____

_____

Why should you review the notes from the previous class? _____

_____

_____

_____

_____

_____

According to research, the average college student listens with about 35% efficiency. Rather than just letting a lecture happen to you, decide to get actively involved. Name some ways that you can become an active listener and participant in your classes.

Explain the acronym LISAN _____

_____

_____

_____

_____

_____

The one minute journal

In a minute or less, jot down one major idea you learned form this chapter.

_____

_____

_____

_____

_____

_____

_____

_____

_____

_____

_____

_____

_____

_____

_____

_____

_____

_____

_____

_____

_____

_____

Will This Be on the Test?: The Essentials of Note Taking

William loved to play pool. Pool was his passion, his hobby, his job, and his first love. Few things ever got in the way of William's pool game. On more than one occasion, William cut class to go to the pool hall with his buddies. "I'll just get the notes from Wanda," he would say. "She's always in class."

When class met on Monday morning, William asked Wanda for her notes.

She told him that her handwriting was not very good and that she took notes in her own shorthand. "Oh, that's all right," William said. "I'll be able to get what I need from them." Wanda agreed to make a copy of her notes and to bring them to William on Wednesday.

Wanda kept her promise and brought a copy of her notes. William put them into his backpack just before class began. The notes stayed in his backpack until the night before the midterm exam. He had not taken them out to look at them or to ask Wanda any questions about them. When he unfolded the notes, he was shocked at what he found. The notes read:

Psy started as a sci. disc. from Phi and Physio. Wihelm Wundt/GERM and Will James/US= fndrs. in lt. 19th cent. APA est. by Stanely Hall in US.
5 mjr Pers in PSY=
  Biopsy. Per
  Psychodym. Per
  Humanistic. Per
  Cog. Per.
  Beh. Per.
Psy wk in 2 mjr. areas 1. Acad. 2. Practicing

William was in trouble. He could not understand Wanda's shorthand, and it was too late to ask her to translate her notes. To add insult to injury, he had lost his textbook a few weeks earlier. After

Psy started as a sci. disc. from Phi and Physio.

trying unsuccessfully to make sense of the notes, he gave up and went to the pool hall to relax and have fun before the test. William failed his midterm.

We've all missed a few classes from time to time, haven't we? Very few students have not missed a class for one reason or another. Still, there are two important reasons for attending every class meeting: first, if you are not there, you will not get the information presented; second, although you may borrow notes from a classmate, there is no substitute for your own notes. William had several problems, including setting priorities, but one of his biggest problems was that he was not in class to take his own notes. To compound this problem, he did not bother to review the notes with Wanda and thus gain some insight into understanding them.

This chapter will address note taking and developing a system of note taking that works for you. At the end of this chapter, you will be able to

- Identify key phrases and words for effective note taking

- Understand why note taking is essential to successful students

- Use the L-STAR system

- Develop and use a personalized, shorthand note-taking system

- Use the outline technique for taking notes

- Use the mapping (or webbing) technique for taking notes

- Use the Cornell (T or modified) technique for taking notes

- Put into practice the cornerstones of effective note taking

Take a moment now to assess your current skills in taking notes.

1. I am an excellent note taker.
   1 2 3 4 5

2. I am a good listener.
   1 2 3 4 5

3. I have a personal note-taking system.
   1 2 3 4 5

4. I use abbreviations when taking notes.
   1 2 3 4 5

5. I use symbols when taking notes.
   1 2 3 4 5

6. I preread each chapter before class.
   1 2 3 4 5

7. I ask questions in class.
   1 2 3 4 5

8. I know how to listen for clues.
   1 2 3 4 5

9. I rewrite my notes after each class.
   1 2 3 4 5

10. I reread my notes before each class.
    1 2 3 4 5

5 = Strongly Agree

4 = Agree

3 = Don't Know

2 = Disagree

1 = Strongly Disagree

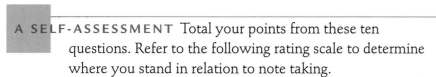

A SELF-ASSESSMENT Total your points from these ten questions. Refer to the following rating scale to determine where you stand in relation to note taking.

0–10   *You do not have a personalized system for note taking and you probably do not take accurate notes.*

11–20   *You have some note-taking skills, but you need to refine your skills by listening and using symbols and abbreviations.*

21–30   *You are an average note taker. You pay some attention to style and content and you probably read over your notes occasionally.*

31–40   *Your note-taking skills are above average. You probably read your notes weekly, correct any mistakes, and make additional notes in the margins.*

41–50 Your note-taking skills are excellent. You rewrite your notes, know how to use symbols and abbreviations, listen well, and probably have a personalized system of note taking.

Now, refer to your journal and respond in writing to your findings. Consider the following questions when writing in your journal.

1. Do you have a personalized note-taking system? What is it?

2. Do you have trouble reading your notes after class? Why?

3. Do you feel you need to upgrade your note-taking skills? Why?

Why Take Notes?

Sometimes it all seems like a big, crazy chore, doesn't it? Go to class, listen, and write it down. Is note taking really important? Actually, knowing how to take useful, accurate notes can dramatically improve your life as a student. If you are an effective listener and note taker, you have two of the most valuable skills any student could ever use. It is important to take notes for several reasons.

■ You become an active part of the listening process.

■ You create a history of your course content when you take notes.

■ You have written criteria to follow when studying.

■ You create a visual aid for your material.

■ Studying becomes much easier.

Preparing to Take Notes

Just as an artist must have materials, such as a brush, palette, canvas, paints, and oils in order to create a painting, you must have certain materials and prepare to become an effective note taker.

Maria D'Angelo-Bray
The University of Montana
Missoula, Montana

The decision to return to university life was not an easy one. After all, I was married and had a job. After extensive discussions with my husband and family, I decided to go back to school. But, unlike the last time, my grades were going to be more important. This time, *I was paying the tuition.*

I have always understood the importance of note taking; however, it was not until late in my college career that I learned how to properly take notes. I was always trying to write down everything the professor said and I would end up missing half the lecture. This made studying for a test from my lecture notes a hard task. I would end up discarding my notes and trying to reread the material. I was not getting the job done and my grades suffered. This went on until I learned several tricks for successful note taking.

One trick was to fold my notebook paper in half, lengthwise, to divide it into two columns. Class notes are written on the right side of the page and review notes that will help me to remember the main lecture points are written on the left half of the page. This gives me the opportunity to review my notes whenever I have time. If I do not get all of the information, I write down the page number where the material is located or ask the instructor where to find the material. Asking questions is an important part of learning.

As I prepare myself for a test, I go over my notes, adding anything that seems important from the text summary section. This helps me determine if I have more questions for the instructor. After I have completed this process, it only takes an hour each night to go over my notes. When test time arrives, I am familiar with the material and do not feel overwhelmed, stressed, or pressured. Advance planning also allows me more fun time with my family and friends. It is much nicer to go into a test feeling calm and knowing that I will do well.

Since an education is a large personal investment, I strive to make good grades. Good notes, planned study time, and discipline are all essential in pursuing my educational goals.

TIPS FOR EFFECTIVE NOTE TAKING

■ **Attend class.** This may sound like stating the obvious, but it is surprising how many college students feel they do not need to go to class. "Oh, I'll just get the notes from Wanda," said William in the opening story. The only trouble with getting the notes from Wanda is that they are Wanda's notes. You may be able to copy her words, but you may very well miss the meaning behind them. If she has developed her own note-taking style, you may not be able to read many of her notes. She may have written something like this:

G/Oke lvd in C/SC for 1yr ely 20c.

Can you decode this? How would you ever know that these notes mean "Georgia O'Keeffe lived in Columbia, South Carolina, for one year in the early part of the twentieth century"? To be an effective note taker, class attendance is crucial; there is no substitute for it.

■ **Come to class prepared.** Do you read your assignments nightly? College professors are constantly amazed at the number of students who come to class and *then* decide they should have read their homework. Doing your homework—reading your text, handouts, or workbooks or listening to tapes—is one of the most effective ways to become a better note taker. It is always easier to take notes when you have a preliminary understanding of what is being said. As a student, you will find fewer tasks more difficult than trying to take notes on material that you have never seen or heard before. Coming to class prepared means doing your homework and coming to class ready to listen.

Coming to class prepared also means bringing the proper materials for taking notes: your textbook or lab manual, at least two pens, enough sharpened pencils to make it through the lecture, a notebook, and a highlighter. Some students also use a tape recorder. If you choose to use a tape recorder, be sure to get permission from the instructor before recording.

■ **Bring your textbook to class.** Although many students think they do not need to bring their textbook to class if they have read the homework, you will find that many professors repeatedly refer to the text while lecturing. Always bring your textbook to class with you. The professor may ask you to highlight, underline, or refer to the text in class, and following along in the text as the professor lectures may also help you organize your notes.

■ **Ask questions and participate in class.** Two of the most critical actions you can perform in class are to ask questions and to participate in the class discussion. If you do not understand a concept or theory, ask questions. Don't leave class without understanding what has happened and assume you'll pick it up on your own. Many professors use students' questions as a way of teaching and reviewing materials. Your questioning and participation will definitely help you, but they could also help others who did not understand something!

Beginning the Building Process

You have been exposed to several thoughts about note taking: first, you need to cultivate and build your active listening skills; second, you need to overcome obstacles to effective listening, such as prejudging, talking during a discussion, and bringing emotions to the table; third, you should be familiar with key phrases used by professors; fourth, you need to understand the importance of note taking; fifth, you need to prepare yourself to take effective notes; and finally, you must scan, read, and use your textbook to understand the materials presented.

THE L-STAR SYSTEM

One of the most effective ways to take notes begins with the L-STAR system.

L Listening

S Setting It Down

T Translating

A Analyzing

R Remembering

This five-step program will enable you to compile complete, accurate, and visual notes for future reference. Along with improving your note-taking skills, using this system will enhance your ability to participate in class, help other students, study more effectively, and perform well on exams and quizzes.

L—Listening. One of the best ways to become an effective note taker is to become an active listener. A concrete step you can take toward becoming an active listener in class is to sit near the front of the room where you can hear the professor and see the board and overheads. Choose a spot that allows you to see the professor's mouth and facial expressions. If you see that the professor's face has become animated or expressive, you can bet that you are hearing important information. Write it down. If you sit in the back of the room, you may miss out on these important clues. Listening was discussed in Chapter 6.

S—Setting it down. The actual writing of notes can be a difficult task. Some professors are organized in their delivery of information, others are not. Your listening skills, once again, are going to play an important role in determining what needs to be written down. In most cases, you will not have time to take notes verbatim. You will have to be selective about the information you choose to set down. One of the best ways to keep up with the information being presented is to develop a shorthand system of your own. Many of the symbols you use will be universal, but you may use some symbols, pictures, and markings that are uniquely your own. Some of the more common symbols are

w/	with	w/o	without
=	equals	≠	does not equal
<	less than	>	greater than
%	percentage	#	number
@	at or about	$	money
&	and	^	increase
+	plus or addition	–	minus or subtraction
*	important	etc	and so on
eg	for example	vs	against
esp	especially	"	quote
?	question	...	and so on

These symbols can save you valuable time when taking notes. Because you will use them frequently, it might be a good idea to memorize them. As you become more adept at note taking, you will quickly learn how to abbreviate words, phrases, and names.

Using the symbols listed and your own shorthand system, practice reducing the following statements. Be sure that you do not reduce them so much that you will be unable to understand them later.

1. It is important to remember that a greater percentage of money invested does not necessarily equal greater profits.

Reduce. _____

_____

2. She was quoted as saying, "Money equals success." Without exception, the audience disagreed with her logic.

Reduce. _____

_____

T—**Translating.** One of the most valuable activities you can undertake as a student is to translate your notes immediately after each class. Doing so can save you hours of work when you begin to prepare for exams. Many students feel that this step is not important, or too time-consuming, and leave it out. Don't. Often, students take notes so quickly that they make mistakes or use abbreviations that they may not be able to decipher later.

After each class, go to the library or some other quiet place and review your notes. You don't have to do this immediately after class, but before the end of the day, you will need to rewrite and translate your classroom notes. This process gives you the opportunity to put the notes in your own words and to incorporate your text notes into your classroom notes. You can correct spelling, reword key phrases, write out abbreviations, and prepare questions for the next class. Sounds like a lot of work, doesn't it? It *is* a great deal of work, but if you try this technique for one week, you should see a vast improvement in your comprehension of material. Eventually, you should see an improvement in your grades.

Translating your notes helps you to make connections between previous material discussed, your own personal experiences, and readings and new material presented. Translating aids in recalling and applying new information. Few things are more difficult than trying to reconstruct your notes the night before a test, especially when they were made several weeks earlier. Translating your notes daily will prove a valuable gift to yourself when exam time comes.

A—**Analyzing.** This step takes place while you translate your notes from class. When you analyze your notes, you are asking two basic questions: (1) What does this mean? and (2) Why is it important? If you can answer these two questions about your material, you have almost mastered the information. Though some instructors will want you to spit back the exact same information you were given, others will ask you for a more detailed understanding and a synthesis of the material. When you are translating your notes, begin to answer these two questions using your notes, textbook, supplemental materials, and information gathered from outside research. Once again, this process is not simple or quick, but testing your understanding of the material is important. Remember that many lectures are built on past lectures. If you do not understand what happened in class on September 17, you may not be able to understand what happens on September 19. Analyzing your notes while translating them will give you a more complete understanding of the material.

R—**Remembering.** Once you have listened to the lecture, set your notes on paper, and translated and analyzed the material, it is time to study, or remember, the information. Some effective ways to remember information include creating a visual picture, speaking the notes out loud, using mnemonic devices, and finding a study partner. Chapter 8 will help you with these techniques and other study aids.

Putting It All Together:
Note-Taking Techniques

There are as many systems and methods of note taking as there are people who take notes. Some people write too small, others too large. Some write too much, others not enough. Some write what is really important, others miss key points. The aim of this section is to help you use the L-STAR system with a formalized note-taking technique. The L-STAR system can be used with any of the techniques presented.

Before examining the three most commonly used note-taking systems, let's review a few principles about basic note taking.

- Always date your notes and use a heading

- Keep notes from each class separate by using dividers or separate notebooks

- Use 8 1/2-by-11 inch paper with a three-hole punch

- Copy any information that is written on the board, used on an overhead, or presented in charts and graphs

- Organize and review your notes the same day you take them

- Do not doodle while taking notes

- Use your own shorthand system

- Clip related handouts to appropriate notes

The three most common types of note-taking systems are: (1) The outline technique; (2) The Cornell, or split-page technique (also called the T system); (3) The mapping technique.

THE OUTLINE TECHNIQUE

The outline system uses a series of major headings and multiple subheadings formatted in hierarchical order. The outline technique is one of the most commonly used note-taking systems, yet it is also one of the most misused systems. It can be difficult to outline notes in class, especially if your professor does not follow an outline while lecturing.

When using the outline system, it is best to get all the information from the lecture and afterward to combine your lecture notes and text notes to create an outline. Most professors would advise against using the outline system of note taking in class, although you may be able to use a modified version in class. The most important thing to remember is not to get bogged down in a system during class; what is critical is getting the ideas down on paper. You can always go back after class and rearrange your notes as needed.

If you are going to use a modified or informal outline while taking notes in class, you may want to consider grouping information together under a heading as a means of outlining. It is easier to remember information that is logically grouped than to remember information that is scattered across several pages. If your study skills lecture is on listening, you might outline your notes using the headings "The Process of Listening" and "Definitions of Listening."

After you have rewritten your notes using class lecture information and material from your the textbook, your pages may look something like this.

The Outline Technique

Study Skills 101	Oct.17 Wednesday
Topic: Listening	
I. The Process of Listening (ROAR)	
A. R = Receiving	
1. W/in range of sound	
2. Hearing the information	
B. O = Organizing & focusing	
1. Choose to listen actively	
2. Observe the origin, direction & intent	
C. A = Assignment	
1. You assign a meaning	
2. May have to hear it more than once	
D. R = Reacting	
l. Our response to what we heard	
2. Reaction can be anything	
II. Definitions of Listening (POC)	
A. P = Listening w/ a purpose	
B. O = Listening w/ objectivity	
C. C = Listening constructively	

THE CORNELL (MODIFIED CORNELL, SPLIT PAGE, OR T) SYSTEM

The basic principle of the Cornell system, developed by Dr. Walter Pauk of Cornell University, is to split the page into two sections, each section to be used for different information. Section A is used for questions that summarize information found in section B; section B is used for the actual notes from class. The blank note-taking page should be divided as shown.

A Blank Cornell Frame

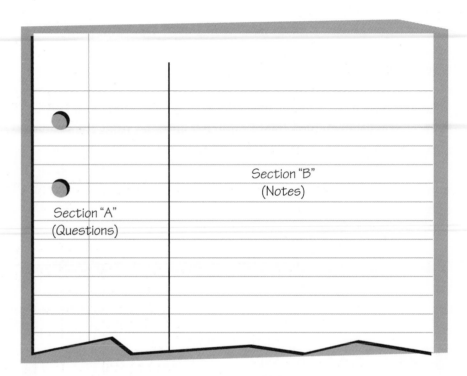

Section "B"
(Notes)

Section "A"
(Questions)

To implement the Cornell system, you will want to choose the technique that is most comfortable and beneficial for you; you might use mapping (discussed later) or outlining on a Cornell page. An example of notes outlined using the Cornell system follows.

Study Skills 101   Oct. 19
Topic: Listening   Friday

What is the listening Process? (ROAR)	*The Listening Process or (ROAR)
	A= Receiving
	1. Within range of sound
	2. Hearing the information
	B = Organizing
	1. Choose to listen actively
	2. Observe origin
Definition of Listening (POC)	*Listening Defined
	A. Listening w/ a purpose
	B. Listening objectively
	C. Listening constructively
Obstacles (PTE)	*What interferes w/ listening
	A. Prejudging
	B. Talking
	C. Emotions

The listening process involves Receiving, Organizing, Assigning & Reacting - Talking, Prejudging & Emotions are obstacles.

THE MAPPING SYSTEM

If you are a visual learner, this system may be especially useful for you. The mapping system of note taking generates a picture of the information. The mapping system creates a map, or web, of information that allows you to see the relationships among facts, names, dates, and places. A mapping system might look something like what follows.

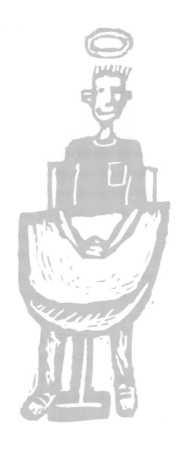

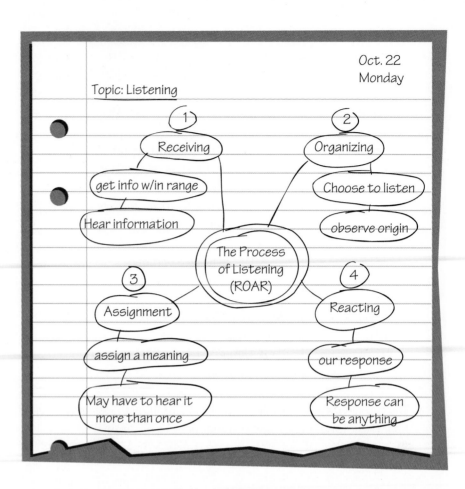

Oct. 22
Monday

Topic: Listening

1. Receiving
- get info w/in range
- Hear information

2. Organizing
- Choose to listen
- observe origin

The Process of Listening (ROAR)

3. Assignment
- assign a meaning
- May have to hear it more than once

4. Reacting
- our response
- Response can be anything

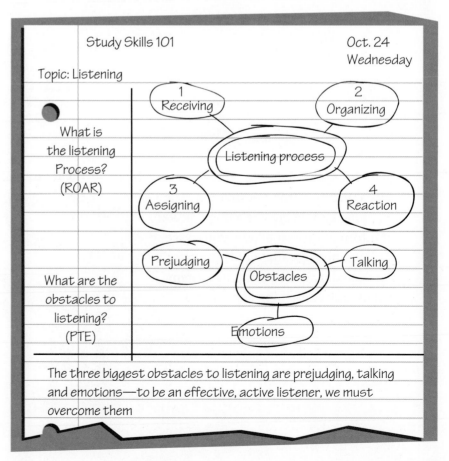

Study Skills 101

Oct. 24
Wednesday

Topic: Listening

What is the listening Process? (ROAR)

1. Receiving
2. Organizing

Listening process

3. Assigning
4. Reaction

What are the obstacles to listening? (PTE)

Prejudging · Obstacles · Talking

Emotions

The three biggest obstacles to listening are prejudging, talking and emotions—to be an effective, active listener, we must overcome them

The most important thing to remember about each note-taking system is that it *must* work for you. Do not use a system because your friends use it or because you feel that you should use it. Experiment with each system or combination to determine which is best for you.

Always remember to keep your notes organized, dated, and neat. Notes that cannot be read are no good to you or to anyone else.

What To Do When You Get Lost

Have you ever been in a classroom trying to take notes and the professor is speaking so rapidly that you cannot possibly get all of the information? Just when you think you're caught up, you realize that he or she has made an important statement and you missed it. What do you do? How can you handle, or avoid, this difficult note-taking situation? Here are several hints:

■ Raise your hand and ask the professor to repeat the information.

■ Ask your professor to slow down.

■ If he or she will do neither, leave a blank space with a question mark at the side margin. You can get this information after class (see the example on the next page). This can be a difficult task to master. The key is to focus on the information at hand. Focus on what is being said at the exact moment.

■ Meet with your professor immediately after class or at the earliest time convenient for both of you.

■ Form a note-taking group that meets after each class. This serves two purposes: (1) you can discuss and review the lecture, and (2) you will be able to get the notes from one of your note-taking buddies.

■ NEVER lean over and ask questions of another student during the lecture. This will cause them to lose the information as well.

■ Rehearse your note-taking skills at home by taking notes from TV news magazines or programs like The History Channel.

■ As a last resort, you can ask the professor's permission to use a tape recorder during the lecture. Do not record a lecture without permission. We suggest that you try to use other avenues, such as the ones listed above, instead of taping your notes. It is a time consuming task to listen to the lecture for a second time. However, if this system works for you, use it.

Public Speaking		Oct. 7
Lecture: Types of Research for Speeches		
*Periodicals	- Magazines, trade & professional	
*Newspapers	Local, state & national (some international as well)	
*Reference materials	Specialized ... (?)	} If you missed it, leave it blank
*Government documents	- Maps, Reports, federal proceedings	

Using Your Computer for Note Taking

i n the age of high-technology, some students prefer to take notes or transfer their notes onto their computers. Some students bring laptops to class while others immediately type and re-organize their notes after class. If you choose to use a computer for note taking, use the following tips:

In class

- Arrive to class in time to set up your computer. Don't disturb others by arriving late.

- Try to sit where you can see the professor and overhead, but also be respectful of other students. Tapping on the keyboard can disturb others' concentration.

- Don't worry too much about spelling or grammar. You can run the spelling and grammar checker after class while "cleaning" up your notes.

- Set your tabs before you begin. You can set them to use an outline format or the Cornell format.

Out of class

- If you are going to enter your notes into the computer program, do so as quickly after class as possible. The information obtained in class needs to be fresh in your mind. Try to re-organize your notes within 24 hours.

- Combine your textbook notes and lecture notes together. This will help you access the big picture of the information.

General hints

- Save your notes on both a disc and the hard drive.

- ALWAYS print your notes after each entry. It can be catastrophic if all of your notes are on one disc or one hard drive and the computer crashes or the disc is lost.

- After you have printed your notes, use a three-whole punch and place your notes in a three-ring binder. Arrange computer notes with related handouts.

A last note about re-copying your notes by hand or onto a computer program: this technique, while valuable to some students, does not constitute studying. Dr. Walter Pauk (1997), creator of the Cornell note-taking system, suggests that "contrary to what most people think, almost no learning takes place during the keyboarding of scribbled notes." Lastly don't be threatened by those who decide to use the computer in class or those who come to class with typewritten, printed notes. *Cornerstone* in general, and this chapter specifically, is about choices. You have to find and use a system that is convenient, easy, and useful to YOU.

CORNERSTONES

of effective note taking

- Attend class.

- Be prepared for every class by doing homework assignments.

- Sit where you can see and hear the professor.

- Recopy your notes after each class.

- If it's on the board or overhead, write it down.

- Use loose-leaf paper.

- Keep the notes for each course separate from one another.

- Have good, straight posture in class.

- Develop your listening abilities and tune out chatter.

- Ask questions.

- Use abbreviations and special notes to yourself.

- Keep your notes neat and clear; do not doodle on your notes.

- Participate in class.

If you remember the concepts of the L-STAR system (listening, setting it down, translating, analyzing, and remembering) and use this system as a study pattern, and if you find a note-taking system that is comfortable and useful for you, then you will begin to see significant improvement in your ability as a note taker and in your performance as a student.

Effective
Note Taking

If you have been using the Internet, you know that URLs change frequently and are sometimes removed. If you cannot locate a particular exercise, try to find one that provides similar information.

Although many professors are changing the ways they deliver information, the great majority still lecture most of the time. Therefore, you *must* be able to take notes to do well in class. You will find that many professors lecture on things that aren't in the textbook, making it even more important that you pay attention and take notes on critical information. Locate the URL (`http://www.d.umn.edu/student/loon/acad/strat/ss_notetaking.html`) for assistance in taking better notes.

What is the main key for good note taking that is discussed in the third paragraph? _____

_____

_____

_____

_____

List the main points included in this article that can help you deal effectively with incoming information.

_____

_____

_____

_____

What do "doodles" in the margins of your notes indicate? _____

_____

_____

_____

_____

The one minute journal

I n a minute or less, jot down one major idea you learned from this chapter.

Live as if you were to die tomorrow. Learn as if you were to live forever.

M. K. Ghandi, political and
religious leader of India

Avoiding the "All-Nighter:" Studying for Success

Tyrone walked into class beaming. He was happy, joking, and smiling, and he spoke to everyone on the way to his seat. He was always a delightful student, but today he seemed even happier than usual. Several classmates asked how he could possibly be so up. They could not understand his jovial attitude because today was test day. How could he be happy today of all days? How could anyone be happy on test day?

Tyrone told his classmates that he was happy because he was prepared. "I'm ready for the world," he said. "I studied all week and I know this stuff." Most of his classmates ribbed him and laughed. In the final moments before the test began, all the other students were deeply involved in questioning each other and looking over their notes. Tyrone stood by the window finishing his soda until time was called.

After all was said and done, Tyrone scored the highest on the exam of all his peers—a 98. Several students asked him how he did so well.

Intrigued by their curiosity, I asked Tyrone to share his secret to successful test taking.

I found his answer extremely useful, especially in light of his active life; Tyrone was on the basketball team, held a part-time job, cared for his elderly grandmother, dated, and worked on the college newspaper.

"You have to do it in steps," Tyrone said. "You can't wait until the night before, even if you have all evening and night." He explained that he incorporated study time into his schedule several weeks before the test.

If the test was to cover four chapters, he would review two chapters the first week and two chapters the second week. "I have a study room at the library because my house is so full of people. I make an outline of my notes, review my text, answer sample questions in the book, and many times I find someone to quiz me on the material."

"You can't wait until the night before, even if you have all evening and night."

s this how you approach studying? Do you have a positive attitude about taking tests? Many of us fear the whole process, and not everyone goes to the trouble that Tyrone did to prepare so well. Unfortunately, lack of study and poor test-taking skills are reflected in grades. Studying is one of the most essential skills a student can master. This chapter will introduce you to a variety of study and memory techniques. At the end of this chapter, you should be able to

- Identify studying strategies

- Identify and use learning styles

- Create a notebook system that works for you

- Determine the proper study environment for successful studying

- Identify new methods of reading, highlighting, and taking notes from texts

- Use the SQ3R method

- Use the READ method

- Create and use mnemonic devices and jingles

- Use cooperative learning

- Identify and use the Cornerstones of Effective Studying

- Use strategies for studying with small children in the house

Why Study? I Can Fake it

didn't have to study very hard in high school, why should I do it now?" This thought may have crossed your mind by this point in the semester. Many students feel that there is no real reason to study. They believe that they can glance at their notes a few moments before a test and fake it. Quite truthfully, some

students are able to do this. Some tests and professors lend themselves to this type of studying technique. More than you imagine, however, this is *not* the case. College professors are notorious for thorough exams, lengthy essay questions, tricky true–false statements, and multiple choices that would confuse Einstein. If you want to succeed in your classes in college, you will need to make studying a way of life.

Effective studying requires a great deal of commitment, but learning how to get organized, take effective notes (see Chapter 7), read a textbook, listen in class, develop personalized study skills, and build memory techniques will serve you well in becoming a successful graduate. Faking it is now a thing of the past. Take a moment to assess your study skills now.

AT THIS MOMENT...

5 = Strongly Agree

4 = Agree

3 = Don't Know

2 = Disagree

1 = Strongly Disagree

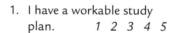

1. I have a workable study plan.   *1 2 3 4 5*

2. I am a very organized person.   *1 2 3 4 5*

3. I use a different notebook for each subject.   *1 2 3 4 5*

4. I know how to use a variety of study techniques.   *1 2 3 4 5*

5. I understand how memory works.   *1 2 3 4 5*

6. I understand the SQ3R study method.   *1 2 3 4 5*

7. I know how to transfer information into long-term memory.   *1 2 3 4 5*

8. I know how to use mnemonics and jingles.   *1 2 3 4 5*

9. I read my notes daily.   *1 2 3 4 5*

10. I know how to survey a chapter.   *1 2 3 4 5*

A SELF-ASSESSMENT Total your points from these ten questions. Refer to the following rating scale to determine where you stand in relation to your study habits and skills.

0–10   *You probably do not have a study plan, spend a great deal of time looking for materials, and have difficulty remembering information.*

11–20   *Your study skills are below average. You probably do not maintain a study plan, you have some trouble remembering information, and you are somewhat unorganized.*

21–30 *Your study skills are average for a new college student. You know the importance of using a study plan, but you probably don't follow it often. You can use memory techniques, and you are somewhat organized.*

31–40 *Your study skills and habits are above average. You probably know exactly where your supplies are, have developed a study plan, and use memory techniques wisely.*

41–50 *Your study skills and habits are excellent. You are probably a very organized person. You keep your supplies together and you know to use memory techniques, read and survey chapters, and take notes from the text.*

Now, refer to your journal and respond in writing to your findings. Consider the following questions when writing in your journal.

1. Is studying easy and exciting for me? Why or why not?

2. Is remembering information difficult for me? Why or why not?

3. I do or do not spend a great deal of time studying. Why?

■ **AN INSIDER'S VIEW**
Christine Latusky
The Community College
of Southern Nevada
Las Vegas, Nevada

I was an individual who returned to college after a 26-year hiatus. I knew from the beginning that the road to success would depend upon my diligent dedication to developing good study habits. In the beginning, the challenge seemed insurmountable, but with the passing of each week, my efforts were paying off.

Studying was the key to my academic success. I wanted to be a good student and have a high GPA. I found that time management was the key to successful studying. I had to learn how to allocate my time for each subject. It was a difficult decision. I had to give up some activities which I enjoyed. Since I was married, I had to balance my home and personal life with this new adventure.

I enrolled in my first classes, listened to each professor about the expectations and, at that point, devised a study plan for success. Before I knew what had happened, studying had become a part of my daily routine. I looked forward to the time I had set aside for me and my growth. Studying introduced me to a wealth of knowledge that has been useful in my everyday life.

I have learned that it takes a great deal of dedication to learn. It is all about persistence and motivation. As a married student, I could have easily found other things to do with my time rather than study, but I had made an emotional and financial commitment to my personal growth. Studying was the only way to reach that goal.

Studying was the key to my academic success.

As I move toward my degree, studying effectively and in a timely manner is still a challenge to me. But the knowledge that I have gained has proved to be a priceless commodity.

Learning Styles

All students learn differently; learning styles are approaches to how we learn. Some enjoy lectures, some enjoy "hands-on," classroom activities. Some enjoy quiet, reflective study time, while still others enjoy studying with a group of people. However, everyone has some learning traits in common. When anyone is learning or processing information, he or she is using one or more of their five senses: touch, taste, smell, hearing, or sight. The most successful students have identified their dominant learning style as either auditory, visual, or tactical. An **auditory learner** is one who learns best by using their sense of hearing. A **visual learner** is one who learns best by using their sense of vision, and a **tactical learner** is one who learns best by touch, or "hands-on." While we all have one dominant learning style, it is best to try to use all senses when receiving new information.

LEARNING STYLES INVENTORY

Before completing this activity, read each statement in each category. For each of the following categories, circle the appropriate number for each statement. Please keep in mind that there are no right or wrong answers.

1 = Least like me

2 = Sometimes like me

3 = Most like me

"A" Learning Styles

1 2 3   In my spare time, I enjoy watching TV or reading a magazine.

1 2 3   When putting something together, I need to look at the drawing.

1 2 3   I like teachers who write on the board and use visual aids.

1 2 3   I need to see things in order to remember them.

1 2 3   When I solve a word problem in math, I draw pictures.

1 2 3   I need a map in order to find my way around.

1 2 3   I can tell how someone feels by the expression on his or her face.

1 2 3   At a meeting, I prefer to watch people.

"B" Learning Styles

1 2 3   In my spare time, I enjoy listening to music or talking on the phone.

1 2 3   When putting something together, I need someone to explain how to do it

1 2 3   I like teachers who lecture about course information.

1 2 3   I need to hear things to remember them.

1 2 3   When I solve math word problems, I need to talk them out.

1 2 3   When getting directions, I need to hear them.

1 2 3   I can tell how people feel by the sound of their voice.

1 2 3   At a meeting, I prefer to listen and talk to people.

"C" Learning Styles

1 2 3   In my spare time, I enjoy physical activities (running, playing ball, etc.).

1 2 3   When putting something together, I need someone to show me how to do it.

1 2 3   I like teachers who provide classroom activities and encourage student involvement.

1 2 3   I need to write things down in order to remember them.

1 2 3   When I solve word problems in math, I prefer that someone show me what to do.

1 2 3   When getting directions, I need to write them down to remember them.

1 2 3   At a meeting, I prefer to take part in the conversation or activities.

Total "A" learning styles = _____
Total "B" learning styles = _____
Total "C" learning styles = _____

"A" learning style is **visual**, the sense of sight.
"B" learning style is **auditory**, the sense of sound.
"C" learning style is **tactical**, the sense of touch.

Source: From Sherfield, R., Williamson, J., and McCandrew, D. (1996). *Roadways to Success.* Allyn and Bacon, Boston.

It is important to note that there are *no* right or wrong answers. We are all different, and we all learn differently. One style is not more important or better than the other, and you may see a little of yourself in all styles. This inventory indicates the style you prefer when studying and learning new material. The following information describes the three types of learners and studying strategies for each.

■ VISUAL LEARNERS Visual learners learn from information through their sense of sight. They need to see in order to understand and remember. This learning style is the most common. The following activities help to develop visual strengths when studying:

■ Reading or studying the written word, pictures, or charts

■ Taking notes (especially in color)

■ Drawing pictures or diagrams of information

■ Visualizing information in your mind

■ Using the mapping system to create a visual of relationships

■ AUDITORY LEARNERS Auditory learners learn information through their sense of sound. They need to hear something to learn and remember it. Approximately 80 percent of the material presented in high school and college is taught in this way. Therefore, it is extremely important that you develop this learning style in order to achieve academic success. The following activities help to develop auditory skills for studying:

■ Stop talking and listen

■ Focus on what your professors are saying

■ Make audio tapes of class lectures and discussions

■ Talk to yourself or others about the information

■ Study in a group

■ TACTICAL LEARNERS Tactical learners learn best through their sense of touch. Students who learn in this way must physically experience the information to understand and remember it. The following activities help to develop the tactical sense while studying:

■ Acting out the information (role playing)

■ Using your hands to experience something

- Making models, charts, diagrams, and so on

- Taking notes

- Adding movement when studying (such as walking, tapping a finger, or rocking in a chair)

- Chewing gum or eating hard candies

- Studying in a group

For some, studying and learning new information can sometimes be difficult; for others, it may be easy. Regardless, to successfully master new material, involve as many of your senses as possible while studying.

As you read the following information concerning your study environment, SQ3R, READ, mnemonics devices, and cooperative learning, keep in mind study techniques that have and have not worked for you in the past. Try to relate each technique to your learning style and determine how you can improve each technique now that you have identified *your* learning style.

> Order and simplification are the first steps toward mastery of a subject.
> Thomas Mann, author

The Importance of Your
Study Environment

You may wonder why your study place is important. The study environment can determine how well your study time passes. If the room is too hot, too noisy, too dark, or too crowded, your study time may not be productive. In a room that is too hot and dimly lit, you may have a tendency to fall asleep. In a room that is too cold, you may spend time trying to warm yourself. Choose a location that is comfortable for *you*.

Different students need different study environments. You may need to have a degree of noise in the background, or you may need complete quiet. You have to make this decision. If you always have music in the background while you are studying, try studying in a quiet place one time to see if there is a difference. If you always try to study

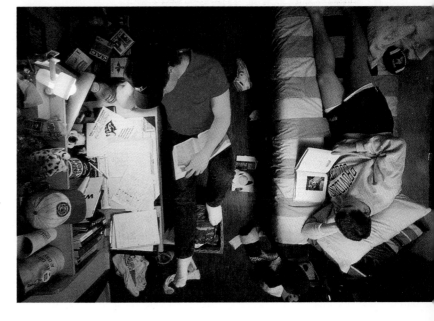

when it is quiet, try putting soft music in the background to see if it helps you. You may have to try several environments before you find the one that is right for you.

Describe your current study environment. _____

_____

_____

_____

_____

_____

_____

Has this environment served you well? Why or why not?

_____

_____

_____

_____

_____

How could this environment be improved? _____

_____

_____

_____

_____

_____

_____

Understanding Memory

hat would happen if you typed your English research paper into the computer and did not give it a file name? When you needed to retrieve that paper, you would not know how to find it. You would have to search through every file until you came across the information you needed. Memory works in much the same way. We have to store it properly if we are to retrieve it easily at a later time.

This section will detail how memory works and why it is important to your studying efforts. Below, you will find some basic facts about memory:

- Everyone remembers some information and forgets other information

- Your senses help you take in information

- With very little effort, you can remember some information

- With rehearsal (study), you can remember a great deal of information

- Without rehearsal or use, information is forgotten

- Incoming information needs to be filed in the brain if you are to retain it

- Information stored, or filed, in the brain must have a retrieval method

- Mnemonic devices, repetition, association, and rehearsal, can help you store and retrieve information

Psychologists have determined that there are three types of memory: sensory memory; short–term, or working, memory; and long-term memory.

Sensory memory stores information gathered from the five senses: taste, touch, smell, hearing, and sight. Sensory memory is usually temporary, lasting about one to three seconds, unless you decide that the information is of ultimate importance to you and make an effort to transfer it to long-term memory. Although your sensory memory bank is *very large*, sensory information does not stay with you for very long (Woolfolk, 1998). Sensory memory allows countless stimuli to come into your brain, which can be a problem when you are trying to concentrate on your professor's lecture. You need to make a conscious effort to remain focused on the words being spoken and not on competing noise. When you make an effort to concentrate on the professor's information, you are then committing this information to short-term memory.

Short-term, or working, memory holds information for a short amount of time. Your working memory bank can hold a limited amount of information, usually about five to nine separate new facts or pieces of information at once (Woolfolk, 1998). Although it is sometimes frustrating to forget information, it is also useful and necessary to do so. If you never forgot anything, you would not be able to function. Educational psychologist Anita Woolfolk suggests that most of us can hear a new phone number, walk across the room, and dial it without much trouble, but that if we heard two or three new numbers, we would not be able to dial them correctly. This is more information than our working memory can handle. If you were asked to give a person's name immediately after being introduced, you would probably be able to do so. If you had met several other new people in the meantime, unless you used some device to transfer the name into long-term memory, you would probably not be able to recall it.

As a student, you would never be able to remember all that your professor said during a 50-minute lecture. You have to take steps to help you to remember information. Taking notes, making associations, drawing pictures, and visualizing information are all techniques that can help you to commit information to your long-term memory bank.

SHORT-TERM MEMORY ASSESSMENT

Theo, Gene, and Suzanne were on their way home from class. As they drove down Highway 415 toward the Greengate subdivision, they saw a 1984 Honda Civic pull out in front of a 1990 Nissan Maxima. There was a crash as the two cars collided. Theo stopped the car. Gene and Suzanne jumped from the car to see if they could help. Suzanne yelled for someone to call 911; Robertina, a bystander, ran to the pay phone at the corner of Mason and Long Streets. Within ten minutes, an ambulance arrived and took Margaret, the driver of the Maxima, to St. Mary's Hospital. Tim, the driver of the Honda, was not badly injured.

Cover this scenario with a piece of paper and answer the following questions.

1. Who was driving the Honda? _____

2. What highway were they driving on? _____

3. Who called 911? _____

4. What hospital was used? _____

5. What year was the Maxima? _____

How many questions did you answer correctly? If you answered four or five questions correctly, your working memory is strong. If you answered only one or two questions correctly, you will need to discover ways to commit more information to your short-term, or working, memory. Some techniques for doing this are discussed later in this chapter.

Long-term memory stores a lot of information. It is almost like a computer disk. You have to make an effort to put something in your long-term memory, but with effort and memory techniques, such as rehearsal and practice, you can store anything you want to remember there. Long-term memory consists of information that you have heard often, information that you use often, information that you might see often, and information that you have determined necessary. Just as you name a file on a computer disk, you name the files in your long-term memory. Sometimes, you have to wait a moment for the information to come to you. While you are waiting, your brain disk is spinning; if the information you seek is in long-term memory, your brain will eventually find it. You may have to assist your brain in locating the information by using mnemonics and other memory devices.

LONG-TERM MEMORY ASSESSMENT

Without using any reference materials, quickly answer the following questions using your long-term memory.

1. *What is your mother's maiden name?* _____

2. *What is the year and make of your car?* _____

3. *What is the state capital of California?* _____

4. *Who wrote* A Christmas Carol? _____

5. *What shape is a stop sign?* _____

6. *What is your social security number?* _____

7. *What is your advisor's name?* _____

8. *Where is his or her office located?* _____

9. *What does the first "R" stand for in the SQ3R method?* _____

10. *Name one character on the TV series, "Friends."* _____

Did the answers come to you quickly? If you review your answers, you will probably find that you responded quickly to those questions whose content you deal with fairly frequently, such as your advisor's name, your social security number, or the year and make of your car. Although you were probably able to answer all the questions, in some instances your brain had to search longer and harder to find the answer. This is how long-term memory works.

There are countless pieces of information stored in your long-term memory. Some of it is triggered by necessity, some may be triggered by the five senses, and some may be triggered by experiences. The best way to commit information into long-term memory and to retrieve it when needed can be expressed through

VCR^3

V—Visualizing

C—Concentrating

R—Relating

R—Repeating

R—Reviewing

VCR^3

To **visualize** information, try to create word pictures in your mind as you hear the information. If you are being told about a Civil War battle, try to see the blue against the gray, try to visualize the battlefield, or try to paint a mind picture that will help you to remember the information.

Concentrating on the information given will help you commit it to long-term memory. Don't let your mind wander. Stay focused.

Relating the information to something that you already know or understand will assist you in filing or storing the information for easy retrieval. Relating the appearance of the African zebra to the American horse can help you remember what the zebra looks like.

Repeating the information out loud to yourself or to a study partner facilitates its transfer to long-term memory. Some people have to hear information many times before they can commit it to long-term memory.

Reviewing the information is another means of repetition. The more you see and use the information, the easier it will be to remember it when the time comes.

Ready, Set, Go!!

In Chapter 5 you got organized, collected all your materials together, and developed a notebook system. In Chapters 6 and 7 you actively listened and developed a note-taking system. So far in this chapter you've found the appropriate study environment. Now it's time to study. That's exciting, isn't it? No? Well, it can be. All it takes is a positive attitude and an open mind. Next you'll learn about several methods of studying that you can use to put yourself in charge of the material. After you've reviewed these methods, you may want to use some combination of them or you may prefer to use one method exclusively. The only set standard in choosing a study plan is that the plan must work for you. You may have to spend a few weeks experimenting with several plans and methods to determine the one with which you are most comfortable. Don't get discouraged if it takes you a while to find what is right for you.

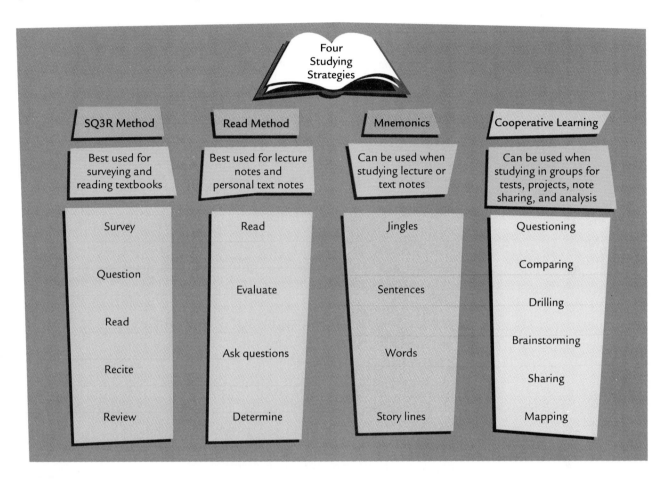

Four Studying Strategies

SQ3R Method	Read Method	Mnemonics	Cooperative Learning
Best used for surveying and reading textbooks	Best used for lecture notes and personal text notes	Can be used when studying lecture or text notes	Can be used when studying in groups for tests, projects, note sharing, and analysis
Survey	Read	Jingles	Questioning
Question	Evaluate	Sentences	Comparing
Read			Drilling
Recite	Ask questions	Words	Brainstorming
			Sharing
Review	Determine	Story lines	Mapping

SQ3R

The most basic and often-used studying system is the SQ3R method, developed by Francis P. Robinson in 1941. This simple, yet effective, system has proved to be a successful study tool for millions of students. SQ3R involves five steps: Survey, Question, Read, Recite, and Review. The most important thing to remember about SQ3R is that it should be used on a daily basis, not as a method of cramming.

1. **Survey.** The first step of SQ3R is to survey, or preread, an assigned chapter. You begin by reading the title of the chapter, the headings, and each subheading. Look carefully at the vocabulary, time lines, graphs, charts, pictures, and drawings included in each chapter. If there is a chapter summary, read it. Surveying also includes

reading the first and last sentence in each paragraph. Surveying is not a substitute for reading a chapter. Reading is discussed later. Before going any further, select a chapter from any book, or one assigned by your professor, and survey that chapter.

▧ CHAPTER SURVEY

1. What is the title of the chapter? _____

2. What is the subheading of the chapter? _____

_____

_____

_____

3. How many sections does the chapter have? _____
List them. _____

_____

_____

_____

4. What are the chapter objectives? _____

_____

_____

_____

5. Does the chapter include vocabulary words? _____
List the words you will need to look up. _____

_____

_____

_____

6. If the chapter contains quotations, which one means the most to you? Why?

_____

_____

_____

7. What is the most important graph or chart in the chapter? Why? _____

_____

_____

_____

2. **Question.** The second step is to question. The five most common questions you should ask yourself when you are reading a chapter are: Who? When? What? Where? and Why? As you survey and read your chapter, try turning the information into questions and seeing if you can answer them. If you do not know the answers to the questions, you should find them as you read along.

3. **Read.** After you survey the chapter and develop some questions to be answered from the chapter, the next step is to read the chapter. Remember, surveying is not reading. There is no substitute for this step in your success plan. Read slowly and carefully. The SQ3R method requires a substantial amount of time, but if you take each step slowly and completely, you will be amazed at how much you can learn and how much your grades will improve.

Read through each section. It is best not to jump around or move ahead if you do not understand the previous section. Paragraphs are usually built on each other, and so you need to understand the first before you can move on to the next. You may have to read a chapter or section more than once, especially if the information is new, technical, or difficult.

Another important aspect of reading is taking notes, highlighting, and making marginal notes in your text-book. You own your textbook and should personalize it as you would your lecture notes. Highlight areas that you feel are important, underline words and phrases that you did not understand or that you feel are important, and jot down notes in the margins.

"If I mark in my text, I may not get much for it when I sell it back to the bookstore," you might say. Right now you need to be concerned with learning the information in the most beneficial and efficient way possible. Don't worry about selling your textbook after the class is over. You might even want to consider keeping your book until you have completed your degree, especially if it relates to your major field of study.

As you begin to read your chapter, mark the text, and take notes, keep the following in mind.

- Read the entire paragraph before you mark anything

- Identify the topic or thesis statement of each paragraph and highlight it

- Highlight key phrases

- Don't highlight too much; the text will lose its significance

- Stop and look up words that you do not know or understand

When you have finished marking in your text, it may look something like this example.

Interacting=
Dynamic
Process

It is not easy to initiate, develop, and maintain positive relationships. It takes work and considerable skill. Interacting with others, for example, is a dynamic process. The interaction is constantly shifting and changing as you and the other person respond and react to each other. Sometimes communication will be clear; other times you may misunderstand each other. Sometimes you will have common goals and needs; other times your goals and needs will conflict. Everything you do will affect the relationship to some degree. Everything the other person does will affect your perceptions and feelings about the other person and the relationship.

Neg feelings
= hard to
lose

There is a general rule that positive perceptions of and feelings toward another person are hard to acquire but easy to lose; however, negative perceptions of and feelings toward another person are easy to acquire and hard to lose. A perception of another person as kind, for example, may develop as you see the person act in sympathetic and generous ways towards others. But one instance of deliberate cruelty can change your perception of the person dramatically. On the other hand, the sight of a person kicking a dog on a single occasion would probably stick in your memory, and repeated evidence of kindness would not wipe out the impression that the person can be cruel.

The complex and constantly changing nature of relationships, the slowness with which positive feelings and impressions are built, and the fragileness of relationships all point to the difficulty in developing friendships. Loneliness, however, pushes most people into the effort to do so. The experience of feeling lonely is a central fact of human existence.

From David W. Johnson, *Reaching Out: Interpersonal Effectiveness and Self-Actualization*, 5/e. © 1993, Allyn and Bacon.

While reading, you will want to take notes that are more elaborate than your highlighting or marginal notes. Taking notes while reading the text will assist you in studying the material and committing it to memory. Among the several effective methods of taking notes while reading are

- Charts

- Outlines

- Key words

- Mind maps

- Flash cards

- Summaries

- Time lines

■ CHARTS Charts assist visual learners in seeing relationships and differences.

Aeschylus	Tragedy	* 7 Against Thebes * Agamemnon * The Persians
Sophocles	Tragedy	* Oedipus The King * Antigone * Electra
Euripides	Tragedy	* Medea * Hippolytus * The Cyclops
Aristophanes	Comedy	* The Clouds * The Birds
Menander	New Comedy	* The Grouch * The Arbitration * The Shorn Girl

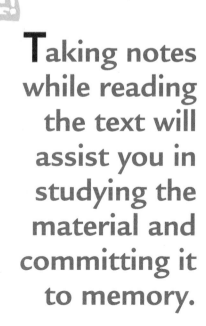

Taking notes while reading the text will assist you in studying the material and committing it to memory.

■ OUTLINES Outlines organize information into clusters or under separate headings.

Internal Sexual Organs   p. 73
(Female)
I. The Vagina
   A. - Extends back & upward from opening
   B. - @ 3 - 5" long at rest
II. The Cervix
   A. - Lower end of the uterus
   B. - Produces secretions (chemical)
III. The Uterus
   A. Pear shaped (called the womb)
   B. Slants forward
IV. The Fallopian Tubes
   A. Extend from upper uterus to ovaries
   B. @ 4" in length
V. The Ovaries
   A. Almond-shaped
   B. @ 1.5" long

■ KEY WORDS Key words help define terminology, phrases, names, and people.

Fat Soluble Vitamins: A, D, E & K (p. 237)

Vitamin A   1st to have been recognized; there
                 are 3 forms: retinol, retinal &
                 retinoic acid

Vitamin D   Different from all other nutrients
                 Body can't synthesize it w/out
                 help of sunlight

■ MIND MAPS Mind maps help show relationships among people, places, and things; they can also help show progression and time.

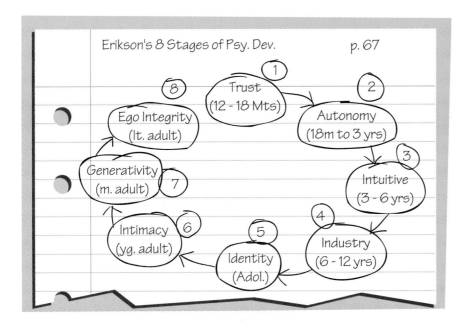

Erikson's 8 Stages of Psy. Dev.   p. 67

1 Trust (12 - 18 Mts)
2 Autonomy (18m to 3 yrs)
3 Intuitive (3 - 6 yrs)
4 Industry (6 - 12 yrs)
5 Identity (Adol.)
6 Intimacy (yg. adult)
7 Generativity (m. adult)
8 Ego Integrity (lt. adult)

■ FLASH CARDS Flash cards are portable and easily accessible. They are useful for remembering key words, phrases, definitions, and procedures. It is best to write the word or phrase on the front and define it on the reverse side.

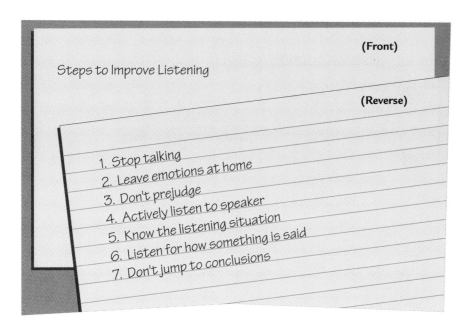

(Front)

Steps to Improve Listening

(Reverse)

1. Stop talking
2. Leave emotions at home
3. Don't prejudge
4. Actively listen to speaker
5. Know the listening situation
6. Listen for how something is said
7. Don't jump to conclusions

■ SUMMARIES Summaries are used for very detailed information that cannot be reduced to note cards, outlines, or time lines.

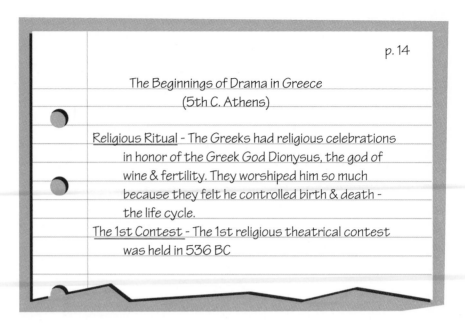

p. 14

The Beginnings of Drama in Greece
(5th C. Athens)

Religious Ritual - The Greeks had religious celebrations
in honor of the Greek God Dionysus, the god of
wine & fertility. They worshiped him so much
because they felt he controlled birth & death -
the life cycle.
The 1st Contest - The 1st religious theatrical contest
was held in 536 BC

■ TIME LINES Time lines are an excellent way to show chronological relationships among events.

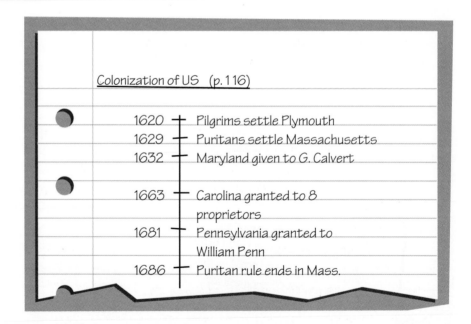

Colonization of US   (p. 116)

1620 ── Pilgrims settle Plymouth
1629 ── Puritans settle Massachusetts
1632 ── Maryland given to G. Calvert

1663 ── Carolina granted to 8
         proprietors
1681 ── Pennsylvania granted to
         William Penn
1686 ── Puritan rule ends in Mass.

As you read through a chapter in your textbook, you may find that you have to use a variety of these techniques to capture information. Try them for one week. Although taking notes while reading a chapter thoroughly is time-consuming, you will be amazed at how much you remember and how much you are able to contribute in class after using these techniques.

4. **Recite.** Recitation is simple, but crucial. Skipping this step may result in less than full mastery of the chapter. Once you have read a section, ask yourself this simple question, "What was that all about?" Find a classmate, sit down together, and ask questions of each other. Discuss with each other the main points of the chapter. Try to explain the information to each other without looking at your notes. If you are at home, sit back in your chair, recite the information, and determine what it means. If you have trouble explaining the information to your friend or reciting it to yourself, you probably did not understand the section and you should go back and reread it. If you can tell your classmate and yourself exactly what you just read and what it means, you are ready to move on to the next section of the chapter.

5. **Review.** After you have read the chapter, immediately go back and read it again. "What?!! I just read it!" Yes, you did. And the best way to determine whether you have mastered the information is once again to survey the chapter, review marginal notes, highlighted areas, and vocabulary words, and determine whether you have any questions that have not been answered. This step will help you store and retain this information in long-term memory.

THE READ METHOD

The READ method works best for studying notes you have taken from the text or in class. It has four steps:

1. **Read the notes.** Many students take notes and never go back to read them. As we pointed out in Chapter 7, the best way to study your notes is to read them the day you take them. It is important to read your notes as soon after you write them as possible so that you can make corrections. You should also read your notes often. For example, if you took notes on the causes of the Civil War last month, you should read those notes before the lecture on the battle of Gettysburg tomorrow. Doing so will refresh your memory and prepare you to participate in class discussions. Reading your notes is an important step in your success plan.

2. **Evaluate what you have read.** After you have read your notes, evaluate the information and prioritize what is most important. People often write too much when taking notes. As you read over your notes, you may find that you have included information that is not important or that you have repeated information. Evaluating will help you to make your notes more concise and to the point. You may want to highlight your handwritten notes or to add marginal notes to your notes.

3. **Ask questions.** As you read and evaluate your notes, ask questions about what you have written: "What was meant by this?" "How does this relate to the textbook information?" "Will I have to use this information on the test or in a paper?" If you have any questions that your notes do not answer, you need to review your text or make yourself a note to ask the professor at the next class meeting. Asking questions of yourself, your notes, your text, and your professors will set you on the road to success as a student.

4. **Determine the main issues.** The last part of the READ method for studying notes is to determine the main issues of what you have written. If you can read your notes and answer the question "What were the main issues covered?" you have a grasp of the material. If you cannot determine the main issues and recite them to yourself, you will need to review your text, ask questions, and maybe rewrite your notes.

USING MNEMONIC DEVICES

Mnemonic devices are memory tricks, or techniques, that assist you in putting information into your long-term memory and pulling it out when you need it. I recently gave a test on the basic principles of public speaking. A student asked if she had to know the parts of the communication process in order. When I replied that she should be able to recall them in order, she became nervous and said that she had not learned them in order. Another student overheard the conversation and said, "Some men can read backwards fast." The first student asked, "What do you mean by that?" I laughed and said that the mnemonic was great! The student had created a sentence to remember source, message, channel, receiver, barriers, and feedback. The relationship worked like this:

Some	=	Source
Men	=	Message
Can	=	Channel
Read	=	Receiver
Backwards	=	Barriers
Fast	=	Feedback

The first student caught on fast; she could not believe how easy it was to remember the steps in order using this sentence. This is a perfect example of how using memory tricks can help retrieve information easily.

The following four types of mnemonic devices may help you with your long-term memory.

■ JINGLES   You can make up rhymes, songs, poems, or sayings to assist you in remembering information, for example, "Columbus sailed the ocean blue in fourteen hundred and ninety-two."

■ SENTENCES   You can make up sentences such as "Some men can read backwards fast," to help you remember information. Another example is "Please excuse my dear Aunt Sally," which corresponds to the mathematical operations: parentheses, exponents, multiplication, division, addition, and subtraction.

■ WORDS   You can create words also. For example, Roy G. Biv may help you to remember the colors of the rainbow: red, orange, yellow, green, blue, indigo, and violet.

■ STORY LINES   If you find it easier to remember stories than raw information, you may want to process the information into a story that you can easily tell. Weave the data and facts into a creative story that can be easily retrieved from your long-term memory. This technique can be especially beneficial if your professor gives essay exams, because the "story" that you remember can be what was actually told in class.

COOPERATIVE LEARNING

There is strength in numbers. Many times, groups of people can accomplish what a single individual cannot. This is the idea behind cooperative learning. We form and use groups in our daily lives in situations like work, worship, and hobbies, and we even group our friends together. We develop groups for inspiration, excitement, and reflection, to advance social causes and to grow. Studying in groups can have the same effect. Cooperative learning can benefit you because you have pulled together a group of people who have the same interests and goals as you: to pass the course. Studying and working in groups can help you in ways such as drilling exercises, brainstorming, group sharing, and mapping.

Before we talk about those specific details, we should examine how to form a study group. The most effective study group will include people with different strengths and weaknesses. It would do little good to involve yourself in an accounting study group with people who are all failing accounting. Here are some tips for forming a cooperative study group:

- Limit the group size to five to seven people

- Search for students who participate in class

- Include people who take notes in class

- Include people who ask questions in class

- Include people who will work diligently

- Include people who do their share for the group

- Invite people who are doing well in a specific area; they may not attend every meeting, but they may be of assistance periodically

When the group is formed, you can engage in several different activities to learn, share, and reinforce information.

- **Questioning.** This technique asks that group members bring several questions to the next session. These may be predicted exam questions, questions about methods or formulas, or questions that the member was not able to answer individually.

- **Comparing.** The study group is a good place to compare notes taken in class or from the text. If you are having problems understanding a concept in your notes, maybe someone in the group can assist you. It is also a good time to compare your notes for accuracy and missing lecture information.

- **Drilling.** This technique assists you with long-term memory development. Repetition is an important step in transferring information to long-term memory. Have a group member drill the other members on facts, details, solutions, and dates. A verbal review of the information will help you and other members retain the information.

- **Brainstorming.** During each session, members can use this technique (discussed in detail in the Critical Thinking chapter) to predict exam questions, review information, and develop topic ideas for research, projects, future study sessions, and papers.

- **Sharing.** The study group is a time when you can give and receive. At the beginning or end of each session, students in the group can share the most important aspect of the lecture or readings. This will assist other members in identifying main points and issues pertaining to the lecture.

- **Mapping.** This technique can be used in a variety of ways. It is similar to the mapping system discussed in the note-taking chapter. On a board or large sheet of paper, let one member write a word, idea, or concept in the center of the board. The next student will add information, thus creating a map or diagram of information and related facts. This can help the group make connections and associations *and* assist members in identifying where gaps in knowledge exist.

Using groups can benefit your study efforts tremendously. If you are asked to participate in a group, take advantage of the opportunity. If you feel that a group could help you master the information, take steps to formulate a cooperative learning group on your campus.

Studying with Small Children in the House

For many college students, finding a place or time to study is the hardest part of studying. Some students live at home with younger siblings; some students have children of their own. If you have young children in the home, you may find the following hints helpful when it comes time to study.

- **Study at school.** Your schedule may have you running from work to school directly to home. Try to squeeze in even as little as half an hour at school for studying, perhaps immediately before or after class. A half hour of pure study time can prove more valuable than five hours at home with constant interruptions.

- **Create crafts and hobbies.** Your children need to be occupied while you study. It may help if you have available crafts and hobbies in which they can be involved while you are involved with studying. Choose projects your children can do by themselves, without your help. Depending on their ages, children could make masks from paper plates, color, do pipe cleaner art or papier-mâché, use modeling clay or dough, or build a block city. Explain to your children that you are studying and that they can use this time to be creative; when everyone is finished, you'll share what you've done with each other.

- **Study with your children.** One of the best ways to instill the value of education in your children is to let them see you participating in your own education. Set aside one or two hours per night when you and your children study. You may be able to study in one place, or you may have separate study areas. If your children know that you are studying and you have explained to them how you value your education, you are killing two birds with one stone: you are able to study and you are providing a positive role model as your children study with you and watch you.

- **Rent movies or let your children watch TV.** Research has shown that viewing a limited amount of educational television, such as *Sesame Street*, *Reading Rainbow*, or *Barney and Friends*, can be beneficial for children. If you do not like what is on television, you might consider renting or purchasing age-appropriate educational videos for your children. This could keep them busy while you study and it could help them learn as well.

- **Invite your children's friends over.** *What¿!!!!* That's right. A child who has a friend to play or study with may create less of a distraction for you. Chances are your children would rather be occupied with someone their own age, and you will gain valuable study time.

- **Hire a sitter or exchange sitting services with another student.** Arrange to have a sitter come to your house a couple of times a week. If you have a classmate who also has children at home, you might take turns watching the children for one another. You could each take the children for one day a week, or devise any schedule that suits you both best. Or you could study together, and let your children play together while you study, alternating homes.

Studying at any time is hard work. It is even harder when you have to attend to a partner, children, family responsibilities, work, and a social life as well. You will have to be creative in order to complete your degree. You are going to have to do things and make sacrifices that you never thought possible. But if you explore the options, plan ahead, ask questions of other students with children and with other responsibilities outside the classroom, you can and will succeed.

CORNERSTONES

for effective studying

- Study your hardest material first.
- Don't cram the night before; plan your time appropriately.
- Overlearn the material.
- Review your classroom and textbook notes daily.
- Set rules for studying.
- Study in a brightly lit area.
- Use the SQ3R method when studying texts.
- Use the READ method when studying lecture notes.
- Use mnemonic devices.
- Take breaks every half hour.
- Have a healthy snack.
- Turn the heat down.

Are You Using Good Study Skills and Time-Management Habits?

If you have been using the Internet, you know that URLs change frequently and are sometimes removed. If you cannot locate a particular exercise, try to find one that provides similar information.

Access the study skills self-help information checklist at this Internet address:

`(http://www.ucc.vt.edu/stdysk/stdyhlp.html)`. Complete the checklist to gain more detailed information about your own study habits and attitudes. The inventory will identify areas in which you are proficient as well as areas in which you could use some improvement.

Name the areas on which you need to focus to improve your study skills. _____

_____

_____

_____

_____

_____

_____

_____

_____

What strong points relative to your study skills did you identify? _____

_____

_____

_____

_____

_____

_____

_____

_____

For more help improving your study skills, you may want to access these additional articles on the Internet:

- Time-Scheduling Suggestions

- Time Scheduling

- Concentration—Some Rules of Thumb

- Reading and Study Skills: Note Taking—The Cornell System

- Editing Lecture Notes

- Constructive Suggestions Regarding Motivation

- Control of the Environment

To determine how good your study skills are, you might want to respond to the Study Skills Survey at this URL (`http://www.d.umn.edu/student/loon/acad/strat/self_test.html`). For still more tips on studying, access this site and respond to the checklist: (`http://www/ucc.vt.edu/stdysk/checklis.html`). As you read these items, note that each point is a tip for improving your study habits.

The one minute journal

in a minute or less, jot down one major idea you learned from this chapter.

The splendid achievements

of the intellect, like the soul,

are everlasting.

The Proving Ground: Strategies for Test Taking

Marchia could tell that something was wrong with her roommate, Ellen. Ellen had been quiet and distant for the past two days. That evening, while walking to the dining hall, Marchia asked Ellen if there was something bothering her. Ellen confided that the first test in her nursing class was in one week and that if she failed the test, she would be asked to leave the nursing program.

Marchia tried to tell Ellen that she had plenty of time to study the material and prepare for the test. Ellen replied that she was not worried so much about knowing the material, but that she was worried because she was a poor test taker. "I can know it from beginning to end," Ellen said, "but when she puts that test in front of me, I can't even remember my name! What am I going to do? This test is going to determine the rest of my life."

Marchia explained to Ellen that she suffered through the same type of anxiety and fear in high school until her math teacher had taught the class how to take a test and how to reduce test anxiety. "It's just a skill, Ellen, like driving a car or typing a research paper. You can learn how to take tests if you're really serious." Ellen asked if Marchia could give her some hints about test taking. As they finished eating, Marchia told Ellen that they could begin working for an hour every morning and an hour every evening to learn how to take exams and to reduce anxiety.

The week of the test rolled around, and Ellen was confident that she knew the material that she was to be tested on. She still had a degree of anxiety, but she had learned how to be in control of her emotions during a test. She had also learned how to prepare herself physically for the exam. She went to bed early the night before the exam. On exam day, she got up early, ate a healthy breakfast, had a brief review session, packed all the supplies needed for the exam, and headed to class early so that she could relax a little before the instructor arrived.

When the exam was passed out, Ellen could feel herself getting somewhat anxious, but she quickly put things into perspective. She sat back and took several deep breaths, listened carefully to the professor's instructions, read all the test instructions before beginning, told herself silently that

This test is going to determine the rest of my life.

she was going to ace the exam, and started.

After one hour and five minutes, time was called. Ellen put her pencil down, leaned back in her chair, took a deep breath, rubbed her aching finger, and cracked the biggest smile of her life. Marchia had been right. The strategies worked. Ellen was going to be a nurse.

T-Day !

The day has finally arrived. Test day! But you are calm and collected because you have learned, as Ellen did, how to listen, take effective, useful notes, apply study habits, and reduce test anxiety. You are ready! You are a success because you planned ahead and because you have convinced yourself that taking a test is a privilege and not a prison sentence.

So, why do you think professors give tests? Are they cruel? Do they love to see you sweat? Do they go home and laugh about it on the weekend? Before going any further, list some reasons that professors give tests.

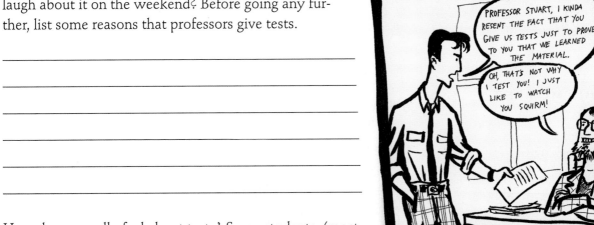

_____

_____

_____

_____

_____

How do you really feel about tests? Some students, (most, to be honest), view tests as punishment and cruel treatment by professors. Some students believe that testing is not necessary and that it is a tool of coercion. Successful students, however, realize that testing is necessary and even useful, that it has several positive purposes. Testing serves to provide motivation for learning, provide feedback to the student and to the professor, and determine mastery of material.

Successful people accept testing as a fact of life. You have to be tested to drive a car, to continue in school, to join the armed services, to become a teacher, a lawyer, a doctor, or a nurse, and often to be promoted at work. To pretend that testing is not always going to be a part of your life is to deny yourself many opportunities.

You may dread tests for a variety of reasons. You may be afraid of the test itself and the questions it may pose. Test anxiety can be over-

come however, and this section will present several ways you can become a more confident test taker and get started on the path to success. At the end of this chapter, you should be able to

- Recognize symptoms of extreme test anxiety
- Put tests into perspective
- Determine your test-anxiety level
- Control test anxiety
- Predict certain test questions
- Identify and use strategies for taking matching tests
- Identify and use strategies for taking true–false tests
- Identify and use strategies for taking multiple choice tests
- Identify and use strategies for taking short-answer tests
- Identify and use strategies for taking essay or discussion tests

AT THIS MOMENT...

5 = Strongly Agree

4 = Agree

3 = Don't Know

2 = Disagree

1 = Strongly Disagree

1. I have a low degree of test anxiety.   1 2 3 4 5

2. I can control my test anxiety.   1 2 3 4 5

3. My mind stays on the material at hand when testing.   1 2 3 4 5

4. I seldom worry about time when testing.   1 2 3 4 5

5. I read all the directions before beginning a test.   1 2 3 4 5

6. I know how to relax before a test.   1 2 3 4 5

7. I know what supplies to bring to a test.   1 2 3 4 5

8. I read the entire test before beginning.   1 2 3 4 5

9. I feel ready to take tests when test day arrives.   1 2 3 4 5

10. I remember test information after the test is over.   1 2 3 4 5

A SELF-ASSESSMENT Total your points from these ten questions. Refer to the following rating scale to determine where you stand in relation to dealing with test anxiety.

0–10   *You probably have very little test-taking training, and you usually experience extreme anxiety.*

11–20   *You may have had some test-taking training, but you still experience high anxiety and dread taking a test.*

21–30 *Your test-anxiety level is average. You probably know a few tech-niques for reducing anxiety.*

31–40 *Your test-anxiety level is lower than that of most students. You know how to take a test, preread the instructions, and reduce anxiety.*

41–50 *You have very little test anxiety. You have learned how to properly prepare for and take a test.*

Now, refer to your journal and respond in writing to your findings. Consider the following questions when writing in your journal

1. Why are so many students uptight about testing?

2. Why do tests mean so much?

3. Describe the best testing situation in which you have been involved. Why was it the best?

Controlling Test Anxiety

A student jokes with a professor, "I have five thousand dollars in my savings account and it is yours if you don't make us take the test!" Well, this may be a bit extreme, but many students would do almost anything to get out of taking exams and tests. Some students have physical reactions to testing, including nausea, headaches, and blackouts. Such physical reactions may be a result of being underpre-pared or not knowing how to take an exam.

Why do you experience test anxiety? _____

_____

_____

_____

_____

Your answer to this question is more than likely nega-tive. You may approach tests thinking

I'm going to fail

I knew I couldn't do this

There is no way I can do well, the teacher hates me

I should never have taken this class

These types of attitudes can cause you to be unsuccessful in testing, but with an attitude adjustment and some basic preparation, you can overcome a good deal of your anxiety about tests. You can reduce anxiety when you are in control of the situation, and you can gain control by convincing yourself that you *can* and *will* be successful. If you can honestly tell yourself that you have done everything possible to prepare for a test, then the results are going to be positive.

It is important to realize that a test is not an indication of who you are as a person or a mark of your worth as a human being. Not everyone can be good at all things. You will have areas of strength and of weakness. You will spare yourself a great deal of anxiety and frustration if you understand from the start that you may not score 100 on every test. If you expect absolute perfection on everything, you are setting yourself up to fail. Think positively, prepare well, and do your best, but also be prepared to receive less than a perfect score on occasion.

TEST-ANXIETY SCALE

Check the items that apply to you when preparing for a test:

_____ I do not sleep well the night before a test.

_____ I get sick if I eat anything before a test.

_____ I am irritable and hard to be around before a test.

_____ I see the test as a measure of my worth as a student.

_____ I black out during the test and am unable to recall information.

_____ I worry when other students are still testing and I am finished.

_____ I worry when others finish and I am still testing.

_____ I am always afraid that I will run out of time.

_____ I get frustrated during the test.

_____ I have a negative attitude about testing.

_____ I think about not taking the test.

_____ I always average my grades before a test.

_____ My body reacts negatively to testing (sweats, nervousness, butterflies).

If you checked off more than five items on this list, you experience test anxiety. It you checked off ten or more, you have severe test anxiety.

PREPARING FOR TESTS

You can take many steps to reduce test anxiety, but one of the most effective ways to reduce anxiety is to know what materials to study in preparation for the test.

Without looking at the answers, can you list the top ten places to find answers to test questions?

1. _____
2. _____
3. _____
4. _____
5. _____
6. _____
7. _____
8. _____
9. _____
10. _____

Answers

- Lecture notes
- Textbook notes
- Textbook highlighting
- Chapters in the textbook
- Sample tests in each chapter
- Previous tests given by the professor
- Handouts given by the professor
- Notes of videos watched in class
- Notes from CD-ROMs or other electronic media
- Study-group notes

Most students can name only four or five of the top ten places to find answers to test questions. One of the most common errors students make when studying for exams is forgetting about handouts and about notes taken from videos and other media. When you are reviewing for an exam, be sure to review *all* information from class, notes, texts, study groups, and media. Professors often test on information other than what they specifically talk about in class.

You can also reduce test anxiety by trying to predict what types of test questions the professor will give. Professors frequently give clues ahead of time about what they will be asking and what types of questions will be given.

Several classes before the test is scheduled, find out from your professor what type of test you can expect. This information can help you study more effectively. Some questions you might ask are

1. What type of questions will be on the test?

2. How long is the test?

3. Is there a time limit on the test?

4. Will there be any special instructions, such as use pen only or use a number 2 pencil?

5. Is there a study sheet?

6. Will there be a review session?

7. What is the grade value of the test?

Asking these simple questions will help you know what type of test will be administered, how you should prepare for it, and what supplies you will need.

PREDICTING EXAM QUESTIONS

You will want to begin predicting questions early. Listen to the professor intently. Professors use cue phrases, such as "You will see this again," and "If I were to ask you this question on the test." Pay close attention to what is written on the board, what questions are asked in class, and what areas the professor seems to be concentrating on more than others. You will begin to get a feel for what types of questions the professor might ask on the test.

It may also be beneficial for you to keep a running page of test questions that you have predicted. As you read through a chapter, ask yourself many questions at the end of each section. When it is time to study for the test, you may have already predicted many of the questions your professor will ask.

Save all quizzes and exams that your professor lets you keep (some professors take the exams back after students have had a chance to review them). These are a wonderful resource for studying for the next exam or for predicting questions for the course final.

Take a moment to try to predict two essay test questions from Chapter 8 on studying.

Question 1. _____

_____

_____

Why do you think this question will be asked? _____

_____

_____

Question 2. _____

_____

_____

Why do you think this question will be asked? _____

_____

_____

Three Types of Responses

to Test Questions

 lmost every test question will elicit one of three types of responses from you as the test taker.

- Quick-time response

- Lag-time response

- No response

Your response is a **quick-time response** when you read a question and know the answer immediately. You may need to read only one key word in the test question to know the correct response. Even if you have a quick-time response, however, *always* read the entire question before answering. The question may be worded in such a way that the correct response is not what you originally expected. By reading the entire question before answering, you can avoid losing points to careless error.

You have a **lag-time response** when you read a question and the answer does not come to you immediately. You may have to read the question several times or even move on to another question before you think of the correct response. Information in another question will sometimes trigger the response you need. Don't get nervous if you have a lag-time response. Once you've begun to answer other questions, you usually begin to remember more, and the response may come to you. You do not have to answer questions in order on most tests.

No response is the least desirable situation when you are taking a test. You may read a question two or three times and still have no response. At this point, you should move on to another question to try to find some related information. When this happens, you have some options:

1. Leave this question until the very end of the test.

2. Make an intelligent guess.

3. Try to eliminate all unreasonable answers by association.

4. Watch for modifiers within the question.

It is very difficult to use intelligent guessing with essay or fill-in-the-blank questions.

Remember these important tips about the three types of responses.

1. Don't be overly excited if your response is *quick*; read the entire question and be careful so that you don't make a mistake.

2. Don't get nervous or anxious if you have a *lag-time* response; the answer may come to you later, so just relax and move on.

3. Don't put down just anything if you have *no response;* take the remaining time and use intelligent guessing.

HELPFUL REMINDERS FOR REDUCING TEST ANXIETY

- Approach the test with an "I can" attitude.

- Prepare yourself emotionally for the test, control your self-talk, and be positive.

- Remind yourself that you studied and that you know the material.

- Overlearn the material—you can't study too much.

- Chew gum or hard candy during the test if allowed, it may help you relax.

- Go to bed early. Do *not* pull an all-nighter before the test.

- Eat a healthy meal before the test.

- Arrive early for the test (at least 15 minutes early).

- Sit back, relax, breathe, and clear your mind if you become nervous.

- Come to the test with everything you need, pencils, calculator, and so on.

- Read the *entire* test first; read *all* the directions; highlight the directions.

- Listen to the professor before the test begins.

- Answer what you know first, the questions that are easiest for you.

- Keep an eye on the clock.

- Check your answers, but remember, your first response is usually correct.

- Find out about the test *before* it is given; ask the professor what types of questions will be on the test.

- Find out exactly what the test will cover ahead of time.

- Ask the professor for a study sheet; you may not get one, but it does not hurt to ask!

- Know the rules of the test and of the professor.

- Attend the review session if one is offered.

- Know what grade value the test holds.

- Ask about extra credit or bonus questions on the test.

- When you get the test, jot down any mnemonic you might have developed on the back or at the top of a page.

- Never look at another student's test or let anyone see your test.

Test-Taking Strategies and
Hints for Success

ouldn't it be just great if every professor gave the same type of test? Then, you would have to worry about content only, and not about the test itself. Unfortunately, this is not going to happen. Professors will continue to test differently and to have their own style of writing. Successful students have to know the differences among testing techniques and know what to look for when dealing with each type of test question. You may have a preference for one type of question over another. You may prefer multiple-choice to essay questions, whereas someone else may prefer essay to true–false questions. Whatever your preference, you are going to encounter all types of questions. To be successful, you will need to know the techniques for answering each type.

The most common types of questions are

- Matching

- True–false

- Multiple choice

- Short answer

- Essay

Before you read about the strategies for answering these different types of questions, think about this: There is no substitute for studying!!! You can know all the tips, ways to reduce anxiety, mnemonics, and strategies on earth, but if you have not studied, they will not help you.

STRATEGIES FOR MATCHING QUESTIONS

Matching questions frequently involve knowledge of people, dates, places, or vocabulary. When answering matching questions, you should

- Read the directions carefully.

- Read each column before you answer.

- Determine whether there are equal numbers of items in each column.

- Match what you know first.

- Cross off information that is already used.

- Use the process of elimination for answers you might not know.

- Look for logical clues.

- Use the longer statement as a question; use the shorter statement as an answer.

■ AN INSIDER'S VIEW

Melissa M. Godi
Northern Michigan University
Marquette, Michigan

As a senior, I suppose you could label me as a late bloomer with regard to taking school seriously. I have always been known to procrastinate, particularly with my studies. I also would waste away my days by repeatedly pushing the snooze button on my alarm clock.

Just a few weeks ago, I was speaking to a close friend of mine on the topic of doing well in school and motivation. We both came to the conclusion that every student in the whole world, with the exception of us, had that driving ambition to achieve high grades *and* juggle nearly a hundred different extracurricular activities at the same time. We, on the other hand, would come up with a hundred excuses for not studying, getting involved, or being motivated. And there we sat, bemoaning our lack of enthusiasm.

Since that conversation with my friend, I have questioned a few students about their habits relating to studying, being motivated, and doing well. Their response was that people who are motivated to study and achieve high grades are usually people who know exactly what they want, where they would like to go, and the fastest way to get there.

I am beginning to realize, as graduation approaches, that they are right. Without direction and having developed the proper study skills, test-taking strategies, and motivation, I would have *never* made it through. I believe that it is something that every student has to do in order to succeed in college—and in life.

Now, when I reflect upon my time and efforts to earn a college degree, I can proudly state that my ability to study, take tests, have ambition, and be motivated helped me make it through college and will help you become a college graduate.

SAMPLE TEST #1

Directions: Match the information in column A with the correct information in column B. Use capital letters.

LISTENING SKILLS

A	B
_____ 1. Listening	a. Within range
_____ 2. Hearing	b. Obstacle
_____ 3. Receiving	c. Voluntary
_____ 4. Objectivity	d. Origin and direction
_____ 5. Prejudging	e. Open-minded
_____ 6. Organizing	f. Involuntary
_____ 7. As a result	g. Key phrase

True–false tests ask if a statement is true or not. True–false questions are some of the most tricky questions ever developed. Some students like them, some hate them. There is a 50/50 chance of getting the correct answer, but you can use the following strategies to increase your odds on true–false tests.

- Read each statement carefully.

- Watch for key words in each statement, for example, negatives.

- Read each statement for double negatives, such as *not un*truthful.

- Pay attention to words that may indicate that a statement is true, such as *some, few, many, often.*

- Pay attention to words that may indicate that a statement is false, such as *never, all, every, only.*

- Remember that if any *part* of a statement is false, the *entire* statement is false.

- Answer every question unless there is a penalty for guessing.

SAMPLE TEST #2

Directions: Place a capital "T" for true or "F" for false beside each statement.

NOTE-TAKING SKILLS

_____ 1. Note taking creates a history of your course content.

_____ 2. "Most importantly" is not a key phrase.

_____ 3. You should always write down everything the professor says.

_____ 4. You should never ask questions in class.

_____ 5. The L-STAR system is a way of studying.

_____ 6. W/O is not a piece of shorthand.

_____ 7. You should use 4-by-6-inch paper to take classroom notes.

_____ 8. The outline technique is best used with lecture notes.

_____ 9. The Cornell method should never be used with textbook notes.

_____ 10. The mapping system is done with a series of circles.

STRATEGIES FOR MULTIPLE-CHOICE QUESTIONS

Many college professors give multiple-choice tests because they are easy to grade and provide quick, precise responses. A multiple-choice question asks you to choose from among usually two to five answers to complete a sentence. Some strategies for increasing your success in answering multiple-choice questions are

- Read the question and try to answer it *before* you read the answers provided.

- Look for similar answers; one of them is usually the correct response.

- Recognize that answers containing extreme modifiers, such as *always, every,* and *never,* are usually wrong.

- Cross off answers that you know are incorrect.

- Read *all* the options before selecting your answer, even if you know that A is the correct response; read them *all.*

- Recognize that when the answers are all numbers, the highest and lowest numbers are usually incorrect.

- Recognize that a joke is usually wrong.

- Understand that the most inclusive answer is often correct.

- Understand that the longest answer is often correct.

- If you cannot answer a question, move on to the next one and continue through the test; another question may trigger the answer you missed.

- Make an educated guess if you must.

- Answer every question unless there is a penalty for guessing.

SAMPLE TEST #3

Directions: Read each statement and select the best response from the answers given below. Use capital letters.

STUDY SKILLS

_____ 1. What are the components of getting organized?

a. supplies, notebook, environment

b. environment, books, residence hall

c. supplies, notebook, lecture notes

d. lecture notes, computer, environment

_____ 2. The best notebook system used for lecture notes is

a. a spiral-bound composition book

b. a legal pad

c. a three-ring binder with loose-leaf paper

d. a collection of Post-it notes

_____ 3. A mnemonic is

a. a note-taking device

b. a memory trick

c. a listening tool

d. a type of harmonica

_____ 4. The first "R" in the SQ3R method stands for

a. read

b. recite

c. review

d. respond

_____ 5. Short-term, or working, memory is

a. great in capacity and lasts for almost 1 hour

b. limited in capacity and holds 5 to 9 pieces of information

c. great in capacity and holds 5 to 9 pieces of information

d. limited in capacity and lasts for almost 1 hour

STRATEGIES FOR SHORT-ANSWER QUESTIONS

Short-answer questions, also called fill-in-the-blanks, ask you to supply the answer yourself, not to select it from a list. Although short answer sounds easy, these questions are often very difficult. Short-answer questions require you to draw from your long-term memory. The following hints can help you answer this type of question successfully.

- Read each question and be sure that you know what is being asked.

- Be brief in your response.

- Give the same number of answers as there are blanks, for example, _____ and _____ would require *two* answers.

- Never assume that the length of the blank has anything to do with the length of the answer.

- Remember that your initial response is usually correct.

- Pay close attention to the word immediately preceding the blank; if the word is *an*, give a response that begins with a vowel (a,e,i,o,u).

- Look for key words in the sentence that may trigger a response.

SAMPLE TEST #4

Directions: Fill in the blanks with the correct response. Write clearly.

LISTENING SKILLS

1. Listening is a _____ act. We choose to do it.

2. The listening process involves receiving, organizing, _____ and reacting.

3. _____ is the same as listening with an open mind.

4. Prejudging is an _____ to listening.

5. Leaning forward, giving eye contact, being patient, and leaving your emotions at home are characteristics of _____ listeners.

STRATEGIES FOR ESSAY QUESTIONS

Most students look at essay questions with dismay because they take more time. Yet essay tests can be one of the easiest tests to take, because they give you a chance to show what you really know. An

essay question requires you to supply the information. If you have studied, you will find that once you begin to answer an essay question, your answer will flow easily. Some tips for answering essay questions are

- Sometimes more is not always better, sometimes more is just more. Try to be as concise and informative as possible. A professor would rather see 1 page of excellent material than 5 pages of fluff.

- Pay close attention to the action word used in the question and respond with the appropriate type of answer. Key words used in questions include

discuss	illustrate	enumerate
compare	define	relate
contrast	summarize	analyze
trace	evaluate	critique
diagram	argue	justify

- Write a thesis statement for each answer.

- Outline your thoughts before you begin to write.

- Watch your spelling, grammar, and punctuation.

- Use details, such as times, dates, places, and proper names, where appropriate.

- Be sure to answer all parts of the question; some discussion questions have more than one part.

- Summarize your main ideas toward the end of your answer.

- Write neatly.

- Proofread your answer.

SAMPLE TEST #5

Directions: Answer each question completely and thoroughly.

STUDY SKILLS

1. Describe the READ study method. _____

_____

2. Discuss why it is important to use the SQ3R method. _____

_____

_____

3. Justify your chosen notebook system. _____

_____

_____

4. Compare an effective study environment with an ineffective study environment. _____

_____

_____

Learning how to take a test and reduce your anxiety are two of the most important gifts you can give yourself as a student. Although there are many tips and hints to help you, don't forget that there is no substitute for studying and knowing the material.

Academic Integrity

If you look in your student handbook, you will more than likely find a "Code of Conduct" for student behavior. This code probably outlines the sanctions for cheating, plagiarism, lying, and other forms of conduct. You may ask yourself, "Who cares if I cheat?" or "Ok, I bought a research paper, so what?" or "No one told me that getting a paper from the Internet was wrong." So, who does care, what does it mean, and what are the ramifications for academic dishonesty? Your student handbook will outline the answers for you. Most institutions are intolerant of academic dishonesty.

Colleges vary in issuing penalties, but they can range from failing the course to being removed from the campus.

Beyond the college campus, dishonesty affects the community at large. Would you want an accountant who had cheated through the CPA exam investing your money? Would you want a construction engineer to build your office building if she had cheated all the way through electrical engineering classes? Would you want a physician to operate on your child or parent if he had cut corners in medical school?

It is important to know what constitutes dishonesty. Below, you will find what most colleges consider academic misconduct:

- Looking on another student's test paper for answers

- Giving another student a test or lab answer

- Using "cheat sheets" on a test or project

- Using a computer, calculator, dictionary, or notes when not approved

- Discussing exam questions with students in classes after yours

- Plagiarism, or using the words or works of others without giving proper credit

- Stealing another student's notes

- Using an annotated instructor's edition of a text

- Having tutors do your homework for you

- Submitting the same paper for more than one class during any semester

- Copying files from lab computers

- Bribing a student for answers or academic work such as papers or projects

- Buying or acquiring papers from individuals or the Internet

- Assisting others with dishonest acts

CORNERSTONES for test taking

- Always write your name on each page of your test.

- Write clearly.

- Check punctuation, spelling, and grammar.

- Use capital letters for true–false and multiple choice.

- Answer all questions.

- Check to see if you skipped a question or a page.

- Ignore the pace of your classmates; some may finish earlier than others.

- Check to see if one question answers another.

- Never use drugs or alcohol to get through a test.

- Watch time limits.

- Ask questions of the professor if allowed.

- Read the entire test before beginning.

- Think positively.

Testing
Tips

If you have been using the Internet, you know that URLs change frequently and are sometimes removed. If you cannot locate a particular exercise, try to find one that provides similar information.

Many college students have a great fear of taking tests, but if you approach the task correctly, you can learn to be successful.

Because you are going to be in college at least four years, you will be taking tests on a regular basis. The sooner you learn to improve your test-taking skills, the more likely you will be to make good grades. Access the URL (`http://www.shsu.edu/~counsel/test_taking.htm`) and answer the following questions related to this article.

How do you make wise use of your time when taking a test? _____

_____

_____

_____

_____

_____

_____

_____

What tips are included that will help you when answering multiple-choice questions? _____

_____

_____

_____

_____

_____

_____

_____

True or False: Research shows that students should not change their answers on multiple-choice questions because their first choices are usually correct. _____

The one minute journal

In a minute or less, jot down one major idea you learned from this chapter.

10

The Serenity Prayer:

God, grant me the serenity to

accept the things I cannot change,

the courage to change the things I

can, and the wisdom to know

the difference.

R. Niebuhr, theologian

I'm Stressed, You're Stressed, We're All Stressed: Controlling Stress

Amanda was a first-generation college student who had overcome tremendous odds to go to college. A single mother and the sole supporter of her three children, she moved back home to live with her own mother so that she could afford to go to school. Amanda's mother cared for the children while Amanda was in class or working. Amanda worked the night shift so that she

could spend time with her children. She attended classes while they were in school, went home and took a nap, and then got up to do homework with the children and help her mother with chores around the house.

Amanda came to my office two weeks after the fall semester began to tell me that she would not be in class because her mother had passed away. We worked out a plan for her to make up her assignments and to take her test at a later date. She was unable to return as quickly as we had hoped because she had trouble finding someone to help her care for her children. Finally, she arranged for her sister to care for the children, and she returned to school.

Amanda made up her assignments and scored one of the highest grades on the exam. Several weeks later, she returned to my office in tears— she had just learned that her son was diagnosed with leukemia. She was devastated, but decided not to drop out of school because it was too late in the semester for her to be reimbursed for the tuition she had paid. She had to take her son to a medical center in another state. After her return, she worked diligently to keep her assignments current.

In spite of all this stress, Amanda completed the fall semester and with very high grades. She preregis-

In spite of all this stress, Amanda completed the fall semester and with very high grades.

tered for the spring semester and eventually completed her degree.

ew students ever have to face this type of adversity or stress. Amanda's story is an example of how some people handle stress. Amanda was able to achieve despite the stress of death and terminal illness in her life; others might not have responded to this stress in as positively a manner. Everyone handles stress differently.

We have written this chapter because most of the students we have counseled during our years in higher education have sought help for stress-related problems, with a class, a test, a professor, or some nonacademic area of their lives. Regardless of the source, students are under incredible stress. We want to share with you some suggestions for dealing successfully with stress.

By the end of this chapter, you should be able to

- Distinguish the different types of stressors

- Determine your own stress level

- Understand how stress is related to your overall health

- Develop a personal stress-management program

AT THIS MOMENT...

5 = Strongly Agree

4 = Agree

3 = Don't Know

2 = Disagree

1 = Strongly Disagree

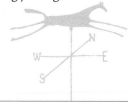

1. Controlling my stress level is important to me now.
   1 2 3 4 5

2. I can define stress.
   1 2 3 4 5

3. I know what situations cause me stress. *1 2 3 4 5*

4. I can recognize the signs when I am getting stressed out.
   1 2 3 4 5

5. I understand how to relieve stress. *1 2 3 4 5*

6. I know how to avoid stress.
   1 2 3 4 5

7. I understand that stress affects all areas of my life.
   1 2 3 4 5

8. I take time out of busy days to take care of myself.
   1 2 3 4 5

9. I practice stress-relief techniques. *1 2 3 4 5*

10. I have a stress-management plan. *1 2 3 4 5*

A SELF-ASSESSMENT Total your points from these ten questions. Refer to the following rating scale to determine where you stand in relation to dealing with stress.

0–10   You have great difficulty dealing with stress.

11–20   You have greater than normal difficulty dealing with stress.

21–30 You have considerable difficulty dealing with stress.

31–40 You have some difficulty dealing with stress.

41–50 You are not negatively impacted by stress.

Now, refer to your journal and respond in writing to your findings. Consider the following questions when writing in your journal.

1. What stressors am I dealing with right now in my life?

2. How am I handling those stressors?

3. Do I want to change how I deal with stress in my life?

What Is Stress?

The word *stress* is derived from the Latin word *strictus,* meaning "to draw tight." Stress is your body's response to people and events in your life; it is the mental and physical wear and tear on your body as a result of everyday life. Stress is inevitable, and it is not in itself bad. It is your response to stress that determines whether it is good stress (eustress) or bad stress (distress). The same event can provoke eustress or distress, depending on the person experiencing the event; just as "one person's trash is another's treasure" (or so you know if you shop at used-clothing stores), so one person's eustress may be another person's distress. For example, if you know that you are going to be graded on oral presentations only in one class, you may experience eustress, while another student may perceive the situation as a fate worse than death and be deeply distressed.

The primary difference between eustress and distress is in your body's response. It is impossible to exist in a totally stress-free environment, in fact, some stress is important to your health and well-being. Only when the stress gets out of hand does your body become distressed. Some physical signs of distress are

Headaches	Abdominal pain and diarrhea
Dry mouth	Impotence
Muscular tension and pain	Menstrual disorders

Hypertension and chest pain	Insomnia
Coughs	Depression
Heartburn and indigestion	Suicidal tendencies
Loss of appetite	Fatigue

Three Types of Stressors

SITUATIONAL STRESSORS

There are two categories of situational stressors—physical environmental and social environmental. A change in your physical environment can be a tremendous source of distress even if you are prepared for it. When you come to college, physical environmental stressors will abound. You may feel a moment of anxiety when you realize that you can't remember how to get from the dorm to your first class, or you lose your syllabus and can't remember the assignment, or you have trouble dealing with living in a crowded environment. The place where you live may change from a warm, quiet, and homey environment to a noisy, institutional environment. At home you might have been able to count on finding a quiet place to curl up with a good book or to study for a test. Your new home, the residence hall, may not provide such an environment. You may be faced with the added pressures of taking care of children while trying to study, or trying to find time to spend with your spouse and still meet the demands of studying and going to class. Whatever your place in life, your age, or your economic status, you can't avoid facing added stressors when you attend college.

You have probably already found that your new social environment is somewhat stressful. New friends, classes, study time, recreational activities, and work-related activities may make conflicting demands on your time and attention. Parents may place added stress on you by expecting you to be home for certain weekends, or they may place great emphasis on grades. You may feel the pressure of trying to maintain a GPA that will enable you to stay in school while you are also juggling family responsibilities and work commitments. The social culture at your college is probably very different from what you are accustomed to. This difference is not necessarily bad, but it is nonetheless the source of some distress. List three examples of situational stressors that affect you.

1. _____

2. _____

3. _____

Later in this chapter you will come back to these situational stressors and develop coping strategies for handling them.

PSYCHOLOGICAL STRESSORS

Psychological stressors have to do with how you perceive and respond to the world around you. If you have to travel a long way to a college, for example, dealing with travel arrangements, tickets, luggage, and airports may all contribute to your level of stress.

Unrealistic expectations can also add to your psychological stressors. Many first-year students are excited about going away to college, but are at the same time confused and upset about the overwhelming sense of homesickness they experience. The expectation that you will not become homesick is probably unrealistic; your new life will be exciting, challenging, frightening, and exhilarating, sometimes all at the same time. When faced with all these new feelings, it is completely natural to experience feelings of homesickness and fear. Don't be afraid to pick up the phone and call your parents or a good friend to talk about your feelings. And don't be afraid to voice your fears to some of your new friends at college. If they aren't experiencing the same feelings you are at the same time you are, they have no doubt felt them before; they will be able to lend a sympathetic ear to your thoughts and perhaps help you get through a difficult time.

Another source of stress for new students comes from trying to do everything. Many students place unrealistic demands on their time by trying to burn the candle at both ends—studying and going to classes all day and partying all night; then, when their grades are not what they expect, they become stressed out.

List three examples of psychological stressors that you are facing.

1. _____

2. _____

3. _____

Later, you'll develop coping strategies for these stressors, too.

BIOLOGICAL STRESSORS

Psychological stressors are closely linked with the third category of stressors, biological stressors. Every stage of your life brings new biological stressors. How you deal with them determines how stressful that period of your life will be. Everyone handles life stages differently.

Your college years put new demands on your body. For many students, going to college coincides with major hormonal changes as well as changes in lifestyle. Physical activity may be replaced by lethargy. The walk from dorm to class may seem so far, even if it is only two blocks long, that you use campus transport buses or drive to class. Your physical activity is likely to be decreasing while your metabolic rate is dropping because of your age. The 15-pound weight gain of first-year students, the "freshman 15," is not a myth—many college students do not understand how all these changes affect them until they have gained weight; then they place unrealistic demands on their bodies as they try to lose the weight.

List some examples of biological changes you may be dealing with now.

1. _____

2. _____

3. _____

4. _____

Financial Pressures

Finances are a source of stress for most college students. Whether you've learned it yet or not, money doesn't grow on trees. The key to alleviating distress caused by finances is planning. Create a budget for each semester. First, total your projected earnings or monthly allowance. Then determine what you will have to pay for tuition, room and board, and other standard fees and subtract it from your total. This will tell you how much disposable income you will have. Work very hard to stick to your budget, because financial worries can constitute a huge stressor, and poor budgeting could result in your having to leave school.

Many students have to work to be able to afford to go to school. If you work, you have to deal with some stressors that do not affect nonworking students. You need to take some time to prioritize your commitments. Obviously work will have to be rather high on your priority list, since most colleges won't allow you to attend if you don't pay the bills. But determine whether you are working for necessities, that is, room and board, tuition, and books, or for luxuries, such as eating out, new clothes, and social functions. If you seem to be struggling under a tremendous financial burden, find out how much of that burden was incurred for luxury items. If attending school and earning good grades is important to you, you will probably have to make some sacrifices. Determine your priorities, then explore your options and work out a plan that enables you to lead a life that is in sync with your priorities.

Your value system may turn out to be the focus of a great deal of stress when you go to college. Values that you may never have questioned will be challenged. You will meet people in classes or at social events who hold beliefs very different from yours. What is taboo for you may be acceptable for them. When you encounter people with different beliefs, listen to their points of view—you may learn something. Don't be afraid to share your own beliefs and to stand firmly by them, but always remember to respect the opinions of others. Everyone does not have to have the same beliefs as you; diversity makes this a much more interesting world to live in.

Unfortunately, recognizing that you will face major stressors when you go to college may not be enough to keep you from suffering from distress. Don't let this get you down. Most people let stress interfere with their lives at some point. The truly happy and healthy people in the world learn how to cope with this stress and how to make stress work for them.

Juggling Responsibilities

In the past, traditional college students had the luxury of leaving home after high school to go to college where they would study full time for four years without having to work and then graduate and start their careers. This is not the case for a large number of today's students. More and more college students are assuming some if not all of the financial responsibilities for their education. Returning students may have chosen to take classes in addition to their full-time career. Learning to juggle work and classes is incredibly difficult. Add to that the family pressures and social pressures, and you have the makings of a very stressful life.

When dealing with students who are struggling academically, rarely have we found that the problem is that the student isn't smart enough for college. Generally the academic problems come as a result of burning the candle at both ends. This problem can be easily remedied if the candle that the student is burning is a social candle, but many times the candle is burning to pay tuition and living expenses, and cutting out the job is not a possibility. In these instances, we suggest the following:

1. Carefully reevaluate your living expenses to determine your *needs* from your *wants.*

2. Review your timeline to ensure that it is realistic. If you must support yourself throughout college, the four-year plan may not be realistic.

3. Prioritize based on your goals. If getting your degree is your number one priority, make the changes necessary to ensure success.

4. Reevaluate your job. If school is your priority, look for a job that

   a. Has little responsibility

   b. Provides opportunity to study during slow times

   c. Provides a flexible schedule so that you can take off time during times of heavy study loads

If school is secondary to your career, then design a realistic time schedule for your graduation date and take a reduced class load.

Building a Stress-Management Program

Learning how to manage stress has become a national hobby. How-to books, audiotapes, videotapes, and self-help seminars are advertised everywhere. Most libraries and bookstores have sections dedicated to stress. People have made fortunes expounding on stress. However, there is no one way of handling stress that is 100 percent effective. Each individual has a unique need and ability to manage stress. To help you manage the stress you will encounter during your college years and for the rest of your life, we offer a variety of techniques and suggestions that you can adapt to your own needs.

Your approach to managing stress should address all three types of stressors—situational, psychological, and biological.

MANAGING SITUATIONAL STRESSORS

To manage situational stressors, you need to understand what it is in your environment that is causing stress for you. If your living arrangements, either the physical facilities or the people around you, are creating stress and you have been unable to work things out, take the necessary steps to change your residence. Since this may take some time, do what you can in the interim to remove stress from the environment. For example, if you are having trouble with the noise level at your dorm, find a quiet place elsewhere to study.

A change of environment can help with stress. We are often so involved in the hustle and bustle of everyday living that we don't even realize how the fast pace is stressing us out. Be aware of your

environment. If you find you are becoming stressed, do an environment check. Look around. Is the stress coming from the obnoxious music your next-door neighbor is playing? Are there too many people walking in and around the room you are in? Are people in your classroom annoying you by constantly coughing, scratching, or clicking a pen? Keep your options open—if your environment gets to you, change it.

Another way to reduce situational stress is to arrange a class schedule that fits your needs and ability to accomplish tasks. If you function better in the morning, try to schedule your classes and study time for early in the day. If you are a night owl, try to avoid early morning classes, but remember to use the evening hours to study and not just to party.

Now, take some time to review the situational stressors you listed earlier in this chapter and come up with some coping strategies you might implement the next time you face them.

1. _____

_____

_____

2. _____

_____

_____

3. _____

_____

_____

MANAGING PSYCHOLOGICAL STRESSORS

Psychological stressors are probably the most prevalent as well as the most difficult to handle. Again, you need first to be able to pinpoint what is causing you stress and then to develop a coping technique to get you through the situation. It is crucial that you do not ignore the stress! You cannot afford to let yourself get run-down. Since you may not be in the best position to recognize exactly what your stressors are when you are in the middle of a stressful time, it is helpful to have a good friend with whom you can talk about your feelings and who can give you feedback about the situation. Choose someone who is positive; some-one who tends to be negative can hurt the situation more than help it. You might also talk with a professor with whom you have developed a special relationship. Professors and mentors can provide insight and compassion. These are people who probably understand your feelings and needed someone to listen to them at one time or another. They are also intimately familiar with the pressures of academia and might be able to offer some concrete suggestions to help you cope with your distress.

Every school has a network of support services. Most colleges and universities provide easy access to counselors, therapists, and psychiatrists at no charge or at a reduced rate. These people are trained to deal with students and are aware of the kinds of stresses you may be experiencing. Remember, talking about your problems is key to relieving stress, and these individuals are trained listeners.

Review the psychological stressors you named earlier in this chapter and list some strategies that might help you deal with these stressors. Why did you choose the strategies you did?

1. _____

_____

_____

2. _____

_____

_____

3. _____

_____

_____

MANAGING BIOLOGICAL STRESSORS

You will have to deal with biological stressors for the rest of your life, as your body ages and changes. You may feel invincible now, but this will change. The physical changes that will take place in your body are not something to dread or despise. There is no one more beautiful or appealing or sexy than a person who is comfortable with his or her body, regardless of age, weight, size, or shape. Still, biological stressors exist and you have to be prepared to deal with them. Learn to eat right by listening to your body. Understand why you are eating. Are you hungry? Most Americans do not allow themselves to feel hunger; they eat not because they are hungry, but because they are happy, sad, nervous, tired, or stressed out and because eating is a social event. Stress can make you ravenous or disinterested in food. Although both

extremes are bad, the former may be preferable. The physical changes brought on by stress cause your body to burn calories; thus your body needs more energy when you are stressed.

Learn to eat right by eating foods such as fresh fruits, vegetables, whole-grain breads, and cereals. Eat adequate amounts of protein and drink lots of water—at least eight 8-ounce glasses per day. Your body will feel better and you will be more capable of handling stressful events.

Exercising is a wonderful coping activity for stress. Exercise releases endorphins, which cause a natural high and help relieve all types of stresses. Aerobic exercises are the best stress reducers. According to Herbert Benson, a physician and author of *The Relaxation Response* (1992), you should exercise vigorously for at least 20 minutes at least three times per week to enable your body to release the pent-up energy caused by stress. You might want to avoid competitive exercises, because they may cause additional stress. Have a friend join you in your exercise program; you can socialize while doing something good for yourselves, rather than share stories over pizza and beer. Exercise prepares your body for stressful situations while it helps you to relieve stress.

Physical activity will also help you avoid the insomnia that is sometimes associated with stress. Adequate sleep is extremely important, although what counts as adequate is different for everyone.

List the types of activities you enjoy. The next time you feel stress, take the time to do one of these activities. _____

_____

_____

Write down some ideas for dealing with the biological stressors you listed earlier in the chapter.

1. _____

_____

_____

2. _____

_____

_____

3. _____

_____

_____

CORNERSTONES for handling stress

- Don't procrastinate.

- Set aside time each day to organize your day.

- Tackle your most difficult and important work first.

- Learn to say no!

- Take time out to be with friends or family.

- Surround yourself with people who are upbeat, kind, sympathetic, funny, and caring.

- Work at your relationships.

- Get involved with the fine arts in your community—music, dance, theater, sculpture, painting, and so on.

- Create variety so that ordinary tasks do not become boring.

- Create study/work area that makes you comfortable—lighting, paintings, colors, plants, and so forth.

- Develop a way to "decompress" after school or work. Find a place where you can go and relax before going home or from school to work. It can be as simple as driving in your car an extra mile, listening to your favorite music.

- Keep yourself healthy with exercise and proper eating habits.

- Explore techniques such as massage or aroma therapy, yoga, or meditation.

Managing
Stress

If you have been using the Internet, you know that URLs change frequently and are sometimes removed. If you cannot locate a particular exercise, try to find one that provides similar information.

Access the address (`http://helping.apa.org/stress3.html`) to find the article, "Six Myths about Stress," by Lyle Miller, Ph.D.

1. What are the six myths about stress?

1. _____

2. _____

3. _____

4. _____

5. _____

6. _____

2. How does managing stress help us? _____

_____

_____

_____

3. How can you plan for stress? _____

_____

_____

_____

4. What are two physical symptoms of stress? _____

_____

_____

_____

Click on the Online Brochure from the American Psychological Association to explore the site.

The one minute journal

in a minute or less, jot down one major idea you learned from this chapter.

People are always blaming their circumstances for what they are. I don't believe in circumstances. The people who get on in this world are the people who get up and look for the circumstances they want, and, if they can't find them, they make them.

*George Bernard Shaw,
playwright*

What Are You Doing for the Rest of Your Life?: Career Planning

I met Wilma when she was a first-year student in college. I was director of student activities and of the Student Government Association and she was a senator representing the first-year class. Her drive and enthusiasm distinguished her from other new students. She wanted to be a teacher. She had not gone to college immediately after high school; instead, she had joined the armed forces and then entered the workforce. During this time, Wilma had given her career a great deal of thought. She told me one day, "I've had many jobs in my life, but I've never had a career."

In the upcoming semesters, Wilma made the president's list and the dean's list, was named to *Who's Who among American College Students*, won several academic scholarships, was elected to the Student Government Association, and even placed second in a dance contest. She was the envy of her peers and colleagues. In addition to energy and drive, she had a desire to have a career, to do something that she loved—to teach. She studied hard, tutored others, and graduated with honors. She received her associate's degree and transferred to a four-year college and became what she had planned for so many years to be. Today, she teaches small children near her hometown.

Wilma's story does not seem extraordinary until you learn that Wilma began her career pursuit in her midsixties. Today, in her seventies,

I've had many jobs in my life, but I've never had a career.

she still teaches. She is an inspiration to all her students and colleagues who learn from her and love her dearly.

Although most of us do not delay our career decisions for more than 50 years, as did Wilma, many students do have a hard time deciding what they want to do for their life's work. Entering the job market often helps people decide what they do not want to do, but people seldom have a clear vision of their career path. Many people search their whole lives to find that certain something that will make them feel worthy, useful, productive, and needed. Yet research suggests that we spend less than 20 hours of our lives in actual career planing (Ellis et al., 1990).

Few people realize that there are 126 million workers in the United States. Even fewer realize that by the year 2000, 90 percent of all jobs will be service oriented and a college or technical degree will be the *basic* requirement for any job with a future (Kleiman, 1992).

This chapter is intended to guide you through a series of questions and thoughts that will start you on the road to thinking about your future.

At the end of this chapter, you will be able to

- Determine the difference between doing and being

- Define the difference between a job and a career

- Identify personal traits that affect job selection and performance

- Use the seven-step plan to decide on a major

- Develop a personal success plan

- Research a career path

- Identify resources for future career study

Take a moment to assess where you are right now in deciding on your life's work.

AT THIS MOMENT...

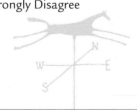

5 = Strongly Agree

4 = Agree

3 = Don't Know

2 = Disagree

1 = Strongly Disagree

1. I have decided on a college major.   *1 2 3 4 5*

2. I know the difference between jobs and careers.
   1 2 3 4 5

3. I have researched a career before.   *1 2 3 4 5*

4. I know how to research a career.   *1 2 3 4 5*

5. I know where the career center is located.
   1 2 3 4 5

6. I have been to an employment agency.   *1 2 3 4 5*

7. I know my personality type.
   1 2 3 4 5

8. I know how my personal interests can affect my career decisions.   *1 2 3 4 5*

9. I know how to use the *Dictionary of Occupational Titles*.
   1 2 3 4 5

10. I know how to develop a success plan.   *1 2 3 4 5*

A SELF-ASSESSMENT Total your points from these ten questions. Refer to the following rating scale to determine where you stand in relation to your career-planning efforts.

0–10   You have given little or no consideration to career planning.

11–20   You have given some thought to career planning.

21–30   You have given a moderate amount of thought to career planning.

31–40   You have given considerable thought to career planning.

41–50   You have given a great deal of consideration to career planning.

Now, refer to your journal and respond in writing to your findings. Consider the following questions when writing in your journal.

1. Have I made a career decision?

2. Have I researched a career?

3. How much thought have I actually put into my career plans?

Do You Want to Do Something or Be Something?

I f you were to ask most people on the street the simple question "What do you do for a living?" they would respond, "I'm a welder" or "I'm an engineer" or "I'm a teacher." Most people answer the question without thinking about what is really being asked.

One of the first questions that you need ask yourself when deciding on a career is "Do I want to *do* something or do I want to *be* something?" The title "welder," or "engineer," or "teacher" does not by itself make you be a welder or engineer or teacher. The art of *being* is a mind-set that you have to develop on your own. There are many people who teach for a living, but there are very few teachers. There are people who do social work, but few are social workers. To be something, you have to make a philosophical decision regarding your future. The questions you have to ask are "How do I want to spend my time?" and "What is my purpose in life?" As an individual, you can do almost anything. You can *do* the work of medicine, you can *do* the work of upholding the law, you can *do* the work of instruction; but in

> I went into the woods because I wished to live deliberately, to front only the essential facts of life, and see if I could not learn what it had to teach, and not, when I came to die, discover that I had not lived.
>
> Henry David Thoreau, author

order to *be* a doctor, lawyer, or teacher, you have to want to *become* the ideal for which those professions stand. Doing is the easy part, but doing the work is not enough to bring fulfillment to your life; it is being the person who heals, protects justice, or teaches that can bring you joy.

Whereas it takes only physical strength to *do* something, it takes vision to *be* something. So, what do you want to *be*? Take a moment to reflect on your dreams for a career.

1. When you were a child, what was the first thing you ever wanted to be? ____

_____

_____

_____

2. Are you considering this same career now? Why or why not? _____

_____

_____

_____

3. Money aside, what would you do if you had the chance to do anything in this world? _____

_____

_____

_____

4. Who is the person in your life who has the career that you want? _____

_____

_____

_____

5. Why do you admire that person and his or her career?

_____

_____

_____

6. How do you best like to spend your time? _____

_____

_____

_____

7. Write a statement detailing what you perceive as your purpose in life. _____

_____

_____

Deepak Chopra, in his book *The Seven Spiritual Laws of Success* (1994), refers to this situation as the Law of Dharma. "Dharma is a Sanskrit word that means 'purpose in life.' According to this law, you have a unique talent and a unique way of expressing it. There is something that you can do better than anyone else in the whole world. . . ." Have you found that something? Have you put your finger on your purpose? If not, don't worry right now. Read on. Maybe we can help.

You've Got a Job, Now You Want a Career

> It is easy to live for others. Everybody does. I call on you to live for yourselves.
> Ralph Waldo Emerson, author

Everyone at some time faces the age-old question "Should I be what others think I should be or should I be what I want to be?" The life's work for many people turns out to be what other people think it should be. Well into the latter half of the twentieth century, women were expected to have traditional female careers, such as teaching, nursing, or homemaking. They had little opportunity to select a profession that suited them; society selected their professions for them. It was uncommon for women to enter the fields of engineering, construction, management, public safety, or politics; the avenues to such choices were not open.

College students, male and female, still face pressures to be what others want them to be. Parents actively guide their children toward professions that suit their ideas of what their children should do. Some students have little choice in deciding what they will do for the rest of their lives.

For nontraditional students, spouses, time, and finances may dictate a profession. Many choose courses of study that can be completed quickly because finances and family considerations pressure them in that direction. Money is often another consideration when choosing a profession. Regardless of the pressures you have in your life, be careful

to research your choices, talk with people already in the profession you are considering, and consider the long-term effects of your decisions. You want your career decisions to be well thought out, well planned, and carefully executed.

You are the only person who will ever be able to determine the answers to the questions "How do I want to spend my time?" and "What is my purpose in life?" No parent, teacher, partner, counselor, or therapist will ever be able to fully answer these questions for you. Another person may be able to provide information that can help you make the decision, but ultimately, you will be the person in charge of your career path, your life's work.

What Do You Want to Be When You "Grow Up"?

> Find a job you like and you'll never have to work a day in your life.
>
> Unknown

More people than you would imagine have trouble deciding what they want to be when they grow up. Studies indicate that more than 20 percent of all first-year college students do not know what their majors will be. That's all right for the time being, but before long you will need to make a decision.

The questions that follow are designed to help you make that decision regarding what you want to do with the rest of your life—your career.

YOUR CAREER SELF-STUDY

■ WHAT IS YOUR PERSONALITY TYPE? You can best answer this question by taking a personality inventory, such as the Myers–Briggs Type Indicator or the Teiger Personality Test. This question is important, because your personality may very well indicate the type of work in which you will be successful and happy. If you are a real people person, for example, in a job with minimal human contact and interaction, you probably will not be very happy. Make an appointment with the career center or a career counselor to learn about your personality type.

After your appointment, describe your personality type. _____

_____

_____

How will your personality type affect your career path? _____

_____

_____

■ WHAT ARE YOUR INTERESTS? Understanding your specific interests may help you decide on a career. If you love working with cars, you might consider being a mechanic for a living. If you love to draw or build things, you might be interested in architecture or sculpting as a career.

What are your major interests? _____

_____

_____

How can these interests be transferred to a career choice? _____

_____

_____

■ DO YOU ENJOY PHYSICAL OR MENTAL WORK? Many people would go crazy if they had to spend so much as one hour per day in an office. Others would be unhappy if they had to work in the sun all day or use a great deal of physical strength. The answer to this question will greatly narrow down your career choices. For example, if you are an outdoor person who loves being outside in all kinds of weather, then you should probably avoid careers that are limited to indoor work. You should also consider whether you have any physical limitations that might affect your career choice.

Do you enjoy physical or mental work or both? Why? _____

_____

_____

What does this mean to your career path? _____

_____

_____

■ DO YOU WANT TO MAKE A LOT OF MONEY? Most people, if asked, "Why do you work?" would respond, "For the money." There is nothing wrong with wanting to make money in your profession, but not all professions, regardless of their worth, pay well. Some of the hardest and most rewarding work pays the least. You have to decide whether to go for the money or to do something that is personally challenging to you. *Many* times, you can find both!

Is your major goal in choosing a profession money or something else? What?

_____

_____

What does your goal mean to your career path? _____

_____

_____

■ WHERE DO YOU WANT TO LIVE? Although this question may sound strange, many careers are limited by geography. If you are interested in oceanography, you would be hard-pressed to live in Iowa; if you love farming, New York City would be an improbable place for you to live. Some people simply prefer certain parts of the United States (or the world) to others. You need to ask yourself, "Where do I eventually want to live?" "What climate do I really enjoy?" "In what size city or town do I want to work?" "Where would I be the happiest?" "Do I want to live near my family or away from them?"

Where do you eventually want to live? Why? _____

_____

_____

What does your preference mean to your career path? _____

_____

_____

■ DO YOU WANT TO TRAVEL? Some jobs require travel; some people love to travel, some hate it. Ask yourself whether you want to be away from your home and family four nights per week or whether you want a job that does not require travel at all.

Do you enjoy travel? Do you want to do a lot of traveling? _____

_____

_____

What does this mean to your career path? _____

_____

_____

■ HOW DO YOU LIKE TO DRESS? Some people enjoy dressing up and welcome the opportunity to put on a new suit and go to work. Others prefer to throw on an old pair of blue jeans and head out the door. Jobs have different requirements in terms of dress, and you will be affected by them every workday, so you will want to consider your own preferences.

How do you like to dress? Why? _____

_____

_____

What does this mean to your career path? _____

_____

_____

■ WHAT MOTIVATES YOU? What are the one or two things in your life that motivate you? Money? Power? Helping other people? The answer to this question is an essential element to choosing a career. You have to find that certain something that gives you energy and then find a profession that allows you to pursue it with fervor and intensity.

What is your motivational force and why? _____

_____

_____

How could this help you in deciding on a career path? _____

_____

_____

■ WHAT DO YOU VALUE? Do you value relationships, possessions, money, love, security, challenges, or power? Once you have identified what you value in your life, you can identify careers that closely match your personal value system and eliminate careers that don't. If you have to constantly compromise your values just to get a paycheck you will be miserable.

What do you truly value in your life? _____

_____

_____

How might these values affect your career decisions? _____

_____

_____

■ WHAT ARE YOUR SKILLS? Are you very good at one or two things? Are you a good typist, a good manager of money, a good carpenter, a good communicator? Your skills will play a powerful part in selecting a career. If you are not good or skilled at using numbers, then you will probably want to avoid careers that require their constant use. If you are not a good communicator, then you probably do not want a career that requires you to give daily presentations. Employers still stress the importance of three basic skills: writing, speaking, and listening. If you have these skills, you are ahead of the pack. If not, you need to enroll in a class that will allow you to become better at all three.

What are your skills? What do you do well? _____

_____

_____

How could your strongest skills help you make a career decision? _____

_____

_____

■ DO YOU LIKE ROUTINE? The answer to this question will narrow down your choices tremendously. If you like routine, you will want a career that is conducive to routine and provides structure. If you do not like routine and enjoy doing different things each day, certain careers will be unrealistic for you.

Do you like routine or do you prefer variety? Why? _____

_____

_____

How does this affect your career path? _____

_____

_____

■ ARE YOU A LEADER? One of the most important questions you must ask yourself is "Do I enjoy leading, teaching, or guiding people?" If you prefer to be a part of the crowd and do not like to stand out as a leader or manager, some careers may not suit you. If you like to take charge and get things done when you are with other people, you will find certain careers better than others. How you relate to leadership will be a part of your personality inventory.

Do you consider yourself a leader? Are you comfortable in a leadership role?

Why or why not? _____

_____

_____

How will your feelings about leadership affect your career path? _____

_____

_____

> Not all who wander are lost.
>
> J. R. R. Tolkien, author

Help Me: I'm Undeclared

No, it isn't a fatal disease. You're not dying. Being undeclared is not a disgrace, nor a weakness. It is a temporary state of mind, and the best way to deal with it is to stop and think. You should not declare a major because you are ashamed to be undeclared, and you shouldn't allow yourself to be pressured into declaring a major. Instead, you can take measures to work toward declaring a major and being satisfied with your decision.

SEVEN STEPS TO CAREER DECISION MAKING

Step 1—Dream! If money were not a problem or concern, what would you do for the rest of your life? If you could do anything in the world, what would you do? Where would you do it? These are the types of questions you must ask yourself as you try to select a major and career. Go outside, lie on the grass, and look up at the sky; think silently for a little while. Let your mind wander, and let the sky be the limit. Write your

dreams down. These dreams may be closer to reality than you think. In the words of Don Quixote, "Let us dream, my soul, let us dream" (Unamuno).

Step 2—Talk to your advisor. Academic advisors are there to help you. But don't be surprised if their doors are sometimes closed. They teach, conduct research, perform community service, and sometimes advise in excess of 100 students. Always call in advance; make an appointment to see an advisor. When you have that appointment, make your advisor work for you. Take your college catalog and ask questions, hard questions. Your advisor will not make a career decision for you, but if you ask the proper questions, he or she can be of monumental help to you and your career decisions.

Use students in your program as advisors, too. They will be invaluable to you as you work your way through the daily routine of the college. Experienced students can assist you in making decisions about your classes, electives, and work–study programs. They can even help you join and become an active member of a preprofessional program.

Step 3—Use electives. The accreditation agency that works with your school requires that you be allowed at least one free elective in your degree program. Some programs allow many more. Use your electives wisely! Do not take courses just to get the hours. The wisest students use their electives to delve into new areas of interest or to take a block of courses in an area that might enhance their career decisions.

Step 4—Go to the career center. Even the smallest colleges have some type of career center or a career counselor. *Use them!* Campus career centers usually provide services for free. The same types of services in the community could cost from $200 to $2,000. The professionals in the career center can provide information on a variety of careers and fields, and they can administer interest and personality inventories that can help you make career and other major decisions.

Step 5—Read, read, read! Nothing will help you more than reading about careers and majors. Ask your advisor or counselor to help you locate information on your areas of interest. Gather information from colleges, agencies, associations, and places of employment. Then *read it!*

Step 6—Shadowing. No, this is not what vampires do when the moon is full! *Shadowing* describes the process of following someone around on the job. If you are wondering what engineers do on the job, try calling an engineering office to see whether you can sit with several of their engineers for a day over spring break. Shadowing is the very best way to get firsthand, honest information regarding a profession in which you might be interested.

Step 7—Join preprofessional organizations. One of the most important steps you can take as a college student is to become involved in campus organizations and clubs that offer educational opportunities, social interaction, and hands-on experience in your chosen field. Preprofessional organizations can open doors that will help you make a career decision, grow in your field, meet professionals already working in your field, and, eventually, get a job.

Where to Learn More About

Careers, Majors, and Work

In your search for opportunity, pursue every avenue that is open to you. So often, we choose only the most obvious paths, unlike the poet Robert Frost, who chose "the road less traveled."

Information regarding careers, majors, and work that you might not have considered can be found in the following resources.

The 100 Best Jobs for the 1990's and Beyond (Berkeley Books)

CAPS (Career Ability Placement Survey)

Career magazines

Chamber of commerce

College or community counseling centers

Computer databases, such as SIGI, DISCOVER

The Dictionary of Occupational Titles (U.S. Department of Labor)

Employment offices

The Guide for Occupational Exploration

Hall Occupational Orientation Inventory

Holland Self-Directed Search

Local and state government offices

Myers–Briggs Personality Indicator

Strong–Campbell Interest Inventory

U.S. armed forces

Vocational Preference Inventory

What Color Is Your Parachute? (Ten Speed Press)

Networking: The Overlooked Source for Career Development

We are often so concerned with books, computerized databases, and interest inventories that we forget to look in our own backyards when thinking about careers. Networking is one of the most important aspects of career development. Look at the person sitting beside you in your orientation class. That person could be a future leader in your field of study. You might be thinking, "No way," but you'd be surprised at how many people lose out on networking opportunities because they do not think ahead. The person sitting beside you is important. You never know where or when you may see this person again—he may be interviewing you for a job in 10 years, or she may be the person with whom you will start a business in 15 years. "Too far down the road," you say? Don't close your eyes—15 years will be here before you can blink.

You've all heard the expression "It's not *what* you know, but *who* you know." Well, few statements could be more true, and college is the perfect place for making many personal and professional contacts. At this moment, you are building a network of people on whom you can call for the rest of your life. Your network may include people you know from

High school and college

Clubs and professional organizations

Student government

Newspaper staff

College committees

Sporting teams and events

Fraternities and sororities

Maria P. Houston
Ohio University
Athens, Ohio

Nothing could have been clearer in my mind. I was going to be a physical therapist! Case closed! I had no doubt that this was going to be my profession in life. I sought out universities that had good physical therapy programs and I made my college choice based on this fact.

Physical therapy required a great deal of math, biology, zoology, chemistry, and physics. Shortly after the semester was under way, I began having major problems with my math classes. Math had never been my strongest subject. One afternoon, a department meeting was held for all potential physical therapy students. We were told that there were 20 openings and over 100 applicants. "If you don't have at least a 3.85 GPA at this time, we suggest that you look into another program, retake some classes, or look at another college." The competition was tough. I was devastated.

Knowing that I did not have the required GPA, I called home to tell my parents that I wanted to drop out. Thankfully, my father talked me out of that notion. He helped me see that there were other options for me. He was able to convince me that I had a purpose in life, if only I would look deeper.

I found a college catalog and began to look for other majors and professions. I knew that I wanted to remain in the health-care profession, but I had been so set on physical therapy that I had never even considered another major. I began to do extensive research in the library and the career center and found a major that I was not familiar with, but one that interested me greatly. I found that speech and language pathology required strong interpersonal skills, strong language skills, and a desire to help people. Speech and language pathology was a health profession that I had never considered.

After much research, questioning, and interviewing, I determined that the attributes of the program matched my personal and professional goals. I returned to school after a weekend at home and changed my major from physical therapy to speech and language pathology. Because I researched the profession carefully, this has been one of the best decisions of my life.

Family connections

Community organizations

Volunteer work

Mentors

A mentor is someone who can help open doors for you, who will take a personal and professional interest in your development and success. Often a mentor will help you do something that you might have trouble doing on your own. It may be too soon for you to determine now whether you have found a mentor, and you may not find that person until you begin to take courses in your field of study.

The student–mentor relationship is unique. You help one another. Your mentor may provide you with opportunities that you might otherwise not have. You may have to do some grunt work, but the experience will usually help you in the long run. While you are helping your mentor, your mentor is helping you by giving you experience and responsibility.

As a young, uncertain first-year college student, Derrick applied for and was awarded a work-study position with Professor Griffon. His job was to help Professor Griffon prepare mailings and other advertising materials for the humanities series. The work was monumental, the pay minimal, and Professor Griffon was not always in the best of spirits. On some days Derrick left the office swearing that he would never return. But he had little choice—the job paid more than unemployment. Derrick stayed with the job, and before too long, Professor Griffon began to give him more challenging work.

One day, an important member of the community came to the office. Derrick and the professor were both working at their desks. As the professor and the guest discussed a lucrative contract for an artist, Derrick overheard Professor Griffon tell the guest he could "bring the contract by tomorrow and leave it with Derrick, my assistant." "Assistant," Derrick thought, "that's interesting."

Before Derrick graduated with his two-year degree, he had a wealth of experience, knowledge, and, most important, contacts! He had learned how to run the lighting board in the theater, he had managed the box office, he had developed a marketing plan for one of the events, and he had been able to shadow many of the artists who came to the auditorium to perform. All this was possible because of his relationship with Professor Griffon. This student–mentor situation was rewarding for both of them. They helped each other, and both profited.

BENEFITS OF HAVING A MENTOR

- Mentors teach, advise, and coach.

- Mentors serve as a sounding board for ideas.

- Mentors serve as constructive critics.

- Mentors can promote you among their peers and contacts.

- Mentors provide information to help with career development.

- Mentors can increase your visibility on campus and in the work arena.

- Mentors introduce you to people who can advance your career.

You can't go shopping for a mentor; you don't advertise; you can't use someone else's mentor. You find a mentor through preparation, work, emotion, and a feeling of being comfortable. The following suggestions may help you find a mentor.

- Arrive at class early and work hard

- Develop an outstanding work ethic

- Seek advice from many professors and staff members

- Ask intelligent, thoughtful questions

- Offer to help with projects

- Convey the impression that you are committed, competent, and hardworking

- Look for opportunities to shadow

- If a professor or staff member gives you an opportunity, take it

- Look at grunt work as glory work

CORNERSTONES for career development

- Always make educated and researched decisions.

- Never be afraid to change your mind.

- Make your own decisions.

- Know your personality type before making major decisions.

- Pinpoint your interests.

- Identify your physical and emotional limitations.

- Know how important salary is to your future aspirations.

- Determine whether you would like to live in a specific geographic region.

- Know whether you want to travel.

- Identify what motivates you to succeed.
- Know your own value and moral system.
- Identify your best skills and sharpen and promote them.
- Shadow and do volunteer work before deciding on a career.
- Determine whether you enjoy leadership roles.
- Find a mentor.

As a mature, rational, caring human being, you should realize that you are a part of a bigger picture. This world does not belong to us; we are only borrowing it for a while. Everything you do affects someone else in some way. You must realize that what you do—not just what you do for your career, but your daily actions—matters to someone. There is value in every job, and there is honor in all professions performed well and honestly. When making career decisions, you need to take into account the fact that other people, strangers and friends, will eventually be looking to you as a mentor, and a role model. This is a major responsibility that you cannot avoid; rather, you should relish the opportunity to inspire and teach. Embrace the moment. Finally, you must realize that unless you are out there, daily, creating a better future for yourself, you have no right to complain about the one that is handed to you.

The 20-Step Career Research Form

1. The career that you have chosen to research is _____

2. Why are you interested in this career? _____
_____
_____

3. What personality type is best suited for this career? _____
_____

4. Does this career require physical or mental work or both? Why? _____
_____
_____

5. What is the average salary for this career? _____
_____

6. Where do most professionals in this occupation live? Is it region-specific? _____
_____
_____
_____

7. Does this career require travel? _____
_____

8. What type of dress is required of people who work in this profession? _____
_____

9. How much training and education are required to work in this career? _____
_____

10. What skills are required to do work in this job? _____
_____

11. Does this career involve routine? _____
_____

12. Does this career require you to be a leader or a participant? _____
_____

13. Does this career require you to work indoors or outdoors? _____
_____

14. What is the call number for this profession in the *Dictionary of Occupational Titles*? _____
_____

15. What are the most positive aspects of this career? _____

_____

_____

_____

_____

16. What is the worst thing about this career? _____

_____

_____

_____

17. Are you still interested in this career? _____

18. Who is a person whom you might be able to shadow in this profession? _____

_____

_____

19. What sources did you use to research this career? _____

_____

_____

_____

20. Whom did you interview to research this career? _____

_____

_____

_____

Great Idea!

If you have been using the Internet, you know that URLs change frequently and are sometimes removed. If you cannot locate a particular exercise, try to find one that provides similar information.

Many first-year college students are a little lost when it comes to choosing a major or deciding what kind of career they want after they graduate. The Internet is a great resource for locating career information.

Use the Internet to research a potential career interest. Using the home page for Career Mosaic (Internet address: `http://www.careermosaic.com:80/cm/cc`), find a list of company names. Select a company name that interests you. Find information about the company and print it. Locate a list of the jobs the company has open.

Do you see a job that interests you? What is it? _____

_____

_____

_____

What major do you think this job requires? _____

_____

_____

Are there summer internships that might give you a taste of what working for this company is like? _____

_____

_____

_____

Write to the company and request information and an application for a summer internship position.

The one minute journal

n a minute or less, jot down one major idea you learned from this chapter.

Glossary

ACADEMIC FREEDOM Academic freedom allows professors in institutions of higher education to conduct research and teach their findings, even if the subject matter is controversial. Academic freedom gives college professors the right to teach certain materials that might not be allowed in high school.

ACCREDITATION Most high schools and colleges in the United States receive accreditation from a regional agency, which ensures that all its members meet or exceed a minimum set of standards. The Southern Association of Colleges and Schools is an accreditation agency.

ADDING Adding a class means enrolling in an additional class. The term is usually used during registration period or during the first week of a semester.

ADMINISTRATION The administration of a college is headed by the president and vice presidents and comprises the nonteaching personnel who handle all administrative aspects of running the college. The structure of the administration varies at each college.

ADVISING An academic advisor is assigned to each student on arrival on campus. It is the advisor's responsibility to guide students through their academic work at the college, to be sure that they know what classes to take and in what order. An advisor is most often a faculty member in the student's discipline or major who will work with the student through the student's entire college career.

AFRICAN AMERICAN STUDIES Courses in African American studies consider the major contributions of African Americans in art, literature, history, medicine, sciences, and architecture. Many colleges offer majors and minors in African American studies.

AIDS This acronym stands for **a**cquired **i**mmuno **d**eficiency **s**yndrome, a disease that is transmitted sexually, intravenously, or from mother to fetus. There is currently no known cure for AIDS, but several medications, such as AZT, DDC, 3TC, DT4, Sequinauir, DDI, and Indinavir, help to slow the deterioration of the immune system. AIDS is the number one killer among people aged 25 to 44 years.

ALUMNA, ALUMNUS, ALUMNI These terms describe people who attended a college. *Alumna* refers to a woman, *alumnus* refers to men, and *alumni* refers to more than one of either or both. The term *alumni* is the most often used.

AMERICA ONLINE America Online (AOL) is the nation's largest commercial on-line computer service. It offers a gateway to the Internet, magazines, software, live interactive services, and financial services, and can be one of the most informative and exciting learning tools for college students today.

ARTICULATION An articulation agreement is a document signed by representatives of two or more institutions that guarantees that courses taken at one of the participating institutions will be accepted by the others. For example, if Oak College has an articulation agreement with Maple College, course work completed at Oak College will be accepted toward a degree at Maple College.

ASSOCIATE DEGREE An associate degree is a two-year degree that usually prepares the student to enter the workforce with a specific skill or trade. It is also offered to students as the first two-years of a bachelor's or four-year degree program. Not all colleges offer the associate degree.

ATTENDANCE Every college has an attendance policy, such as "any student who misses more than 10 percent of the total class hours will receive an F for the course." This policy is followed strictly by some professors and more leniently by others. Students should know the attendance policy of each professor with whom they are studying.

AUDITING Most colleges offer the option of auditing a course. Whereas a student enrolled in a course pays a fee, must attend classes, takes exams, and receives credit, a student auditing a course usually pays a smaller fee, does not have to take exams, and does not receive credit. People who are having trouble in a subject or who simply want to gain more knowledge about a subject but don't need or want credit are the most likely candidates for auditing. Some colleges charge full price for auditing a course.

BACCALAUREATE The baccalaureate degree, more commonly called the bachelor's degree, is a four-year degree granted in a specific field, although it can be completed in as few as three or as many as six or more years. This degree prepares students for careers in such fields as education, social work, engineering, fine arts, and journalism.

BOARD OF TRUSTEES The board of trustees is the governing body of a college. For state schools, the board is appointed by government officials (usually the governor) of the state. The board hires the president, must approve any curriculum changes to degree programs, and sets policy for the college.

CAMPUS The term *campus* refers to the physical plant of a university or college, including all buildings, fields, arenas, auditoriums, and other properties owned by the college.

CAMPUS POLICE All colleges and universities have a campus police or security office. Campus security helps students with problems ranging from physical danger to car trouble. Every student should know where this office is in case of emergency.

CARREL A carrel is a booth or small room, often large enough to accommodate one person only, located in the library. Students and faculty can reserve a carrel for professional use by the semester or the week. Personal belongings and important academic materials should never be left in a carrel, because they could be stolen.

CATALOG The college catalog is a legal, binding document that states the degree requirements of the college. It is issued to all students at the beginning of their college career and it is essential to developing a schedule and completing a degree program. Students must keep the catalog of the year in which they entered college.

CERTIFICATE A certificate program is a series of courses, usually lasting one year, designed to educate and train an individual in a specific area, such as welding, automotive repair, medical transcription, tool and die, early childhood, physical therapy, and fashion merchandising. Although certified and detailed, these programs are not degree programs. Associate and bachelor's degrees are also offered in many of the areas that have certificate programs.

CLEP The College Level Examination Program (CLEP) allows students to test out of a course. The exams are nationally averaged and are often more extensive than a course in the same area. If a student CLEPs a course, it means the student does not have to take the course in which he or she passed the CLEP exam.

COGNATE A cognate is a course or set of courses taken outside of the student's major but usually in a field related to the major. Some colleges call this a minor. A student majoring in English, may take a cognate in history or drama.

COMMUNICATIONS College curricula often mandate nine hours of communications, which commonly refers to English and speech (oral communication) courses. The mixture of courses is typically English 101 and 102 and Speech 101; the numbers vary from college to college.

COMPREHENSIVE EXAMS Exams that encompass materials from the entire course are comprehensive exams. That is, a comprehensive exam covers information from the first lecture through the last.

CONTINUING EDUCATION Continuing education or community education courses are designed to meet specific business and industry needs or to teach subjects of interest to the community. These courses are not offered for college credit, but continuing education units may be awarded. Continuing education courses range from small engine repair to flower arranging, from stained glass making to small-business management.

CO-OP This term refers to a relationship between a business or industry and the educational institution that allows a student to spend a semester in college and the next semester on the job. Co-ops may be structured variously, but the general idea of a co-op is always to gain on-the-job experience while in college.

COREQUISITE A corequisite is a course that must be taken at the same time as another course. Science courses often carry a corequisite, for example, Biology 101, may have as a corequisite the lab course, Biology 101L.

COUNSELING Most college campuses have a counseling center. Staffed by counselors trained to assist students with problems that might arise in their personal lives, with their study skills, and with their career aspirations. Counseling is different from advising—academic advisors are responsible for helping students with their academic progress. Some colleges combine the two, but in most cases the counselor and the advisor are two different people with two different job descriptions.

COURSE TITLE Every course has a course title. A schedule of classes may read: ENG 101, SPC 205, HIS 210, and so on. The college catalog defines what these terms mean. For example, ENG 101 usually stands for English 101, SPC could be the heading for speech, HIS could mean history. Headings and course titles vary from college to college.

CREDIT HOUR A credit hour is the amount of credit earned for a class. Most classes are worth three credit hours; science, foreign language, and some math courses that require labs are worth four credit hours. A class that carries three credit hours typically meets for three hours per week. This formula varies in summer sessions or midsessions.

CRITICAL THINKING Critical thinking is thinking that is purposeful, reasoned, and goal directed. It is the type of thinking used to solve problems, make associations, connect relationships, formulate inferences, make decisions, and detect faulty arguments and persuasion.

CURRICULUM The curriculum is a set of classes that the student must take to earn a degree in an area of study.

DEAN *Dean* is the title given to the head of a division or area of study. The dean is the policy maker and usually the business manager and final decision maker for that area. A college might have a dean of arts and sciences, a dean of business, and a dean of mathematics. Deans usually report to a vice-president or provost.

DEAN'S LIST The dean's list is a listing of students who have achieved at least a 3.5 (B+) on a 4.0 scale (these numbers are defined under "GPA"). Although it varies from college to college, the dean's list generally comprises students in the top 5 percent of the college.

DEGREE A student is awarded a degree for completing an approved course of study. The type of degree depends on the college, the number of credit hours in the program, and the field of study. A two-year degree is called an associate degree, and a four-year degree is called a bachelor's degree. A student who attends graduate school may receive a master's degree (after two to three years) and a doctorate (after three to ten years). Some colleges offer postdoctorate degrees.

DIPLOMA A diploma is awarded when an approved course of study is completed. Diploma requirements are not as detailed or

comprehensive as the requirements for an associate degree and usually consist of only 8 to 12 courses specific to a certain field.

DROPPING Students may elect to drop a class if they are not enjoying it or think that they will not be able to pass it because of grades or absenteeism. A class that has been dropped will no longer appear on the student's schedule or be calculated in the GPA. Rules and regulations governing dropping courses vary from college to college and are explained in the college catalog.

ELECTIVE An elective is a course that a student chooses to take outside his or her major field of study. An elective can be in an area of interest to the student or in an area that complements the student's major. For example, an English major might choose an elective in the field of theater or history because these fields complement one another. An English major might also elect to take a course in medical terminology because of an interest in that area.

EMERITI This Latin term applies to retired college personnel who have performed exemplary duties during their professional careers. A college president who procured funding for new buildings, enhanced curriculum programs, and increased the endowment might be named president emeritus (singular of emeriti) on retirement.

EVENING COLLEGE An evening college program is designed to allow students who have full-time jobs to enroll in classes that meet in the evening. Some colleges offer an entire degree program in the evening; others offer only some courses in the evening.

FACULTY The faculty is the body of professionals at a college who teach, conduct research, and perform community service. Faculty members prepare for many years to hold the responsibilities carried by the title. Some may have studied for 25 years or more to obtain the knowledge and skill necessary to train students in their specific fields.

FALLACY A fallacy is a false notion. It is a statement based on false materials, invalid inferences, and incorrect reasoning.

FEES Fees refer to the money charged by colleges for specific items and services. Fees may be charged for tuition, meal plans, books, health care, and activities. Fees vary from college to college and are usually printed in the college catalog.

FINANCIAL AID Financial aid is money awarded to a student from the college, the state, or federal government, private sources, or places of employment on the basis of need or of merit. Any grant, loan, or scholarship is formally called financial aid.

FINE ARTS The fine arts encompass a variety of artistic forms, such as theater, dance, architecture, drawing, painting, sculpture, and music. Some colleges also include literature in this category.

FIRST-YEAR STUDENT The term "first-year student" is used by colleges and refers to a student who has not yet completed 30 semester hours of college-level work.

FOREIGN LANGUAGE Almost every college offers at least one course in foreign languages, and many colleges offer degrees in this area. Some of the many foreign languages offered in U.S. colleges are Spanish, French, Russian, Latin, German, Portuguese, Swahili, Arabic, Japanese, Chinese, and Korean.

FRATERNITY A fraternity is an organization in the Greek system. Fraternities are open to male students only. Induction for each is different. Many fraternities have their own housing complexes on campus. Honorary fraternities, such as Phi Kappa Phi, are academic in nature and are open to men and women.

GPA The grade point average, GPA, is the numerical grading system used by most colleges in the United States. A student's GPA determines his or her eligibility for continued enrollment, financial aid, and honors. Most colleges operate under a 4.0 system: an A is worth 4 quality points, an B 3 points, a C 2 points, a D 1 point, and an F 0 points. To calculate a GPA, for each course the number of quality points earned is multiplied by the number of credit hours carried by the course; the numbers thus obtained for all courses are added together; finally, this total is divided by the total number of hours carried.

Example: A student is taking English 101, Speech 101, History 201, and Psychology 101, all of which carry three credit hours. If the student earns all A's, the GPA is 4.0; if the student earns all B's, the GPA is 3.0. However, if he or she had a variety of grades, you would calculate as such:

COURSE	GRADE	CREDIT HRS.		QUALITY POINTS		TOTAL POINTS
ENG 101	A	3	×	4	=	12 points
SPC 101	C	3	×	2	=	6 points
HIS 201	B	3	×	3	=	9 points
PSY 101	D	3	×	1	=	3 points

GPA = 30 points divided by 12 hours = 2.5 (C+)

GRADUATE TEACHING ASSISTANT In some larger colleges and universities, students working toward master's and doctorate degrees teach lower-level undergraduate classes under the direction of a senior professor in the department.

GRANT Usually a grant is money that goes toward tuition and books that does not have to be repaid. Grants are most often awarded by the state and federal governments.

HIGHER EDUCATION This term applies to any level of education beyond high school; all colleges are considered institutions of higher education.

HONOR CODE Many colleges operate under an honor code, which demands that students perform all work without cheating, plagiarizing, or engaging in any other dishonest actions. A student who breaks the honor code may be expelled from the institution. In some cases, a student may be expelled if he or she does not turn in a fellow student whom he or she knows has broken the code.

HONORS Academic honors are based on a student's GPA. Academic honors may include the dean's list, the president's list, and departmental honors. The three highest honors, summa cum laude, magna cum laude, and cum laude, are awarded at graduation to students who have maintained a GPA of 3.5 or better. Although the breakdown varies from college to college, these honors are usually awarded as follows: cum laude, 3.5 to 3.7; magna cum laude, 3.7 to 3.9; and summa cum laude, 4.0.

HONORS COLLEGE The honors college is a degree or a set of classes offered for students who performed exceptionally in high school.

HUMANITIES The humanities are sometimes as misunderstood as the fine arts. Disciplines in the humanities include history, philosophy, religion, cultural studies, and sometimes literature, government and foreign languages. The college catalog defines what a college designates as humanities.

IDENTIFICATION CARDS An identification (ID) card is an essential possession for any college student. An ID card allows students to use the library, participate in activities, use physical fitness facilities, and often to attend events free of charge. ID cards can also be useful beyond the campus borders. Admission to movie theaters, museums, zoos, and cultural events usually costs less and is sometimes free for students with IDs. ID cards also allow access to most area library facilities with special privileges. Some colleges issue ID

cards at no charge, and some charge a small fee. ID cards are usually validated each semester.

INDEPENDENT STUDY Many colleges offer some independent study options. Independent study courses have no formal classes and no classroom teacher; students work independently to complete the course under the general guidelines of the department and with the assistance of an instructor. Colleges often require that students maintain a minimum GPA in order to enroll in independent study classes.

INFERENCE An inference is a thought that is arrived at by logical evidence. An inference does not include opinion, hearsay, illogical thought, or unjust reasoning.

JOURNAL In many classes, such as English, orientation, literature, history, and psychology, students are required to keep a journal of thoughts, opinions, research, and class discussions. The journal often serves as a communication link between the student and the professor.

JUNIOR A student who is in his or her third year of college or who has completed at least 60 credit hours of study is a junior.

LEARNING STYLE A learning style is one's preferred method of processing information and learning new material. There is no right or wrong learning style. The three styles are visual, auditory and tactile. A visual learner learns best by seeing new information. An auditory learner learns best by hearing new information and a tactile learner learns best by doing, touching, and feeling.

LECTURE The lecture is the lesson given by an instructor in a class. Some instructors use group discussions, peer tutoring, or multimedia presentations. The term *lecture* is usually used when the material is presented in a lecture format, that is, when the professor presents most of the information.

LIBERAL ARTS A liberal arts curriculum ensures that the students are exposed to a variety of disciplines and cultural experiences, that they take courses beyond those needed for a specific vocation or occupation. A student at a liberal arts college who is majoring in biology would also have to take courses in fine arts, history, social sciences, math, hard sciences, and other areas, for example.

LOAD The number of credit hours or classes that a student is taking is the student's load. The normal load is between 15 and 18 hours or five to six classes. In most colleges, 12 hours is considered a full-time load, but a student can take up to 18 or 21 hours for the same tuition.

LOGICAL A logical thought is a thought that is based on evidence, reasoned and critical thought, and proven past events and situations. Logical thoughts avoid fallacies, manipulation, opinions, and invalid inferences.

MAJOR A major is a student's intended field of study. The term *major* indicates that the majority of the student's work will be completed in that field. Students are usually required to declare a major by the end of their sophomore (second) year.

MEAL PLAN A student purchases a meal plan at the beginning of a semester that allows the student to eat certain meals in the cafeteria or dining hall. These plans are regulated by a computer card or punch system. Meal plans can be purchased for three meals a day, breakfast only, lunch only, or a variety of other meal combinations.

MENTOR A mentor is someone who can help a student through troubled times, assist in decision making, and provide advice. A mentor can be a teacher, staff member, fellow classmate, or upper-level student. Mentors seldom volunteer. They usually fall into the role of mentor because they are easy to talk with, knowledgeable about the college and the community, and willing to lend a helping hand. Sometimes students are assigned mentors when they arrive on campus.

MINOR A student's minor usually comprises six to eight courses in a specific field that complements the student's major area of study. A student majoring in engineering might minor in math or electronics, subjects that might help later in the workforce.

NATURAL SCIENCES The natural and physical sciences refer to a select group of courses from biology, chemistry, physical science, physics, anatomy, zoology, botany, geology, genetics, microbiology, physiology, and astronomy.

ORIENTATION All students are invited and many are required to attend an orientation session when they enter college. These sessions are extremely useful. They present important information about college life as well as details of the rules of the specific college.

PLAGIARISM Plagiarism refers to the act of using another person's words or works as one's own without citing the original author. Penalties for plagiarism vary and can include asking the student to withdraw from the institution. Most institutions have strict guidelines for dealing with plagiarism. Penalties for plagiarism are usually listed in the student handbook.

PREFIX The code used by the Office of the Registrar to designate a certain area of study is called a prefix. Common prefixes are ENG for English, REL for Religion, THE for Theater, and HIS for History. Prefix lettering varies from college to college.

PREPROFESSIONAL PROGRAMS Preprofessional programs usually refer to majors that *require* further study at the master's or doctoral level in order to be able to practice in the field. Such programs include law, medicine, dentistry, psychiatry, nursing, veterinary studies, and theology.

PREREQUISITE A prerequisite is a course that must be taken *before* another course. For example, in most colleges students are required to take English 101 and 102 (Composition I and II) before taking any literature courses. Therefore, English 101 and 102 are prerequisites to literature. Prerequisites are listed in the college catalog.

PRESIDENT A college president is the visionary leader of the institution. He or she is usually hired by the board of trustees. The president's primary responsibilities include financial planning, fund-raising, developing community relations, and maintaining the academic integrity of the curriculum. Every employee at the college is responsible to the president.

PROBATION A student who has not performed well in his or her academic studies, usually manifested by a GPA below 2.0 in any given semester or quarter, may be placed on academic probation for one semester. If the student continues to perform below 2.0, he or she may be suspended. The rules for probation and suspension must be displayed in the college catalog.

PROFESSOR Not all teachers at the college level are professors. The system of promotion among college teachers is adjunct instructor, instructor, lecturer, assistant professor, associate professor, and full professor, or professor. A full professor is likely to have been in the profession for a long time and usually holds a doctorate degree.

PROVOST The provost of a college is the primary policy maker with regard to academic standards. The provost usually reports directly to the president. Many colleges do not have provosts, but have instead a vice-president for academic affairs or a dean of instruction.

READMIT A student who has stopped out for a semester or two, usually has to be readmitted to the college, but does not lose previously earned academic credit unless the credit carried a time limit. Some courses in psychology, for example, carry a five- or ten-year limit, which means that the course must be retaken if a degree is not awarded within that time period. Students who elect not to attend summer sessions do not need to be readmitted. There is typically no application fee for a readmit student.

REGISTRAR The registrar has one of the most difficult jobs on any college campus, because the registrar is responsible for all student academic records as well as for entering all grades, recording all drops and adds, printing the schedule, and verifying all candidates for graduation. The Office of the Registrar is sometimes referred to as the records office.

RESIDENCE HALL A residence hall is a facility on campus where students live. Residence halls can be single sex or coeducational. Many new students choose to live in residence halls because they are conveniently located and they provide a good way to meet new friends and to become involved in extracurricular activities. Each residence hall usually has a full-time supervisor and elects a student representative to the student council. In addition, a director of student housing oversees the residence halls.

RESIDENCY REQUIREMENT Many colleges have a residency requirement, that is, they require that a minimum number of credits must be earned at the home institution. Many two-year colleges require that at least 50 percent of credits applied toward graduation must be earned at the home college. Many four-year colleges, require that the last 30 hours of credits must be earned at the home college. All residency requirements are spelled out in the college catalog.

ROOM AND BOARD Room and board refers to a place to stay and food to eat. Colleges often charge students who live on campus a fee for room and board. Students may opt to buy a meal plan along with their dorm room. Issues involving room and board are usually discussed during orientation.

SCHOLAR *Scholar* typically refers to a student who has performed in a superior manner in a certain field of study.

SECTION CODE When many sections of the same course are offered, a section code identifies the hour and instructor of the student's particular class. A schedule that includes section codes may look something like this:

> English 101 01 MWF 8:00–8:50 Smith
> English 101 02 MWF 8:00–8:50 Jones
> English 101 03 T TH 8:00–9:15 McGee

The numbers 01, 02, 03, and so on refer to a specific section of 101.

SENIOR Senior refers to a student who is in the last year of study for the undergraduate degree. To be a senior a student must have completed at least 90 credit hours.

SOCIAL SCIENCES The social sciences study society and people. Social science courses may include psychology, sociology, anthropology, political science, geography, economics, and international studies.

SOPHOMORE *Sophomore* refers to a student who is in the second year of study and who has completed at least 30 credit hours.

SORORITIES A sorority is an organization in the Greek system open to women only. Many sororities have on-campus housing complexes. Initiation into a sorority differs from organization to organization and from campus to campus.

STAFF College personnel are usually divided into three categories: administration, staff, and faculty. The staff is responsible for the day-to-day workings of the college. People who work in admissions, financial aid, the bookstore, housing, student activities, and personnel, for example, usually hold staff titles, whereas the people who head these departments are usually in administration.

STUDENT GOVERNMENT ASSOCIATION One of the most powerful and visible organizations on the college campus, the

Student Government Association (SGA) usually comprises students from all four undergraduate classes. Officers are elected annually. The SGA is the student voice on campus and represents the entire student body before the administration of the college.

STUDENT LOAN A student loan is money that must be repaid. Student loans generally have a much lower rate of interest than do bank loans, and the payment schedule for most student loans does not begin until six months after graduation. This delayed start is intended to allow the graduate to find a secure job and a steady income before having to make payments. If a student decides to return to school, the loan can be deferred, with additional interest, until the graduate degree is completed.

SUSPENSION Students may be suspended for a variety of reasons, but most suspensions are for academic reasons. Again, GPA requirements vary, but students are usually suspended if their GPA falls below 1.5 for two consecutive semesters. The college catalog lists the rules regarding suspension.

SYLLABUS In college, a syllabus replaces the class outline of high school. A syllabus is a legally binding contract between the student and the professor; it contains the attendance policy, the grading scale, the required text, the professor's office hours and phone number(s), and important, relevant information about the course. Most professors include the class operational calendar as a part of the syllabus. The syllabus is one of the most important documents that is issued in a class. Students should take the syllabus to class daily and keep it at least until the semester is over.

TENURE Tenure basically guarantees a professor lifelong employment at an institution. Tenure is usually awarded to professors who have been with the college for many years in recognition of their successful efforts in research, their record of having books and articles published, and their community service.

TOEFL The Test of English as a Foreign Language, TOEFL, is used to certify that international students have the English skills necessary to succeed at the institution or to become a teaching assistant. Some colleges allow international students to use English to satisfy their foreign language requirement if they score high enough on the TOEFL.

TRANSCRIPT A transcript is a formal record of all work attempted and/or completed at a college. A student has a transcript for every college attended. Many colleges have a policy of listing all classes, completed or not, on the transcript. Some colleges allow Ds and Fs to be removed if the student repeats the course and earns a better grade, but many others retain the original grade and continue to calculate it in the GPA. Rules regarding transcripts vary from col-

lege to college. Many employers now require that a prospective employee furnish a college transcript.

TRANSIENT A transient student is a student who is taking one or two courses at a college other than his or her home institution. For example, a student who enrolls in a college near home for the summer while maintaining student status at his or her chosen college is a transient student.

TRANSITIONAL STUDIES Many colleges have an open admission policy, meaning that the door is open to any student, and colleges frequently offer a transitional studies program to help students reach their educational goals. For example, a student who has not performed well in English, math, or reading may be required to attend a transitional studies class to upgrade basic skills in that area.

TRANSFER The term *transfer* can refer to course work as well as a students. A student who enrolls in one college and then moves to another is classified as a transfer student. The course work completed at the original college is called transfer work. Many colleges have rules regarding the number of credit hours that a student can transfer. Most colleges will not accept credit from another college if the grade on the course is lower than a C.

VETERANS' AFFAIRS Many colleges have an Office of Veterans' Affairs to assist those students who have served in the military. Colleges often accept credit earned by a veteran while in the service. Veterans' financial packages are also often different because of the GI Bill.

VICE PRESIDENT Many colleges have several vice-presidents who serve under the president. These are senior-level administrators who assist with the daily operations of the college and may include vice presidents of academic affairs, financial affairs, and student affairs, among others.

VOLUMES A volume refers to a book or a piece of nonprint material that assists students in their studies. If a college library has 70,000 volumes, it means that the library has 70,000 books *and* other pieces of media. Many colleges have millions of volumes.

WHO'S WHO This is the shortened title of *Who's Who in American Colleges and Universities*. Students are nominated by the college for this national recognition because of their academic standing and their achievements in cocurricular activities and community service.

WOMEN'S STUDIES Some colleges offer majors and minors in women's studies. The curriculum is centered on the major contributions of women in art, literature, medicine, history, law, architecture, and sciences.

References

Adler, R., Rosenfeld, L., and Towne, N. *Interplay. The Process of Interpersonal Communication.* New York: Holt, Rinehart and Winston, 1989.

American College Testing Program. *National Drop Out Rates.* ACT Institutional Data File, Iowa City, 1995.

Astin, A. *Achieving Educational Excellence.* San Francisco: Jossey-Bass, 1985.

Beebe, S., and Beebe, S. *Public Speaking: An Audience Centered Approach.* 2d ed. Englewood Cliffs, NJ: Prentice Hall, 1994.

Benson, H. *The Relaxation Response.* New York: Caral Publishing Group, 1992.

Benson, H., and Stuart, E. *The Wellness Book: The Comprehensive Guide to Maintaining Health and Treating Stress-Related Illness.* New York: Birch Lane Press, 1992.

Benson, H., and Stuart, Eileen. *Wellness Encyclopedia.* Boston: Houghton Mifflin, 1991.

Berenblatt, M., and Berenblatt, A. *Make an Appointment with Yourself: Simple Steps to Positive Self-Esteem.* Deerfield Beach, FL: Health Communication, 1994.

Beyer, B. *Developing a Thinking Skills Program.* Boston: Allyn and Bacon, 1998.

Bosak, J. *Fallacies.* Dubuque, IA: Educulture Publishers, 1976.

Boyle, M., and Zyla, G. *Personal Nutrition.* St. Paul, MN: West Publishing, 1992.

Bozzi, V. "A Healthy Dose of Religion," *Psychology Today* (November, 1988).

Buscaglia, L. *Living, Loving, and Learning.* New York: Ballantine, 1982.

Chickering, A., and Schlossberg, N. *Getting the Most out of College.* Boston: Allyn and Bacon, 1995.

Christian, J., and Greger, J. *Nutrition for Living.* Redwood City, CA: Benjamin/Cummings Publishing, 1994.

Chopra, D. *The Seven Spiritual Laws of Success.* San Rafael, CA: New World Library, 1994.

Cohen, L. *Evaluating Internet Resources.* University of Albany Libraries; Internet http://www.albany. edu, 1996.

Cohen, L. *Conducting Research on the Internet.* University of Albany Libraries; Internet http://www.albany.edu, 1996.

Cooper, A. *Time Management for Unmanageable People.* New York: Bantam Books, 1993.

Donatelle, R., and Davis, L. *Health: The Basics.* Englewood Cliffs, NJ: Prentice Hall, 1994.

Ellis, D., Lankowitz, S., Stupka, D., and Toft, D. *Career Planning.* Rapid City, SD: College Survival, Inc., 1990.

Elrich, M. "The Stereotype Within." *Educational Leadership* (April 1994), p. 12.

Fulghum, R. *All I Really Need to Know, I Learned in Kindergarten.* New York: Ivy Books, 1988.

Gardenswartz, L., and Rowe, A. *Managing Diversity: A Complete Desk Reference and Planning Guide.* New York: Irwin/Pfeiffer, 1993.

Gardner, J., and Jewler, J. *Your College Experience.* Belmont, CA: Wadsworth, 1995

Grilly, D. *Drugs and Human Behavior.* Boston: Allyn and Bacon, 1994.

Gunthrie, H., and Picciano, M. *Human Nutrition.* Salem, MA: Mosby, 1995.

Hales, D. *Your Health.* Redwood City, CA: Benjamin/Cummings Publishing, 1991.

Helpern, D. *Thought and Knowledge: An Introduction to Critical Thinking.* NJ: Lawrence Erlbaum, 1996.

Kleiman, C. *The 100 Best Jobs for the 90's and Beyond.* New York: Berkley Books, 1992.

Lecky, P. *Self-Consistency: A Theory of Personality.* Garden City, NY: Anchor, 1951.

Nevid, J., Fichner-Rathus, L., and Rathus, S. *Human Sexuality in a World of Diversity.* Boston: Allyn and Bacon, 1995.

Olesen, E. *Mastering the Winds of Change.* New York: Harper Business, 1993.

Ormondroyd, J., Engle, M., and Cosgrave, T. *How to Critically Analyze Information Sources.* Cornell University Libraries; Internet http://www. library.cornell. edu/, 1996.

Ormondroyd, J., Engle, M., and Cosgrave, T. *Distinguishing Scholarly Journals from Other Periodicals.* Cornell University Libraries; Internet http://www.library. cornell.edu/, 1996.

Pauk, W. *How to Study in College.* 6th ed. New York: Houghton Mifflin; 1997.

Paul, R. *What Every Person Needs to Survive in a Rapidly Changing World.* Santa Rosa, CA: The Foundation for Critical Thinking, 1992.

Popenoe, D. *Sociology,* 9th ed. Englewood Cliffs, NJ: Prentice Hall, 1993.

"Retention Rates by Institutional Type," Higher Education Research Institute, UCLA, Los Angeles, 1989.

Rathus, S., and Fichner-Rathus, L. *Making the Most out of College.* Englewood Cliffs, NJ: Prentice Hall, 1994.

Rogers, C. *On Becoming Partners: Marriage and Its Alternatives.* New York: Delacorte Press, 1972.

Romas, J., and Sharma, M. *Practical Stress Management.* Boston: Allyn and Bacon, 1995.

Sciolino, E. World Drug Crop Up Sharply in 1989 Despite U.S. Effort. *New York Times,* March 2, 1990.

Shaffer, C., and Amundsen, K. *Creating Community Anywhere.* Los Angeles: Jeremy P. Tarcher Publishing, 1994.

Warnick, B., and Inch, E. *Critical Thinking and Communication—The Use of Reason in Argument.* New York: Macmillan, 1994.

Whitfield, C. *Healing the Child Within.* Deerfield Beach, FL: Health Communication, 1987.

Woolfolk, A. *Educational Psychology.* 6th ed. Boston: Allyn and Bacon, 1995.

Yale Study of Graduating Seniors. Yale University, New Haven, CT, 1953.

Index